NEW DIMENSIONS SERIES

Teaching About War and War Prevention

by William A. Nesbitt
for the Foreign Policy Association

The Foreign Policy Association

The Foreign Policy Association is a private, nonprofit, non-partisan educational organization. Its objective is to stimulate wider interest, greater understanding, and more effective participation by American citizens in world affairs. However, as an organization, it takes no position on issues of United States foreign policy. In its publications the FPA strives to insure factual accuracy, but the opinions expressed are those of the authors and not of the organization.

In preparing this book, we are grateful for the advice and assistance of Dr. Jerome D. Frank of the Johns Hopkins University School of Medicine, Professor Richard C. Snyder of the University of California at Irvine, and Professor Lee F. Anderson of Northwestern University. We should also like to thank Betty Reardon, Saul Mendlovitz, and Lawrence Metcalf of the World Law Fund, Monsieur and Madame André Goenaga of the American Consulate in Bordeaux, Professor Jack R. Fraenkel of San Francisco State College, and Professor Charles Barker of the Johns Hopkins University. The author thanks Helen Nesbitt for kind assistance. For editorial direction and supervision of the series, the Foreign Policy Association thanks David C. King, Editorial Director.

JAMES M. BECKER
DIRECTOR
School Services
Foreign Policy Association

CONTENTS

Introduction:
Why Teach About War and War Prevention?

YOUNG PEOPLE TODAY ARE DEEPLY AWARE OF THE ELEMENTS
that make up what Richard Falk has referred to as our
"high-risk environment." They are troubled and anxious
over problems of environmental health, social justice,
population control, and the prevention of war. We
shouldn't need campus (and high school) unrest or public demonstrations to remind us that their awareness is
combined with a deep sense of commitment, as well as
with confusion and frustration.

Perhaps the overriding issue facing teachers today is
how to provide the sort of education our youth need in
order to cope with this high-risk environment. How do
we go about making our courses truly relevant to the

lives of our students? How do we devise the "survival curriculum" demanded of us in this decade? These questions are of particular importance to the social studies which have long been under attack as among the least relevant parts of our educational system.

Education for the closing decades of this century might well include a systematic, interdisciplinary study of war —its causes, its nature, the possible means of its prevention. We know enough of the dangers of war to know that failure to solve this problem may preclude solutions to the other problems facing mankind. We are also gradually becoming aware that the cost of the current security system is so great that it seriously hampers our ability to deal with other domestic and world crises. The U.S. Arms Control and Disarmament Agency reports that "global military expenditures take more than 7% of the world's gross product. In money terms they are equivalent to the total income produced by the one billion people living in Latin America, South Asia, and the Near East. They are greater by 40 percent than world expenditures on education at all levels of government and more than three times world-wide expenditures on public health." And, the report concludes, military allocations continue to grow at a faster rate than do expenditures for these other needs.

If schools are to help students to deal with any of the problems of our high-risk environment, then the subject of war and the cost of the security system cannot be ignored. A realistic approach to this subject may also help young people avoid the negativism with which they frequently react to the problems we face. They may come to see that the objective of war-prevention involves all of us, not just a handful of government leaders, and that it is an objective that is obtainable.

The systematic study of war and the means of its

eventual abolition is increasingly recognized as a legitimate part of the curriculum of the social sciences, history, law, and other fields. More than a generation of
research has resulted in a deepening understanding of
the causes of war, what a warless world might resemble
and how it might be achieved. This book is an attempt
to translate some of the findings in the war/peace field
into a conceptual framework of value to teachers, as well
as to provide some practical classroom suggestions. By
using the concepts developed here as the starting point
for teaching units or, preferably, for an entire course, the
teacher will be able to help students grapple with such
questions as

1. What have social scientists learned about the causes
of human conflict, violence, and war?

2. What is national security? Is it confined to armaments? Are foreign aid and international trade related to
security?

3. Can a single nation be secure—can there be a "for-
tress America"?

4. Is our present security system adequate? What are
the risks of the current system? What are the alternatives
and the risks involved with them?

5. Are we spending too much or too little on defense?
Should we reduce our defense expenditures, and if so,
how can this be done without reducing security?

6. What changes are needed to produce a world that
is relatively safe and capable of reducing the other pressures of our high-risk environment? What changes are
already taking place that provide clues to possible shifts
in the international system?

The chapters that follow are not designed to answer
these questions, but rather to provide a framework for
dealing with them in an intelligent and responsible way.

Much of the treatment may seem overly ambitious or superficial. We cannot isolate and analyze *all* the causes of war; we can't offer students more than an oversimplified understanding of what we do know. But neither can we wait until the many disciplines involved have discovered all the answers, or until we have developed all the best teaching strategies, before we attempt to help our students wrestle with these complex and essential issues. The purpose of this book, then, is to outline some ideas and suggestions in the hope that they will serve as a starting point for creative and imaginative teachers. None of the ideas presented or the materials mentioned are offered as the definitive word on how to go about teaching war/peace issues; they are suggestions only.

In general, we have followed the framework used by Kenneth Waltz in *Man, The State, and War*. We have examined some of the causes of war that lie within the nature of man, and then we have tried to understand how the nation-state and the international system create an environment in which large-scale violence and war are possible and probable. Part III outlines proposals that have been made for changes within the current system, and also some of the models developed for creating alternative systems. Part IV offers some alternative ways of approaching these concepts by plugging them into traditional course offerings. Throughout, an attempt has been made to offer as objective and balanced a view as is possible, without advocating any particular cause or solution.

We have also attempted to make the treatment of war/peace issues as flexible as possible, in order to fit the needs of the individual teacher. Teachers who feel comfortable with an inquiry approach, for example, can use the questions raised as the basis for hypothesis formation; others will prefer to use them as discussion questions or as the basis for research assignments. The framework is also expandable—particular concepts or units may be fitted into traditional course offerings, or the entire framework may be used as the basis for part or all of a new course.

Limitations of space make the bibliographies highly selective. In choosing sources, we have tried to offer materials that will present a balanced view, with an emphasis on brief and inexpensive materials and collections of readings. Wherever possible, we have included the number of pages and the price of books and pamphlets as an aid in planning. To deal with these subjects adequately, the teacher will probably find that a considerable amount of self-training is necessary; consequently we have attempted to offer a brief summary of the basic concepts, as well as certain titles in the bibliographies specifically for the teacher. A special section at the end of the book lists resource organizations that offer films, publications, simulations, and other teaching aids.

BIBLIOGRAPHY

On methods and rationale, *Social Science Concepts in the Classroom* (Syracuse University Press, 1968, 64 pages, $1.50) by Verna Fancet and others, is particularly useful for ideas on teaching concepts of "multiple causation." *Teaching Public Issues in the High School* (Houghton Mifflin, 1966, 330 pages, $4.50), by Donald Oliver and James Shaver, offers a justification and methodology for dealing with values and ethical commitments in social studies.

Some basic works on the interrelatedness of man's problems, and on the causes and nature of war are: Walter Clemens, Jr. (ed.), *Toward a Strategy of Peace* (Rand McNally, 1965, 264 pages, $3.95); Stanley Hoffman, *The State of War* (Praeger, 1965, 276 pages, $2.25); William H. McNeil, *Past and Future* (Chicago University Press, 1954, 217 pages, $1.75); Kenneth N. Waltz, *Man, The State and War* (Columbia University Press, 1965, 263 pages, $2.95); Quincey Wright, *A Study of War* (University of Chicago Press, 1964, 461 pages, $2.95).

PART I

DEVELOPING AN UNDERSTANDING OF THE CAUSES AND NATURE OF WAR

One can't study the course of human history without studying something about wars. In our traditional history courses, however, the treatment of war is fragmentary; each one is presented as a separate and isolated phenomenon. While we might follow the usual pattern of looking at the causes, the events, and the results of each war, the student emerges with only the cloudiest notion of what war is or why wars happen. If he remembers these studies at all, it's likely to be a vague recollection of "one damned war after another," and an equally vague notion that wars are things that happen—events beyond the control of man.

One of the basic objectives of dealing with war/peace concepts as a separate course of study is to enable us to examine war as a social phenomenon. Certain factors common to all wars can be isolated and studied, giving the student some grasp of the nature and causes of war as well as possible means of war prevention.

1

Conflict, Violence, and War

WITHOUT BECOMING INVOLVED IN THE SEMANTICS OF PRO-
viding a precise definition of war (e.g., does American
involvement in Southeast Asia constitute a "war"? Are
the Black Panthers at "war" with the Establishment?),
it will be helpful if the students begin their study of war
with an exploration of the relationship between *conflict*
and war.

One can make a good case, in fact, for devoting a con-
siderable amount of social studies time to a more system-
atic study of human conflict. In a booklet titled *Major
Concepts for the Social Studies* (Syracuse University
Press, 1965, 62 pages, $1.50), published by the Syracuse
Social Studies Curriculum Center, the authors contend

that "to ignore conflict as a social force worthy of recognition in curricular revision is an unrealistic view of how man's destinies have been shaped. Conflict has been a powerful, if not the most powerful, force structuring the world of today. It is ever present and ever operative in society."

The teacher might begin by simply asking the class what they think conflict is. He can help them sort out some of the different levels of meaning by asking specific questions and encouraging them to give examples in their answers. Here are some sample questions:

1. Have you ever had a conflict within yourself? What are some forms of "inner conflict"?

2. What are some examples of conflicts between individuals? between groups? within groups?

3. Is conflict synonymous with violence? What are some forms of nonviolent conflict?

4. Is conflict always unhealthy? That is, is there a distinction between *functional* and *dysfunctional* conflict?

5. Does the outcome of conflict always mean that whatever one party gains the other must proportionately lose?

6. Would it be possible to have a society without conflict? What might such a society be like?

7. Are there times when conflicting groups cooperate? Give examples.

8. In what human situations is conflict most likely? least likely? impossible?

9. How do interdependence and density affect human beings in regard to conflict?

Although much will become clear by simply handling these questions in a controlled bull-session fashion, it will be much better if the students have some solid material to apply these questions to. The teacher might, for example, use some of the questions as the basis for a writing or tape-recording assignment. Working individually or in small groups, they might build scenarios that will illustrate some of the different aspects of the subject. These scenarios can be actual events or fictionalized; they could be constructed from personal or family situations, or from larger settings such as the school community or society as a whole. Research assignments are another possibility for focusing on these questions; for instance, a student report on the experiments that have been conducted with rats placed in an overcrowded environment would give the class some insights into the possible effect of population density on conflict.

An alternative or additional introduction to the suggestions outlined above, is to use one or more simulation games. Some simulations, like *Sunshine, Ghetto,* or *Star Power,* concern conflict between individuals and subnational groups.[1] They are useful in helping the class deal with the following questions:

1. Is conflict more intense when the parties are of different color, social position, or nationality? Why or why not?

2. How do communication and perception (or misperception) influence conflict?

3. How do differing ideologies affect conflict?

4. How do these differences lead to stereotyping and misperception? Having labeled someone, can we do things to them we wouldn't do otherwise?

5. How does denial of rights and opportunities affect conflict?

[1] A comprehensive listing of simulations designed for use in the social studies classroom will be found in *Simulation Games for the Social Studies Classroom,* by William A. Nesbitt, New Dimensions Series (Thomas Y. Crowell, 1971).

Still another approach to conflict would be to have the class read an account of the Robbers Cave Experiment[2]—or, an inventive teacher might even try a modified version of the situation. In this experiment, eleven-year-old boys at a camp were divided into two groups, which were kept isolated from each other for a few days. Each group developed its own organizational structure, with definite leadership roles and customs emerging. They were then brought together in a competitive atmosphere, in which one side's victory spelled defeat and some sense of humiliation for the other. In describing the experiment, psychiatrist Jerome Frank wrote, "To their own groups the children attributed self-glorifying qualities, but to the other they assigned traits that justified treating it as an enemy. They improvised and hoarded weapons, and indulged in other shows of power."

Attempts were made to create peace between the two groups, but it proved difficult to overcome the stereotyping and misperception that marked their mutual hostility. The leader of one side, for example, who attempted peaceful overtures, was rebuffed by his opponents who thought he was trying to trick them, and his efforts were derided by his own companions who interpreted them as a sign of weakness. Only when cooperative action was made necessary by the counselors (through such methods as interrupting the camp water supply) was hostility lessened.

From any of these exercises, the students should begin to gain an idea of the major elements of conflict at the personal and group level, and, by analogy, at the community and international level. They should see that conflict is unavoidable when people are in contact, but that such conflict is not necessarily something undesirable

---

[2] The experiment is described in Jerome Frank's *Sanity and Survival* (Vintage Books, 1967, $1.95), pp. 250–252.

that should be eliminated in a healthy society. The teacher should be careful to point out that, not only would it be impossible to eliminate conflict, but that conflict frequently has a positive value. As H. L. Nieburg wrote, "Conflict, in functional terms, may be viewed as the means of discovering consensus, of creating agreed terms of collaboration. . . . [It] constitutes a great force in keeping things loose, capable of adaptation and adjustment. . . ."

Another important distinction that should emerge is that conflict is not only people seeking something tangible, but intangible goals as well, such as the triumph of an ideology. Conflict may also be about something illusory—an accident or a misunderstanding.

Escalation is another concept of great importance in understanding the nature of conflict. In any of the exercises mentioned above, the teacher can point out situations in which there was a spiral of reciprocal actions along a scale toward violence. Sometimes violence occurred; usually it did not. In the escalation process, the underlying cause often becomes secondary and may even be forgotten. In World War I, for instance, atrocities and the mounting death toll were a greater reason for the war in the minds of many participants than were the original issues.

At some point, the students are likely to raise some questions about why conflict sometimes leads to violence, while at other times it is resolved peacefully or even through cooperative action. Although there are no clear answers to such questions, the class should develop an awareness of the complexities involved and the directions in which current research is pointing. A readable and brief review of what has been learned about the causes and function of violence can be found in a Special Report for the *1969 World Book Year Book*, entitled "The Riddles of Violence." In the space of a few pages, highlighted by some impressive pictures, the students will begin to see why the authors conclude that ". . . we know so little at this point about the nature of violent persons, and the dynamics of violence in any society, that our attempts to design public policies against violence may prove utterly futile. Research into violence is so primitive that there is not even agreement among many authorities about the sources of violent behavior in man."

In other words, we have no way of isolating the factors that determine whether a conflict situation will become violent. If students wish to explore this matter further, an excellent source is the Kerner Commission Report. Some mention should also be made of the fact that many people feel that violence, like conflict itself, is not only inevitable, but even desirable and necessary. Students could read some selections from Frantz Fanon's *The Wretched of the Earth* (Grove Press, 1963, 225 pages, $1.25), to learn something of why radical elements in the Third World feel that violence on a large scale is absolutely necessary in order to bring about the sort of sudden and drastic changes that are necessary. A little research will also disclose that radical elements of the extreme left in this country are quite in agreement with Fanon: they are convinced that "the system" will not reform itself and therefore must be destroyed.

If the class finds that it has been in murky waters in trying to determine why conflict sometimes leads to violence, they will discover that it is just as difficult to assess why conflict is sometimes resolved through peaceful or cooperative effort. In examining some of the material mentioned below, the students will see that parties in conflict have a number of options open to them; violence is one. Rational examination of the issues, for example, might disclose that misperception has exaggerated points of difference, and thus such examination may lead to the resolution of the conflict. If the parties have irreconcilable goals and values, they might continue the conflict but peaceably. One of the parties might be willing to give up something that the other feels it must have. One party or both might decide to change goals. Or, one or both sides may find that the cost of continuing the conflict is so great that a peaceful resolution seems preferable, even if it means the surrender of certain goals.

A simple classroom device for getting at some of the factors involved is through an "interaction brief" called the *Cooperation Squares* game. In a single class period, the students are placed in a conflict situation in which it appears that what enables one individual to win necessitates a loss for others. But the game cannot end until the individuals in each group find the means of cooperating with each other, without verbal communication.

Here is the procedure as described in the October, 1969 issue of the *NEA Journal*[3]:

Before class, prepare a set of squares and an instruction sheet for each five students. A set consists of five envelopes containing pieces of stiff paper cut into patterns that will form five 6″ x 6″ squares as shown in the diagram. Several individual combinations will be possible but only one total combination.

Cut each square into the parts *a* through *j* and lightly pencil in the letters. Then mark the envelopes *A* through *E* and distribute the pieces thus: Envelope *A*, pieces *i*, *h*, *e*; *B*, pieces *a*, *a*, *a*, *c*; *C*, pieces *a*, *j*; *D*, pieces *d*, *f*; and *E*, pieces *g*, *b*, *f*, *c*.

Erase the small letters from the pieces and write

---

[3] The game was developed by D. Nylen, J. R. Mitchell, and A. Stout for the NTL Institute for Applied Behavioral Science, an autonomous organization associated with NEA.

instead the envelope letters *A* through *E*, so that the pieces can be easily returned for reuse.

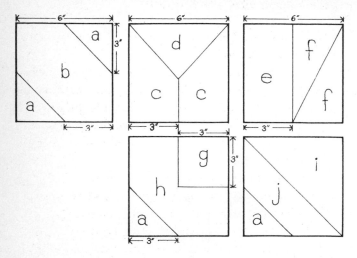

By using multiples of 3 inches, several combinations will form one or two squares; but only one combination will form five 6" x 6" squares.

Divide the class into groups of five and seat each group at a table equipped with a set of envelopes and an instruction sheet. Ask that the envelopes be opened only on signal.

Describe the experiment as a puzzle involving conflict and cooperation. Read the instructions aloud, point out that each table has a reference copy of them, then give the signal to open the envelopes.

The instructions are as follows: Each person should have an envelope containing pieces for forming squares. At the signal, the task of the group is to form five squares of equal size. The task is not completed until everyone has before him a perfect square and all the squares are of the same size.

These are the rules: No member may speak. No member may ask for a card or in any way signal that he wants one. Members may give cards to others.

When all or most of the groups have finished, call time and discuss the experience. Some of the following questions may provoke discussion:

1. How did you feel when someone held a piece and did not see the solution?

2. What was your reaction when someone finished his square and then sat back without seeing whether his solution prevented others from solving the problem?

3. What were your feelings if you finished your square and then began to realize that you would have to break it up and give away a piece?

4. How did you feel about the person who was slow at seeing the solution or who misunderstood the instructions? If you were that person, how did you feel?

5. Was there a climate that helped or hindered?

6. In our previous study, have you encountered situations that were similar to this experiment? Explain.

A more sophisticated example of the same sort of experiment is provided by a simulation called *The Road Game* (Herder & Herder, 232 Madison Ave., N.Y., N.Y., teacher's guide, $1.45, student book, $1.25), in which the players have to map out a road through territory that belongs to others, setting up conflict situations that require peaceful resolution and cooperation.

An excellent way to pull these strands together and to make a transition from personal and group conflict to conflict among nations is to have the class read William Golding's *Lord of the Flies* (Putnam, 1959, $1.25). Better still, let them view the film. Whichever is used, the teacher will gain great assistance from a brief (two-page) discussion guide developed by the World Law Fund. Here is a sample of the sort of questions raised in the guide:

The boys were beset by fear, fear of not being res-
cued, fear of the Beast, fear of Jack, fear of starving,
fear of the unknown. What similar fears haunt people
and nations today? What origins do these fears have in
the realities of world affairs?

It has been said that fear can cause both cooperation
and conflict. The fears of the boys helped them to form
a cohesive group around Jack, who promised protection.
When mass hysteria, helped along by Roger, made
Ralph appear to be a hostile figure, Jack consolidated
his power. Finally, Ralph seemed to be the Beast, as
Simon before him. Does such a phenomenon exist in
the political behavior of nations? If you think it does,
give specific examples.

A *Teacher's Guide To Three Films and World Peace*
(World Law Fund, 1968, 28 pages, $.75).

Scenarios and simulations offer excellent ways for students to grasp some of the ways in which conflict operates between groups and between nations. They will
see how factors such as escalation and misperception
can lead a conflict to violence. They will also see that
such things as assessment of the costs involved will frequently lead to the peaceful resolution of conflict. *Dare
To Reconcile: Seven Settings For Creating Community*
by John Oliver Nelson (Friendship Press, 1968, 127
pages, $1.50) offers a series of scenarios dealing with
various kinds of conflict (war, race, generation gap),
with a heavy emphasis on peaceful resolution.

Simulations are particularly useful because they place
the students in the role of decision-makers. In making decisions, they have to cope with communications
problems, misinformation, escalation, and misperception.
Once a decision is made, they learn the consequences of
the decision, and discover whether they have moved the
situation toward violence or toward peaceful resolution
of the conflict. *Dangerous Parallel* and *Crisis* are good

examples of simulations that call for decision-making; a third simulation, appropriately titled *Conflict*, places the players in a futuristic crisis that occurs in a disarmed world.

Although this introductory study will create some sense of the relationship between war and conflict, it leaves unanswered some essential questions: Is there something in the nature of man or of society that produces violence and war? Is violence unavoidable? If it is, what levels of violence can be tolerated? Are there ways of keeping violence within certain limits? Is there something inherent in the nation-state system that makes war inevitable? How can wars be controlled or avoided? The chapters which follow will suggest some ways of getting at these questions.

BIBLIOGRAPHY

The Sociological Resources for the Social Studies has produced a number of useful booklets dealing with conflict and conflict resolution, including *Simulating Social Conflict* and *Small Group Processes*. For more information write to SRSS, 503 First National Building, Ann Arbor, Mich. 48108.

Bondurant, Joan V. (ed.), *Conflict: Violence and Nonviolence* (Atherton Press, 1970), 200 pages, $2.45.

Graham, Hugh, *et al.* (eds.), *Violence in America: Historical and Comparative Perspective* (A Report to the National Commission on the Causes and Prevention of Violence) (The New American Library, 1969), 795 pages, $1.25.

Griffith, Priscilla and Betty Reardon, *Let Us Examine Our Attitude Toward Peace* (World Law Fund, 1969),

47 pages, $1.00. A reader designed for high school use. On conflict and violence, see Lin Piao, "Long Live the Victory of the People's War."

McNeil, Elton B. (ed.), *The Nature of Human Conflict* (Prentice-Hall, 1965), $7.95.

FOR TEACHER PREPARATION

Arendt, Hannah, *On Revolution* (Viking, 1963), 344 pages, $1.65.

Boulding, Kenneth, *Conflict and Defense: A General Theory* (Harper & Row, 1963), 349 pages, $1.95.

Coser, Lewis, *The Functions of Social Conflict* (Macmillan, 1964), 188 pages, $1.95.

Nieburg, H. L., *Political Violence: The Behavioral Process* (St. Martin's Press, 1969).

International Encyclopedia of the Social Sciences (Crowell, Collier & Macmillan, 1968). See headings "Conflict," "Violence," "War."

2

Is Man the Cause?

ARE VIOLENCE AND WAR CAUSED BY SOMETHING INHERENT in man's nature? Do we have a natural propensity toward violence? Does something happen to people in groups that makes them more prone to violence?

These questions have troubled Americans for some time, especially in the wake of assassinations and urban riots in the 1960's. We began to wonder whether our society was more violent than others. Commissions were established to explore the causes of violence and to search for answers to the following questions: Why are there more murders in the borough of Manhattan each year than there are in the nation of England? Why does our rate of violent crime continue to rise at such an alarming pace?

No one came up with any final answers. Perhaps there are none. But researchers continue to explore theories that can lead us to a better understanding of our behavior. Some of these hypotheses will strike the students as eminently logical and valid; others will seem bizarre or improbable. In any case, the students' experience with these often conflicting theories will be exciting as well as rewarding.

A good introduction to the complex question of why individuals engage in violence and wars would be a showing of the film *The Ox-Bow Incident* (Brandon Films, N.Y.). This classic western is a dramatic and well-acted tale of the lynching of three innocent men. The class will have little difficulty identifying such factors as stereotyping, misperception, escalation. In addition, other elements, which may not have emerged in their previous study of conflict, may become evident— elements such as the role of leadership and the force that operates on people in a group which makes them capable of acts they would shun as individuals.

Very little preparation is needed to build a highly stimulating unit around the question of whether or not there is something innate in man that produces aggression, violence, and war. The work of three men, who have drawn conclusions from their observations of animal behavior and from archaeological evidence, should be used to support the theory that man is innately aggressive:

Konrad Lorenz, *On Aggression* (Bantam Books, 1969), 306 pages, $1.25.

Desmond Morris, *The Naked Ape* (Dell Publishing Co., 1969), 205 pages, $.95.

Robert Ardrey, *The Territorial Imperative* (Atheneum, 1966), 390 pages, $2.45.

If there isn't time for the class to read all three, individuals or groups could read separate titles and report the major findings to the rest of the class. Another alternative would be to select certain portions of each for all the students to read.

Even a brief sampling of any one of the titles frequently converts students to the persuasive evidence being presented. To offer them a more balanced view, it is suggested that they also read some of the arguments opposing these theories. *Man and Aggression*, edited by Ashley Montague (Oxford University Press, 1968, 178 pages, $1.95), provides a collection of essays that di-

"You shouldn't feel bad if you don't win this war. There'll be other wars."

rectly challenge the conclusions of Lorenz, Ardrey, and Morris.

The work of ethnologist Konrad Lorenz has been especially influential in lending scientific credence to the view that not only are animals innately aggressive, but so is man. Lorenz believes that aggression, which he defines as a fighting instinct against members of the same species, has been bred into many animals in the course of evolution and serves certain positive functions. Fighting among male primates over females, for example, results in a kind of selective breeding, and helps in the social organization of the group by establishing a hierarchy or "pecking order." But, Lorenz argues, most species stop short of fatal combat, which could decimate the species and lead to extinction, by what he calls "appeasement gestures." In effect, the defeated animal signals to the victor, "I give up." For example, a wolf who has lost a fight against another will bare his throat, which acts as an inhibitory cue to his opponent.

In the course of evolution, man also developed an adaptive aggression, or what Lorenz refers to as "militant enthusiasm." But men—and rats—failed to develop instinctive mechanisms against killing their own kind. Lorenz sees the advent of weapons as a turning point. Before weapons, men were probably given to flight rather than aggression, but as tools and weapons developed, he increasingly became a killer of his own species.

Some authorities believe that a crucial factor in human aggression was the distance between the combatants that weapons permitted. As Desmond Morris wrote in *The Naked Ape,* "The moment that attacking is done from such a distance that the appeasement signals of the losers cannot be read by the winners, then violent aggression is going to go raging on." Modern weapons, he adds, allow for aggression at such distances that "the result is wholesale slaughter on a scale unheard of in any other species."

Lorenz describes aggression as being a "true autonomous instinct: it has its own appetitive behavior, its own releasing mechanisms, and, like sexual urge or any other strong instinct, it engenders a specific feeling of intense satisfaction. The strength of its seductive lure explains why men may behave as irrationally and immorally in their political as in their sexual lives. . . ."

Lorenz and Morris pretty much agree that aggression explains why men go to war. War provides an object for releasing aggression against a hated enemy, whether concrete or abstract—Jews, tyrants or capitalism, fascism, etc. Under some inspiring leader, surrounded by members of the group with similar feelings, war sanctions man's desire to kill. Lorenz recognizes that war can sometimes be justified as purely a matter of self-defense, but he emphasizes that war can also be a situation for the release of a "mechanism of behavior whose animal properties bring with them the danger that he will kill his brother" without reason, but persuaded that he is doing so in pursuit of the highest and most noble motives.

Many ethnologists, including Lorenz, have observed in some animals an instinct to stake out a territory and to defend it against either all intruders, or, in some cases, only against intruders of the same species. Whereas many scientists have been reluctant to posit such an instinct in man, Robert Ardrey, a journalist with some scientific credentials, created quite an impact with *Territorial Imperative*, which is based on the theory that man is no different from other animals in his instinctive protection of territory. "If we defend the title to our land or the sovereignty of our country," he wrote, "we do it for reasons no different, no less innate, nor less ineradicable, than the lower animals. The dog barking at you from behind his master's fence acts from a motive indistinguishable from that of his master when the fence was built."

As the territorial imperative serves physiological and psychological functions in animals, Ardrey explains, so it does in man. He speculates that for *homo sapiens* the staking out and defense of territory serves three needs: identity, security, and stimulation. And war is particularly well-suited for the gratification of these needs. "In a subtle fashion, war provides identity for all, from commanding general to private"; even those at home feel a greater sense of group identity than at other times. War also serves to satisfy the need for security: "The predator fights for a net gain in security, whether in loot, land, slaves, or the confusion of enemies. The defender, on the other hand, fights to conserve security, and to destroy those forces that threaten it."

On the opposition side, the contributors to *Man and Aggression* present a variety of arguments and evidence. Several authorities, for example, question the accuracy of analogies between animals and man. Kenneth Boulding points out that very little can be gleaned from what prehistoric man left that tells us much about his behavior, and he raises the question of whether the study of a monkey today tells us what a monkey was like two million years ago. "In jumping from monkeys to man, therefore, we are really making two leaps in the dark, one from the monkey back to man's common ancestor, and again from this ancestor to man." In this essay, titled "Am I a Man or a Mouse—or Both?", he concludes: "We have not learned aggression, however, from our remote biological ancestors, nor have we learned territoriality from them. Insofar as aggression or territoriality play a part in human culture—and they do—each generation learns them from the previous generation and perhaps in a lesser degree from its own physical environment and random events."

Anthropologist Geoffrey Gorer, in "Man Has No 'Killer' Instinct," states that there is no doubt that man "has no inhibitions against killing his fellowmen who do not belong to the same pack. . . ." But, he argues, this does not mean that killing is based on instinct. If there were a killer instinct, then societies universally would exhibit similar patterns of violence, which is not the case. He mentions a number of primitive cultures as examples of societies that do not kill each other within their own tribe or others, even though they possess the weapons to do so. The reason for this pacifism is that these peoples are not reared to violent behavior. Their values emphasize enjoyment and peace; demonstrations of bravery and virility and forms of aggressiveness are frowned upon.

Because the nature versus nurture controversy is still unresolved, the teacher shouldn't expect the class to come to any definite conclusions about what theories are valid and which should be discarded as unproved. To draw the opposing arguments together, it does seem clear that man can have a capacity for aggressiveness, including killing members of his own species as individuals or in groups, and that the nature and intensity of the aggressive behavior is largely determined by the social environment. Most social scientists would agree with anthropologist Napoleon Chagnon that "cultural systems define and regulate the circumstances under which expressions of aggression are permitted, what form they take, against what or whom they are directed and the legitimate means of such expressions." In some cultures, the threshold of violent conflict is low; in others it is high. For example, the National Commission on the Causes and Prevention of Violence found that the United States has the highest rate of violent crime of all "modern stable nations."

Although man's aggressive tendencies give us some clues to an understanding of violence, they do not explain the large-scale violence that occurs among nations. As Gordon Allport wrote, "however pugnacious or frustrated an individual may be, he himself lacks the capacity to make organized warfare. He is capable of temper tantrums, also of chronic nagging, biting sarcasm, or personal cruelty, but he alone cannot invade an alien land or drop bombs upon a distant enemy to give vent to his emotions." World War I did not begin because the population of the opposing states reached a level of hostility that spilled over into war. A nuclear war between the United States and the Soviet Union would hardly result from a crescendo of aggressive feelings in hundreds of millions of people in the two countries. It may be that war depends upon the hostile attitudes of important segments of people who sanction the action of leaders in going to war; and, once war has begun, it is clear that its prosecution over an extended period of time requires sustained aggressive feeling among masses of people. The next chapter will outline ways of helping students to understand some of the psychological factors involved in creating and sustaining hostility among people—hostility that enables them to condone or participate in large-scale violence.

BIBLIOGRAPHY

The World Law Fund is preparing a book of *Readings in World Order*, edited by Gerald Hardcastle, which will include selections from Lorenz, Ardrey, *et al.* (See Resources section, page 164, for address.) The Education Development Center, in its material for *Man: A Course of Study,* includes a number of "Seminars For Teachers," one of which is on the subject "Is Man Innately Aggressive?" The booklet offers brief selections from a number of different points of view.

Fried, Morton, *et al.* (eds.), *War: The Anthropology of Armed Conflict and Aggression* (Natural History Press, 1968), 262 pages, $2.95.

Fromm, Erich, *War Within Man* (American Friends Service Committee, 1963), 56 pages, $.35.

3

Some Psychological
Factors in War

Why to Teach Them and How

HUMANS RESPOND TO STIMULI AND EVENTS AROUND THEM
in ways that shed some light on why men fight and kill
each other. These psychological "mechanisms" are by
no means innate, and do not, in themselves, any more
than aggression, adequately explain why millions of people can be mobilized into groups to fight other groups
in the complex phenomenon called war. Although they
don't provide all the answers, an awareness of these
mechanisms is important to an understanding of the
causes and nature of war.

So much of the literature in this area consists of scholarly studies by psychologists, social psychologists, and sociologists, that it would be very difficult to put together a selection of readings that students could understand. Consequently, it might be best for the teacher to outline for the students the concepts mentioned here. These concepts by no means include all of the findings on the psychological bases for men's ability to wage war. The presentation does not have to be strictly lecture, since the students will certainly be able to contribute examples of the behavior described. For this reason, a set of possible discussion questions are included in this chapter.

What Are They?

Perception

A basic factor in determining our attitudes towards others is, naturally enough, our perception of them— what we believe them to be, whether the belief is accurate or not. In other words, if we perceive someone as an "enemy," we will have certain negative feelings concerning everything about him; if we consider another country as the "enemy," even the symbols (flag, etc.) of that country will evoke a negative response. The role of perception will be discussed more fully in the next chapter in connection with the role of nationalism in war. At this point, it should be sufficient to point out that if we are perceiving another group as an enemy, this enables us to act towards them in certain ways we would not otherwise be inclined to act. On the basis of their previous experience with conflict, students should be able to point out examples of how the perceptions of opposing forces influenced behavior.

Displacement

Displacement is a term psychologists use to explain the common mechanism by which people may vent aggressive feelings on someone or something more acceptable than was the source of such feelings. This behavior is well illustrated by the child who "for no reason" gets angry at a toy rather than a parent, for whom he is ex-

"On the bright side, the Chinese are not so inscrutable as they used to be."

Drawing by Joseph Mirachi.
Copyright © 1967 Saturday Review, Inc.

pected to express affection and gratitude and from whom he may fear punishment.

The object of such displaced anger is frequently referred to as a scapegoat. It may be some weaker or "different" child in the playground; among nations, it may be a group or country that appears to have the attributes of weakness or of being "different." The most familiar historical example, of course, was the treatment of Jews in Nazi Germany. For many Germans, encouraged by a government policy, the Jews were a convenient and defenseless target against which individuals could vent personal frustrations or could compensate for the sense of humiliation engendered by defeat in World War I and years of economic chaos. Moreover, guilt for feelings and behavior toward Jews could be largely obviated by the official stereotyped view that they were not really "human."

The phenomenon of displacement and the corollary of stereotyping have been observed in the war in Vietnam. American soldiers, suffering from the bitterness of seeing friends killed and from the exhaustion of long and brutal fighting, have been guilty of killing Vietnamese civilians. Jonathan Schell, in an article in *The New Yorker*, observed a willingness on the part of some Americans to bomb and shell by artillery fire Vietnamese villages that were suspected of being pro-Viet Cong. One private that Schell interviewed said, "The trouble is, no one sees the Vietnamese as people. They're not people. Therefore, it does not matter what you do to them."

Remote Killing

The war in Vietnam, and modern warfare in general, provide many examples of human insensitivity to what is remote or beyond the sense of sight and sound. Much of the killing in war is now accomplished in such a way that the individual dropping a bomb or firing an artillery weapon does not have to witness the human suffering that results. James Reston pointed out, in a *New York Times* editorial on the alleged atrocity at My Lai, that B-52 bombers and long-range artillery have hit many similar villages in the "free fire zone." "The only difference," Reston said, "in the attack of Company C was that they saw the human beings in the village, and killed them with their M-16s anyway, and then told their story on TV. But, in other ways, in long-distance artillery fire and high-flying B-52 bombers, the same thing happens all the time and it never gets into the newspapers or on the television."

In World War II, remote killing was far more common than that in which the soldier witnessed the effect of his weapons; the nuclear bombs over Hiroshima and Nagasaki were dramatic examples. Future warfare may be expected to become even more remote. In a speech before the Association of the United States Army, General William Westmoreland stated: "On the battlefield of the future, enemy forces will be located, tracked, and targeted almost instantaneously through the use of datalinks, computer-assisted intelligence evaluation and automated fire control." He estimated that "no more than ten years should separate us from the automated battlefield." And, of course, ICBM's permit massive destruction on "targets" thousands of miles from the firing line.

The Megadeath Syndrome

Psychologists have observed that people possess an enormous capacity to become used to something unpleasant extended over a period of time. For example, people can live next to a subway or railroad track and gradually become able to ignore the sound of rumbling cars day and night. Television has now made it possible for people to experience vicariously violent and agonizing death in such places as Vietnam and Biafra almost on a daily basis. People, understandably, will not allow themselves to suffer continuously from witnessing the suffering of others. Somehow, the mind develops the capacity to block out the unpleasantness it is exposed to, especially when that unpleasantness is on a large scale. An editorial in the *Washington Post*, dealing with the diminishing concern over the situation in Biafra, where perhaps a million or two had died of starvation, described this mechanism as the "megadeath syndrome," which "goes to work, dulling compassion, reducing human suffering to the tolerable dimensions of 'politics.'"

Selective Inattention

Another mechanism related to war, especially to the possibilities of a nuclear World War III, is the screening out of unpleasant or threatening information, a process that psychiatrists have labeled "selective inattention." In its more positive function, this mechanism may enable people to live without the constant anxiety of their own frail existence or the possibility of death on every hand from, say, automobile accidents or diseases. On the other hand, this screening out process can also allow us to deny reality. Many Germans, for example, in the period after World War II refused to accept the fact that millions of Jews had been put to death in concentration camps during the war. In a similar fashion, many people deny the widely destructive force of nuclear weapons that threaten their own existence as well as the lives of millions of others, and continue to speak of "winning" a war between nuclear powers.

A closely related means of avoiding unpleasant realities has been pointed out in an article by Jerome Frank

contained in the World Law Fund's collection of readings for schools. In "Let Us Examine Our Attitude Toward Peace," Dr. Frank points out that people frequently
employ comforting words that do not convey an accurate
meaning. The word *defense,* for example, is applied to
our arsenal of nuclear weapons with the implication that
the word means "to protect from violence or attack;"
but, "It is perfectly clear that there is no defense against
atomic weapons. . . ." He cites other examples of such
words as *shield, balance of power, national security,* and
stalemate. One can add such expressions as *nuclear um-
brella* and *bomb-shelter,* which suggest protection in
nuclear war that is misleading but comforting. Also, a
number of words have come into use that tend to de-
humanize the effect of war. The word *target* is used to
refer to people; certain types of bombs are *anti-personnel*
weapons; the word *enemy* may be applied to a village
of Vietnamese peasants.

Discussion Questions

1. What are some examples from your own experience
of "displacing" feelings of anger, frustration, or hostility?
For example, did you ever blame a teacher for giving
an "unfair" test that you did poorly on?

2. What are some examples of scapegoats frequently
used in our society? How might a political figure—a
mayor or governor or president—become a scapegoat
for dissatisfied factions in the country? How have racial
and ethnic minorities been used as scapegoats?

3. In a recent riot in the predominantly black section
of a southern city, six people (all blacks) were killed,
scores were injured and dozens of fires were set by
rampaging mobs. In explaining the situation, the governor of the state said, "It's clear this was the work of the

Communists. It's all part of a plot and we all know it."
What psychological mechanism was the governor using?
Why did he blame the Communists?

4. Every year some 50,000 Americans are killed in
automobile accidents, but we are generally more affected by a picture of a single fatal accident. How would
you explain this? Can you think of other situations in
which we tend to ignore the statistics of suffering or
death?

BIBLIOGRAPHY

Farrell, John C. and Asa P. Smith (eds.), *Image and
Reality in World Politics* (Macmillan, 1965), 238 pages,
$2.45.

Frank, Jerome, *Sanity and Survival: Psychiatric Aspects
of War and Peace* (Random House, 1967), 330 pages,
$1.95.

Nesbitt, William, *Interpreting the Newspaper in the
Classroom: Foreign News and World Views* (Thomas Y.
Crowell Co., 1968, 1971), 128 pages, $2.50.

White, Ralph K., *Nobody Wanted War: Misperception in
Vietnam and Other Wars* (Doubleday, 1968), 346 pages,
$5.95.

FOR TEACHER PREPARATION

Group for the Advancement of Psychiatry, *Psychiatric
Aspects of the Prevention of Nuclear War*, Vol. 5, Report
No. 57, Sept., 1964, 96 pages.

Klineberg, Otto, *The Human Dimension in International
Conflict* (Holt, Rinehart & Winston, 1964), $4.25.

Lasswell, Harold D., *World Politics and Personal In-
security* (Macmillan, 1965), 238 pages, $2.45.

4

Do Nation-States Cause War?

THE SURVEY OF SOME OF THE PSYCHOLOGICAL BASES FOR violence and war may seem to imply that wars are caused by people acting in some capacity as a group. To some extent this is true, but what about the actual decision to go to war? When we speak of nations deciding to fight, we don't really mean that people *en masse* suddenly pick up weapons and head for the enemy. Instead, the outbreak of war involves decision-makers in government who, usually with the expectation that their people will support them, make the decision, mobilize the country, and conduct the war.

There is a tendency, in fact, to believe that the citizenry of a country is not responsible for war; they are simply led into it by the rulers of the country. One of the defense arguments used at the Nuremberg trials, for example, was that the defendants were only acting under orders—they had no responsibility for the acts they committed. Similarly, American involvement in Southeast Asia has raised questions about whether or not the decisions being made are subject to the traditional checks of our democratic system. But if an individual feels that war, or a particular war, is wrong or unjust, does he have to obey those leaders who order him to participate?

There are other questions involved in how wars are decided upon and how and why they are supported by the populace. Do the leaders of a country respond to the will of the people? Can any government, even a totalitarian one, force its people into war without first persuading them that the cause is just? On the other hand, in an age of push-button warfare, and in the complexity of an international crisis, is it possible for the leaders of a country to leave the decision-making up to the people, or even the people's elected representatives?

Social scientists, statesmen, journalists, and "ordinary" citizens have debated these questions for years. There are sound arguments on both sides of each question and probably no clear answer to any of them. The classroom ideas outlined here are not designed to provide those answers, but rather to help the student clarify his own thinking.

The Role of Decision-Makers: A Case Study

A good percentage of our young people are convinced that our country is run by the "Establishment," an amorphous group of industrialists, generals, and politicians who make decisions in their own selfish interests with little regard for the will of the people or the welfare of the nation. Although minds may not be changed by this study, it is important that students attempt a systematic and objective analysis of the subject. They should learn something of what is involved in the decision-making process, especially in a crisis situation. They should examine the motives and objectives of those involved. And they should see how difficult it is to assess the available information and to act on that information in a manner consistent with personal and national values, as well as with a consideration of "public opinion."

Any number of case studies would be satisfactory to illustrate the pressures placed on decision-makers, and the difficulties involved in making war/peace decisions in the modern international system. Some suggestions for using World War I as a case study are offered in Part IV of this book. It is a case study that is particularly useful in illustrating such factors as escalation and misperception. The Cuban Missile Crisis of 1962 is offered as a sample here because it illustrates certain aspects of the modern international system and also because there is a wealth of useful resources available.

Students should keep in mind the following questions:

1. Did the decision-makers on each side accurately perceive the intentions of the other side?

2. What actual steps were involved in the escalation of the crisis?

3. In what ways did time (or the lack of it) place added pressure on the men involved?

4. Did President Kennedy have access to all the information he needed?

5. To what extent did he have to rely on the advice of

his military advisors? What misgivings did he express about this advice?

6. What factors prevented the President from leaving the decisions up to Congress or the people?

7. How were international organizations (U.N., O.A.S.) involved? Could they have played a larger role in the crisis? Why or why not?

For classroom use, an excellent multi-media package, titled *Confrontation: The Cuban Missile Crisis,* has been produced by School Marketing, Inc. (1414 Sixth Ave. New York, N.Y. 10019). The unit includes readings from Soviet and Cuban sources as well as American, a sound-filmstrip and a simulation-game. The total effect of the package is to give the students a feeling of actually being involved in the crisis situation, creating a sort of gut-level awareness of the pressures involved.

Additional readings should include the following: Robert Kennedy's *Thirteen Days* (Mentor, 1968, 224 pages, $.95), which provides personal insights into the crisis; *The Missile Crisis* (Lippincott, 1966) by Elie Abel, a dramatic and well written account; and Theodore Sorenson's *Decision-Making in the White House* (Columbia University Press, 1963, 94 pages, $1.25), a book that covers some of the broader aspects of the decision-making process in addition to this particular event, and is particularly useful for examining the role of public opinion. The legal questions involved are explored in Quincey Wright's "International Law: The Cuba Quarantine of 1962," in *Power and Order: Six Cases in World Politics* (Harcourt, Brace & World, $3.75), edited by John G. Stoessinger and Alan F. Westin.

In a sense, the Cuban missile incident is atypical of international crises because both sides operated with constraint and reason. The teacher may want to raise some questions about how a future crisis might be different:

1. Might a future crisis find men less willing to act in such a sober fashion? Can you think of examples in history (e.g., Munich) where one side did not correctly perceive the intentions of the other; or where constraint seemed to give way to panic?

2. Will there always be time for reason to prevail? Can you construct a hypothetical incident in which time would force a decision-maker to act too hastily?

3. In future crises, will each side be willing to back down? Will one side or both be willing to allow the other to "save face"?

4. Is the international system as now constituted the best way to keep a lasting peace? Why or why not?

An interesting and useful essay or research project could be based on the following quotations from an article by Emile Benoit:

> Few truly comprehend that we are now in the strange position of being militarily dependent upon our opponents. . . . In effect, what has occurred is a *mass exchange of hostages,* leaving the population of the world's major cities subject to sudden slaughter by hostile governments. This is interdependence on a new plane of intensity: to an unbelievable and gruesome degree we now depend on each other's leaders to be rational, to be predictable, to be sane.
>
> "Interdependence on a Small Planet," *Columbia Journal of World Business,* Spring, 1966, p. 10.

The essay should be built around such questions as the following: Do you agree or disagree with Benoit's assessment? To what extent do you think he exaggerates? Does the Cuban Missile Crisis support or deny his arguments? Explain your answers with specific examples.

As we mentioned earlier, simulation games offer students at least the vicarious experience of being in the roles of decision-makers. *Dangerous Parallel,* for example, makes the players acutely aware of the dangers of misperception, of how difficult it is to determine what the other side intends to do, or how they might react to any decision you make. They also gain some experience with the problems of time and of communicating with one's own advisors as well as with representatives of the other "nations" involved. The "Decision-Maker's Checksheet," an integral part of the simulation, provides a conceptual framework to help the student consider such factors as whether or not his country has the resources to carry out a proposed decision, what the effect might be on public opinion, and whether or not the decision is a step toward peaceful resolution of the conflict.

An aspect of the decision-making process not directly dealt with in the above case study should certainly be the topic of a separate unit of study, namely, the question of where the decision-making power should lie in a democracy.

For many years, Americans have been concerned about the problems of executive decision-making. In an age when split-second decisions are needed, involving complex questions of diplomacy and strategy, is it possible for anyone but the President to make the decisions that may involve the fate of the nation or of the entire world? On the other hand, is it safe or wise to invest such awesome power and responsibility in one man? Does the nation have satisfactory checks over such situations as the war in Vietnam, or could executive (or military) decisions lead us into a much larger war contrary to our will or the national interests?

While no one has been able to establish a perfect

balance between executive and Congressional decision-making, the students can gain valuable insights by an analysis of both sides of the question, and by examination of some of the attempts at compromise. The subject is a natural for a debate topic.

For a brief analysis of both sides of the issue, as well as the attempts at compromise, the class could use Number 171 in the Foreign Policy Association's Headline Series, *Making Foreign Policy in a Nuclear Age: 1. Government and Public Opinion* (Foreign Policy Association, 64 pages, $1.00). The booklet deals with the following questions: Does the President have adequate authority to conduct the nation's foreign policy effectively? What is the proper role of Congress in the foreign policy making process? How might it be helped to play its role more effectively? Are secret intelligence agencies —the CIA and others—necessary to the conduct of our foreign policy?

For books dealing with arguments in favor of greater Congressional control, students can select from a number of available paperbacks: J. W. Fulbright's *The Arrogance of Power* (Vintage Books, 1967, 264 pages, $1.95); George McGovern's *A Time of War, a Time of Peace* (Vintage Books, 1968, 203 pages, $1.65); or *American Militarism 1970* (The Viking Press, 1970, 150 pages, $.95), edited by Erwin Knoll and Judith Nies McFadden, a book consisting primarily of statements by a number of Senators and Congressmen.

For arguments in favor of strong executive control over foreign policy, appropriate selections could be taken from the following: Robert Goldwin (ed.), *Readings in American Foreign Policy* (Oxford University Press, 1959, 709 pages, $2.20); James Rosenau (ed.), *Domestic Sources of Foreign Policy* (Macmillan, 1967, 354 pages, $8.50);

Alan F. Westin (ed.), *The Uses of Power: Seven Cases in American Politics* (Harcourt, Brace & World, 375 pages, $4.25).

The Role of the People: Nationalism and War

Traditional courses in world or modern history normally include some mention of the emergence of modern nationalism, associating it with the "age of revolution," and giving some indication of its relationship with the changing nature of war (e.g., the popular armies of the French Revolution replacing the professional armies of the Middle Ages). Most texts also indicate that nationalism itself is frequently a contributing cause of international conflict and war. The Spanish-American War and World War I are frequently cited as cases in which a heightened sense of patriotism was an underlying, if not a direct, cause of the wars.

Students, of course, readily grasp these analyses, and they well understand the quasi-religious nature of national loyalty, such as is typified in this description by John Good:

> As a citizen of a nation-state, the individual associates himself with other individuals in common loyalty and action, as he does in an organized religion. Like religion, nationalism is developed through symbols. The national flag replaces the Christian cross, and the national anthem becomes the foremost hymn of the new religion. The hundreds of thousands of Americans who visit Washington, D.C. are, in a way, making a pilgrimage to a national shrine. The heroes of a nation's history become the saints of this new religion. Nationalism has also proved as intolerant of non-conformists as

religion, and, like religion, the nation asks men to sacrifice their property and their lives.

John Good, *The Shaping of Western Society* (Holt, Rinehart & Winston, 1968).

Young people today, however, are likely to feel that such strong feelings do not apply to them; they are too "sophisticated" to feel such blind loyalty to the state, and they are quick to criticize their texts and their teachers for trying to indoctrinate them with patriotic slogans and symbols. To some extent, their criticism is just—our educational structure does place a preponderant importance on building loyal citizens. If the study of the role of nationalism in war/peace matters is conducted in an objective and rational way, they will come to understand that national perspectives (including their own) do differ, and that these differences have a bearing on war/peace questions.

Most of us, for example, including our students, are not even aware of the ethnocentric goggles through which we look at the world. National groups tend to have an image of their country as having a monopoly on virtue and certain other countries as having a monopoly on evil. Through a human need to make sense out of the world, people tend to filter or interpret incoming "messages" to fit their preconceptions.

To illustrate this "strain toward consistency" in our perception of images, the teacher might repeat a frequently used experiment, in which American fifth and sixth graders were asked to respond to a photograph of a Russian road lined with trees. When asked why the trees were there, typical answers were "so that people won't be able to see what is going on beyond the road" and "it's to make work for prisoners." However, when asked why American roads had trees, the answers were very different—"for shade" or "to keep the dust down." Considering the changing nature of the Cold War, it might be useful to try a variation by indicating that the road is in Cuba or China, rather than the Soviet Union, since stereotyped impressions of the two former countries tend to be more rigid.

The New Dimensions book, *Interpreting the Newspaper in the Classroom: Foreign News and World Views* contains a number of classroom exercises designed to illustrate how previous learning and experience influence our perceptions. One of these exercises, developed for The High School Curriculum Center in Government at Indiana University, is particularly useful in showing how national perspectives influence one's view of reality, a somewhat more sophisticated version of the experiment mentioned above. Here is a description of the exercise as presented in the New Dimensions book:

> In the Indiana project, students are shown ten 35 mm color slides of political symbols: the American flag, the Communist Chinese flag, the Statue of Liberty, the Presidential Seal, the Lenin Medal, a Nazi poster, a United States Marine monument, a Soviet political rally, President Nixon, and St. Basil's Cathedral in Moscow. (Other symbols may, of course, be substituted for these.) As the slides are shown, the student records his response on a scale, using one for each slide, or ten scales in all.

Very bad feeling	Bad feeling	Little or no feeling	Good feeling	Very good feeling

After the slides have been shown and students have recorded their reactions, the teacher can build a frequency distribution scale. It is important, however, that this be done in such a way that students do not know how other individual members of the class have reacted. A typical scale might look like the following:

	VBF	BF	LNF	GF	VGF
American flag				10	15
Communist Chinese flag	10	12	3		
Statue of Liberty				18	7
Presidential Seal			5	15	5
Lenin Medal	4	15	6		
Nazi poster	2	8	15		
U.S. Marine monument			4	18	3
Soviet political rally		10	15		
President Nixon	1	2	2	15	5
St. Basil's Cathedral		2	22	1	

With the results visible on the blackboard or projected on a screen, the teacher may begin to inquire into the meaning of the data. In the example, several patriotic American symbols with responses on the right-hand columns in the frequency distribution scale are clear. But what about President Nixon (or some other political figure)? Students will soon discover that their responses have to do with political attitudes—usually acquired from their family.

Some slides in the example were clearly recognized as Communist symbols, and students indicated a strong negative response. The Nazi poster did not evoke the response that might have been expected, because Nazism is ancient history to ninth graders. St. Basil's was not recognized as a Russian Church by most students. The students might be told that the church is in Red Square in Moscow and then asked how they would change their responses.

The exercise should vividly demonstrate to the student that his response to symbols that represent or are threatening to American cultural values is influenced by past learning, stereotypes and expectations. They may also come to realize that they would have responded differently to the symbols had they been brought up in another country, especially a Communist one. In sum, they may learn the profound fact that they have "pictures in their heads" to which they respond. They differ among themselves in their pictures, and the group's pictures may be very different from those of students their own age in another nation.

William H. Nesbitt, *Interpreting the Newspaper in the Classroom: Foreign News and World Views* (Thomas Y. Crowell, 1971).

Other mechanisms of perception that influence how one views other nations and cultures are described in Jerome Frank's *Sanity and Survival.* It would be worthwhile to have one or more students read Chapter Seven, "The Image of the Enemy," and report to the rest of the class some of the things psychologists are learning about this subject. The description of some recent experiments in such areas as fear of the unknown will be especially intriguing. One experiment described by Frank, for example, involved an attempt to increase anxiety by putting the subjects through a "stress interview." Preparation for the experiment required putting the subjects in a laboratory and attaching electrodes to their arms and legs to measure the physiological response. The experimenters were surprised to discover that the students showed more anxiety about the preparations than the stress interview, because "they were apparently frightened by the strange room full of equipment and by uncertainty as to what was going to happen to them." Similarly, Frank concludes, "it has been suggested that mutual anxiety at the international level is greatest when each country knows enough about the other to recognize that it has the power to inflict harm, but does not know enough to be sure of its intent or of how much power it actually has."

Another way of treating this subject, and at the same time of counterbalancing the ethnocentric approach of most social studies texts, would be to have the students compare accounts in any standard American history text, with selections about the same events in *As Others See Us: International Views of American History*. This book covers some of the major events in American history as described in high school texts of other countries, both nations that are friendly with the United States and some that are not.

Some of the accounts will show a sharply different interpretation of an event than the students will find in the American text, because the national and ideological viewpoints are so different. A selection from an East German textbook, for example, opens with this paragraph on the subject of U.S. relations with Cuba:

> After the United States imperialists had been unable to prevent victory of the people's revolution in Cuba in 1959–1962, and when the landing of Cuban counter-revolutionaries met with bloody failure in April, 1961, the anti-Communist hysteria in the United States rose to the point of preparation for an attack against socialist Cuba. Piratical attacks along the Cuban coast increased; subversives were parachuted from airplanes; Havana was shelled by artillery. The reactionary circles in the United States attempted to justify their planned aggression with the ridiculous assertion that Cuba threatened the security of the United States.
>
> *As Others See Us: International Views of American History* (Houghton Mifflin, 1969), p. 171.

In some cases, the nationalistic or ideological shading will be considerably more subtle, such as this excerpt from a selection in a Finnish textbook, dealing with the Vietnam war:

> The United States began to give technical aid to South Vietnam, but when it began to lose in battle in spite of everything, the United States itself entered the struggle. In 1965 large numbers of American troops

were sent to South Vietnam. At the same time air attacks were carried out almost daily against North Vietnam.

Thus, the United States staked its entire military and political prestige on a war where the danger was constantly growing that the conflict could develop into a Third World War.

As Others See Us: International Views of American History (Houghton Mifflin, 1969), p. 174.

The point to stress in these comparisons is not the veracity of each account, but the ways in which nationalistic and ideological factors influence the way the event is treated. Discussions could center around the following questions: What particular words or phrases indicate a particular slant? Are some facts exaggerated, toned down, or left out in some of the accounts; how are these facts treated differently in other accounts? Which of the selections you read seemed most fair or objective? Why?

A somewhat similar exercise has been developed by the Foreign Policy Association in a case study analyzing how national and ideological perspectives influence news accounts of an event. Titled *The Nationalization of the Suez Canal Co., 1956: A Case Study in Analyzing News Accounts* (Foreign Policy Association, $2.50 for classroom kit), the classroom kit contains seventeen articles and editorials from various countries, all dealing with the same international crisis. In the introductory exercise, the students do not know the source of the account they are given, but must try to analyze what country it might be from on the basis of the nationalist or ideological interpretation presented.

In addition to understanding some of the ways in which a sense of identity with the nation influences behavior and attitudes, the class should also gain some awareness of how leaders use national loyalties to gain support and, on the other side of the coin, how much influence the people may have over specific decisions made by Congress or the President. As illustrations of the former, the teacher could analyze some of the persuasive methods used by Franklin Roosevelt, or President Nixon's Vietnam speech of November 3, 1969. The students will see how presidents can rally the support of the people in time of crisis by appealing to their national loyalties. The opinion polls[1] taken immediately before and after Nixon's speech would provide some indication of the degree of success, however temporary, achieved by that particular effort.

Examples of popular influence on a decision could be drawn from accounts of the debate over President Woodrow Wilson's futile struggle to persuade Congress and the American people that the United States should be a member of the League of Nations. A more current case is provided by the coalescence of anti-Vietnam war feeling in this country in the spring of 1968, which may have been the major factor in Lyndon Johnson's decision not to seek re-election.

The debate over U.S. involvement in Southeast Asia might also be used as a case study in exploring the influence of interest groups and the mass media on both public opinion and on governmental decision-making. Some political scientists argue that pressure groups or the news media can affect a decision by swinging patriotic feelings either for or against the government's position. Other observers, while recognizing that these two sources have *some* influence, raise serious questions about

---

[1] Two of the major polling services who will supply results of their national opinion surveys are Information Services, Louis Harris and Associates, Inc., One Rockefeller Plaza, New York, N.Y. 10020; and Dr. George Gallup, The Gallup Poll, 53 Bank Street, Princeton, New Jersey 08540.

how decisive that influence can be. Students should have some acquaintance with the arguments on both sides. If an historical case study is preferred, perhaps the classic example used by social scientists is the role played by pressure groups and newspapers in stirring up public feeling against the Spanish prior to the Spanish-American War, creating popular pressure on President McKinley that, some argue, made it difficult for him to avoid going to war. *The Splendid Little War* (Little Brown, 1958, $12.50) by Frank Freidel, has some excellent material on this subject.

War and Personal Values

This generation of high school students has grown up with the seemingly endless debate over U.S. involvement in South Vietnam. The questions involved are rather symbolic of the ambiguity young people must learn to live with in the closing decades of this century. World War II, the Korean War, and the confrontations of the Cold War didn't present such a cloudy picture; we could still visualize international conflicts as being between "the good guys" and "the bad guys," and few people questioned the morality of their government's policies.

The debate over Vietnam, of course, has been quite different and has raised serious questions about whether or not our government is doing what is right. Even before they reach draft age, young people have wrestled with this issue, and with the draft and actual participation in the conflict so close to many of them, it's little wonder that they're concerned. If school curriculums are to be relevant, this is clearly one of the topics we must help students deal with as intelligently as possible.

Some good classroom material on the moral issues of war has been developed by the Harvard Social Studies Project, and published in a 63-page booklet titled *The Limits of War; National Policy and World Conscience.* Brief historical background is offered on the evolution of the methods of war and on man's efforts to place certain limits on war. The major portion of the text deals with the Nuremberg Trials and the decision to use the atomic bomb in 1945. Following the pattern used in the other booklets in the Project's series, the principles established by the readings are then applied to other cases. In connection with the Nuremberg Trials, for example, the students read three short "analogous cases": one, on the handling of the resettlement of the Creek Indians by the United States Government in the 1830's; the second, describing the case of Captain Howard Levy, a U.S. Army medical officer who refused to train medical aid-men for the Green Berets; and the third, presenting a fictionalized account of a free-speech controversy based on an incident at the University of California at Berkeley.

Specific questions help the students see how complex the issues are, as in this sample from the accompanying teacher's guide:

> When students use the word "people" in discussions of international violence, they sometimes mean Americans; they sometimes mean all mankind. It is useful to make this ambiguity explicit. For example, a student might decide that the atomic bomb should have been dropped on Japan because doing so "saved lives." But whose lives were saved: American? Japanese? Both? Suppose that the bombs saved some American lives at the expense of many Japanese lives? Does it really make a difference that the Japanese are racially different? Would it have been more difficult to drop the atomic bomb on Rome? Would students feel differently

about the bombing of Nagasaki after learning that it had a large Catholic population?

A teacher's guide to *The Limits of War; National Policy and World Conscience* (Harvard Social Studies Project, 63 pages).

The concluding section of the booklet presents a hypothetical war situation in the future, developing out of a crisis in Brazil in the year 1981.

Other materials dealing with the issue of war and individual conscience have been suggested in a special issue of *Intercom* titled *Conscience and War: The Moral Dilemma* (vol. 11, November/December, 1969, Center For War/Peace Studies, 218 East 18th Street, New York, N.Y., 10003, $1.50). The booklet covers such topics as "Historical Notes on Conscience and Conscription in America" and "Types of Responses to War and the Draft." It could profitably be read by the class as well as the teacher. There is also a good bibliography of books, articles, and films, including a section on "Justifications of War and Violence."

BIBLIOGRAPHY

Carr, Albert Z., *A Matter of Life and Death: How Wars Get Started—Or Are Prevented* (Viking, 1966), $4.50.

Galt, Thomas F., *Peace and War: Man-Made* (Beacon Press, 1963), $3.95.

Handlin, Oscar, *et al.*, *Dissent, Democracy and Foreign Policy: A Symposium* (Foreign Policy Association, 1968), 47 pages, $1.00.

Hollins, Elizabeth J. (ed.), *Peace Is Possible: A Reader on World Order* (Grossman, 1967), 350 pages, $2.00;

also available: "A Study Guide for Peace Is Possible," by Robert S. Hirschfield (World Law Fund, 1967).

King, Edward, Jr., *War and Conscience in America* (Westminster Press, 1968), 144 pages, $1.65.

O'Brien, William, *War and/or Survival* (Doubleday, 1968), 216 pages, $4.95.

Schlissel, Lillian (ed.), *Conscience in America: A Documentary History of Conscientious Objection in America, 1795–1967* (E. P. Dutton, 1968), 444 pages, $2.75.

FOR TEACHER PREPARATION

Almond, Gabriel, *The American People and Foreign Policy* (Praeger, 1960), 269 pages, $2.75.

Holsti, K. J., *International Politics: A Framework for Analysis* (Prentice-Hall, 1967), $8.50.

Niebuhr, Reinhold, *Moral Man and Immoral Society* (Scribners, 1960), 248 pages, $1.45.

Mark, Max, *Beyond Sovereignty* (Washington, D.C., Public Affairs Press), 1965.

Patrick, John, *Political Socialization of American Youth: Review of Research with Implications for Secondary Social Studies* (Washington, D.C., National Council for the Social Studies, 1968).

Pruitt, Dean G., and Richard C. Snyder (eds.), *Theory and Research in the Causes of War* (Prentice-Hall, 1969), 314 pages, $4.95.

PART II

WAR AND THE INTERNATIONAL SYSTEM

In organizing a conceptual framework for the study of war/peace concepts, the materials presented so far have concentrated on man and the state. In this section, we will deal with some of the ways in which the international system creates an environment in which war is not only possible, but some would say, inevitable. Our objectives should be to create some understanding of the modern international system, the ways in which it is changing, and the elements within it that are conducive to violence as well as those that may be steps toward peace and stability.

1

Understanding the International System

AN ADEQUATE UNDERSTANDING OF THE INTERNATIONAL system is not something that can be achieved within the confines of a single course, or even within the span of the individual's school years. Major curriculum reforms, including courses other than the social studies, are needed to help our young people understand how the system functions, how the different parts of it are interrelated, and how it affects their daily lives. The need for sweeping changes in our concept of, and approaches to, international education is the subject of the New Dimensions book, *International Education for Spaceship Earth* (Thomas Y. Crowell Co., 1968, 1970, 128 pages).

For our purposes here, it will be sufficient to concentrate on three concepts that seem particularly important for an understanding of war/peace issues:

1. the growing interrelatedness of man, including the development of something that might be called "global society";

2. the persistence of the nation-state system as the basic political fact of the world system;

3. changes that have occurred, or are occurring, in the international system that have a direct bearing on war/peace questions.

In other words, students should see that there is increased contact and communication among the peoples of the world, because of and as a result of a growing body of rules, laws, and customs to regulate this growing interrelatedness. At the same time, the nation-state system represents something of a counter-trend, isolating people into separate and frequently conflicting groups. The combination of the forces of nationalism and internationalism creates constant changes and stresses within the international system—changes that are of vital importance to issues of war and peace.

To understand the full implications of man's growing interrelatedness, we should try to develop an understanding of the "systemness" of the emerging global society. The teacher will have little difficulty putting across the idea of a system as any set of interrelated parts. A simple and obvious example is the heating system of a house, with its interconnected elements, furnace, fuel supply, pipes, thermostat, etc. If there is a breakdown in one part of the system, it will affect the other parts of the system.

The students will easily make the transition from this simple illustration to other, more complicated systems—systems that they are familiar with, but probably haven't thought of as being a set of interrelated parts. Ask them to point out ways in which a family functions as a system, and from there go on to other examples in the local community to give them the idea that we live in a complex network of systems—social, political, transportation, communications, etc.

On a global level, students should see that man's growing interrelatedness involves more than simply the interaction among political units. To give them some idea of the many levels involved in this global society, the teacher might read to the class the following excerpt from an editorial in *The Saturday Review*:

> A new musical comedy erupts into success on Broadway and within a matter of weeks its tunes are heard all the way from London to Johannesburg, as though they had pre-existed and were waiting only for a signal from the United States to spring to life. Or a new movie about the Russia of a half-century ago will be made from a book and all over the world the theme song from *Doctor Zhivago* will be a request favorite of orchestras in far-off places, from Edmonton to Warsaw.
>
> Few things are more startling to Americans abroad than to see youngsters affect the same unconventionalities of dress and manner, whether in Stockholm, Singapore or Sydney. The young girls with their flashing thighs on Carnaby Street in London or on the ginza in Tokyo; the young rakes with their long hair and turtleneck sweaters (with or without beads) in Greenwich Village or the Left Bank or Amsterdam or Hong Kong—all seem to have been fashioned by the same stylists of alienation and assertion.
>
> Or a fashion designer in Paris will decide to use spikes instead of heels on women's shoes, and women across the world will wobble with the same precarious gait. Then, almost as suddenly, the designer will decide to bring women back to earth again, flattening the heels and producing square or wide toes that only a

few years earlier would have been regarded as acceptable only for heavy work in the fields—and once again the world's women will conform.

The same sort of interrelatedness operates in the area of international conflict. An event in one part of the globe can have almost instantaneous ramifications elsewhere. The point is well illustrated in the following:

> Civil disturbances in the Congo and in South Vietnam have their repercussions in New York, Moscow, and Peking; crop failure in India calls forth a response from the American midwest; nuclear explosive power unites men around the world in the fear of holocaust and the dread of environmental contamination; physical changes on the surfaces of the sun affect man's ability to communicate with his fellow men; complex sensors located in artificial earth satellites reveal guarded secrets concerning the capabilities of another group; a desert war east of Suez threatens to bring the industrial machinery of Europe to a grinding halt; new ideological notes struck on the taut strings of Balkan societies set up entirely new patterns of harmony and disharmony in world affairs.
>
> Raymond E. Platig, *International Relations Research* (Carnegie Endowment, 1966), p. 2.

A good exercise to bring home to the students the interrelatedness of the system is to have them list, from reading a good daily newspaper or a weekly news magazine, the events occurring in various parts of the globe that set off reverberations elsewhere. A more elaborate approach is to have them code these events, place the codes on a world map, and then draw lines to the other parts of the planet where some reaction occurred. Usually, the events will be fairly easy to trace—an anti-war demonstration in Washington causes reactions in Hanoi, Saigon, Peking, Moscow and perhaps a few other political capitals. If you asked them, however, to locate the areas affected by a change of price or policy by some large multinational corporation—say, Standard Oil or IBM—they would find that an impossible cobweb of lines would be needed. (Some international airlines will supply maps of their air routes, significant in themselves, and these maps would be particularly useful when national boundaries aren't shown.)

As contacts across national boundaries have increased, so has the body of rules by which nations and groups operate within the international system. This cooperative side of history has been much neglected in social studies textbooks, perhaps because—as in news broadcasts—the dramatic and violent are more interesting.

A brief survey of the development of international law, and the growing areas of cooperation in such areas as economics and technology is important for the students to see that nation-states (or their governments) are not the only actors on the world stage, and even within the nation-state system there are important instances of cooperation. To fill this gap, individual students could be assigned short readings in *Peace Is Possible: A Reader on World Order* (Grossman, 1967, 350 pages, $2.00) edited by Elizabeth J. Hollins. Reports to the rest of the class would create at least some feeling for the important developments that have been taking place and what possibilities they might offer for the future.

But, as we mentioned earlier, students should also see that there is something of a counter-trend, a splintering of the world into separate groups that limits the extent of world integration. An objective and balanced picture of these opposing forces is presented by Lincoln Bloomfield. Here is a brief excerpt from Bloomfield's analysis:

> Clearly, some of the trends . . . do argue for more integration. All the technically based trends toward

more bigness, for example, call for larger-than-national units. Some require the creation of customs unions and common markets, as in Western Europe and Central America today. Others involve the transfer of limited political authority to a central power, whether the UN or some other institution, as a practical means of tackling such worldwide problems as deteriorating ecological conditions, or the need for rules regulating the use of outer space and the seabed. Finally, developments in modern weaponry urgently call for arms limitation and reduction, although national sensitivity and mistrust make supranational control least promising in this area, however desirable in theory.

But some of the trends cited also argue for less integration, and even disintegration, accompanied by greater tribal exclusiveness, clannishness, nationalism and xenophobia. . . . No doubt narrow nationalism is the unmistakable enemy of a greater sense of world community. But nationalism can also be a creative force. In Eastern Europe nationalism is likely to express itself not so much in exclusivism as in filling a vacuum left by the failure of communism as an ideology.

Lincoln Bloomfield, *The U.N. and World Order* (Foreign Policy Association, Headline Series, No. 197, 1969, 62 pages, $1.00), pp. 30–31.

In addition to nationalism and internationalism, the class should also be aware of other significant trends and forces that shape the international system. Most American and world history texts present coverage of some of the significant patterns that have occurred over the course of this century: the shifting balance of power; the changing nature of national power, with the Soviet Union and the United States emerging as the superpowers; the division of the world into Cold War blocs, and the resulting confrontations; the efforts to achieve security through military strength and alliances; the struggle for independence and nationhood on the part of the peoples of the Third World. Background knowledge of all these developments should be included in any course covering war and war prevention.

Another development that may have significant bearing on the subject of war/peace is the widening gap between the rich nations and the poor nations—a gap that many observers feel raises more serious threats to world peace and stability than does the division of the globe into Communist and non-Communist camps. The pressures of population increase and the "revolution of rising expectations" are threats to the industrialized nations as well. But the developing countries also face other pressures that lead to instability and unrest; for many, the desperate struggle for modernization requires the breakdown of traditional social structures, value systems, village life, and so on. For others, like Kenya or Nigeria, the attempt to create a nation in more than name only sets up frequently violent conflicts involving tribalism, localism, or racial issues.

Since few texts relate this growing dichotomy to the possibilities of large-scale violence or war, some additional readings are suggested. Selections from the works of economists like Barbara Ward, Gunnar Myrdal, and Kenneth Boulding are available in paperback form, and all three present their arguments in highly readable prose, offering insights that the students will find stimulating and thought-provoking. Frantz Fanon's *The Wretched of the Earth* will make vividly clear how the world looks to radical elements in the developing nations, as would the testimony of guerrilla fighter Regis Debray (available in a reprint titled "Revolution: Violent and Nonviolent," *Liberation* Magazine, February 1968, 28 pages, $.35).

A good collection of essays on the subject of the rich/poor gap is *Man Against Poverty: World War III*, which stresses the threat the gap poses to world peace and stability. The book includes selections by Senator J. William

Fulbright, Michael Harrington, Oscar Lewis, Robert L. Heilbroner, and Barbara Ward. The following excerpt indicates how serious the problem looks to one contributor and how it is related to the danger of war:

> Today the issue is above all one of keeping faith. Better shares and progressive taxation helped to raise up the poor and create the modern market *inside* domestic society. We have to believe that similar policies, conducted as steadily, will have the same economic effect on the world at large—and will in addition profoundly influence political attitudes by ending the picture of wealthy white colonialists exploiting the "helpless" peoples of the developing world. Such a change is not a matter of policy or machinery. These are largely available. The World Bank, the International Development Authority, the International Monetary Fund, the United Nations Special Fund—all these organizations contain enough skilled and experienced men to run the economic organs of a world authority. The sums involved are relatively puny—some $12 billion a year, compared with the $120 billion the developed world, Capitalist and Communist together, spend on a system of armed security which threatens them both with extinction. As the only means available to counter the grievances which lead to war, it looks positively cheap.
>
> *Man Against Poverty: World War III* (Vintage Books, 1968, 456 pages, $2.45), pp. 434–435; reprinted from Barbara Ward's *Nationalism and Ideology*.

The class should also examine the idea that the drive for national independence and modernization in the Third World nations has changed the nature of power in the modern world. Although there is no agreement on this, some observers feel that the enormous military power of even the United States is ineffective in the sort of ferment and unrest that exists in various parts of the developing world. The war in Vietnam is offered as the prime example of the inability of the superpowers to impose their will on other nations through military strength. A reading of portions of *The Crisis of Confidence* by Arthur M. Schlesinger, Jr. will illustrate how persuasive this argument is. Here is a brief portion of Schlesinger's thesis:

> The pathos of the present situation is that, just as America cannot unilaterally impose its will in Southeast Asia and Russia cannot unilaterally impose its will on the Middle East, so America and Russia together, even if they agreed on every detail of policy and worked together to put a common policy over, can no longer settle affairs in Southeast Asia and the Middle East. The events in the rest of the world have developed a life of their own—a future as well as a past of their own—and they are passing beyond the reach even of joint American-Russian dictation.
>
> Arthur M. Schlesinger, Jr., *The Crisis of Confidence* (Bantam, 1969, 237 pages, $1.25), pp. 140–141.

Because of the instability and unrest of much of the world, plus the steady development of increasingly destructive weapons that seem to be the only way the superpowers could exert their superior strength, many people have come to question whether the present nation-state system is capable of preventing war or of providing security. Many would agree with Kenneth Waltz in his statement that "With many sovereign states, with no system of enforceable law among them, with each state judging its grievances and ambitions according to the dictates of its own reason or desire—conflict, sometimes leading to war, is bound to occur." Kenneth Boulding put this pessimism in even stronger terms: "I believe the present international system to be one which has a significant probability built into it of irretrievable disaster for the human race." The following chapters will suggest some ways of studying some of the factors that make large-scale violence possible in the present international system.

BIBLIOGRAPHY

Benoit, Emile, "Interdependence on a Small Planet," *Columbia Journal of World Business*, 1966, 18 pages, $.15.

Stavrianos, Leften S. (ed.), *Readings in World History* (Allyn & Bacon, 1965), Unit 12: "Our World Today," pp. 843–896.

FOR TEACHER PREPARATION

Burton, John W., *Systems, States, Diplomacy and Rules* (Cambridge U. Press, 1968), $7.00.

Deutsch, Karl W., *The Analysis of International Relations,* Foundations of Modern Political Science Series (Prentice-Hall, 1968), $2.95.

Emery, Fred, *Systems Thinking* (Penguin Books, 1969).

Frankel, Joseph, *International Relations* (Oxford U. Press, 1964), $2.00.

Luard, Evan, *Conflict and Peace in the Modern International System* (Little, Brown & Co., 1968), $4.50.

Russett, Bruce M., *Trends in World Politics* (Macmillan, 1967), $1.95.

Scott, Andrew M., *The Functioning of the International Political System* (Macmillan, 1967), $3.25.

2

The Military System and Arms

IN AN ATTEMPT TO ACHIEVE SECURITY IN A CHAOTIC international system, the nations of the world have placed their major reliance on strong military structures. Although the students probably have at least vague notions that an arms race exists, it will be helpful if they look at the dimensions of this contest in some detail, particularly in order to understand how it affects efforts to cope with other aspects of our high-risk environment. They should also become aware of the rationale for a powerful military structure, as well as how the very existence of such structures tends to increase tensions between nations.

Perhaps the best way to understand the nature and

extent of the world's military systems is to have the class analyze the pertinent data. They should be able to answer the following questions:

1. What is the size of each of the military establishments in terms of men under arms? Is the size increasing or decreasing? by how much?

2. What is the annual cost of defense for the major countries of the world? Is this increasing or decreasing? by how much?

3. In the developed countries, what percentage of per capita spending is used for the military budget? in the underdeveloped countries?

4. How do world military expenditures compare to appropriations for education, public health, foreign economic aid?

5. What are the estimated nuclear capabilities of the United States and the U.S.S.R.?

Of course, the very search for such data can be a useful exercise. If class time is limited, however, the teacher can make use of the following tables for most of the figures needed. These figures can be reproduced and given to the students, or simply copied on the chalk board.

The class should also explore some of the current literature concerning chemical and biological warfare (CBW), and the continuing debate over the development and deployment of ABM's. The teacher should make it clear that the creation of new weapons and defense systems is a self-perpetuating process. If the "balance of terror" is to be maintained, neither side dares to allow the other to gain an advantage—a "first-strike capability." The ever-increasing sophistication of weaponry has led many people, including some members of Congress, to wonder if the question of defense is not becoming largely an academic exercise. The arsenal of germs, for example, includes such items as botulism toxin, one ounce of which could kill 60 million people, and pneumonic plague,

Table 1: World's Largest Regular Armed Forces, and Changes from 1966–68

COUNTRY	1966 SIZE	1968 SIZE	CHANGE
United States	3,094,000	3,500,000	+406,000
Soviet Union	3,165,000	3,220,000	+ 55,000
China	2,486,000	2,761,000	+275,000
India	879,000	1,033,000	+154,000
Turkey	450,000	514,000	+ 64,000
France	523,000	505,000	− 18,000
West Germany	440,000	456,000	+ 16,000
Britain	438,000	427,000	− 11,000
Italy	376,000	365,000	− 11,000
Indonesia	352,000	340,000	− 12,000
Pakistan	278,000	324,000	+ 46,000

Institute for Strategic Studies, London, "The Military Balance, 1968–69."

Note: These figures do not include reserves (of which China alone may possess more than 200 million), or paramilitary and guerilla forces. Further exploration of these data can be found in Murray Thompson's *Militarism 1969: A Survey of World Trends* (Peace Research Reviews, Peace Research Institute, Oakville, Ontario, Canada, No. 5, Oct., 1968).

against which there is no known vaccine. And, while there is considerable debate over the potential effectiveness of ABM's, most experts agree that a nuclear battle between Russia and the U.S. would result in the death of somewhere between 50 and 100 million people in each country.

In the past decade, the rising level of armaments and armed forces, with their supporting industries, scientists, and technicians, have given rise to concern about the spread of militarism. Those who see grave danger in the very existence of such a system, frequently quote President Eisenhower's warning, given in a speech near the

Table 2: National Military Expenditures

	1967	1968	CHANGE
United States	73.0 billion	79.6 billion	+6.6 billion
U.S.S.R.	44.0 "	50.0 "	+6.0 "
Mainland China	6.9 "	7.0 "	+ .1 "
Britain	5.3 "	5.5 "	+ .2 "
France	5.5 "	6.1 "	+ .6 "
West Germany	5.3 "	5.1 "	− .2 "
Italy	1.89 "	1.94 "	+ .05 "
Canada	1.56 "	1.59 "	+ .03 "
India	1.37 "	1.45 "	+ .08 "
Japan	1.07 "	1.17 "	+ .10 "
Poland	1.66 "	1.83 "	+ .17 "
Sweden	.97 "	1.01 "	+ .04 "
Czechoslovakia	1.45 "	1.54 "	+ .09 "
Australia	1.28 "	1.37 "	+ .09 "
Spain	520 million	540 million	+ .02 "

Institute for Strategic Studies, London, "The Military Balance, 1968–69"; reprinted from Murray Thompson, *Militarism 1969: A Survey of World Trends*, p. 16.

end of his term of office: "In the councils of government, we must guard against the acquisition of unwarranted influence, whether sought or unsought, by the military-industrial complex. The potential for this disastrous rise of misplaced power exists and will persist. . . ."

Many people are convinced that some sort of military-industrial conspiracy exists and is bent on continuing and expanding the war system. Part of the dissent of youth, of course, is directly aimed at such a conspiracy. Although it would be difficult to prove or disprove this sort of charge, it is important that young people try to

Table 3: World Military and Other Public Expenditures, 1967

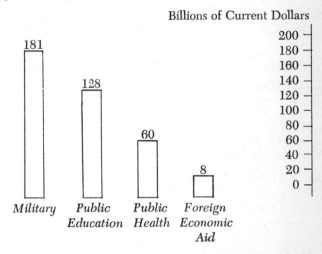

U.S. Arms Control and Disarmament Agency, *World Military Expenditures, 1969* (Washington, 1970), p. 6. This booklet, available from the Superintendent of Documents, U.S. Government Printing Office, $.60, contains many useful charts and tables, although the latest year for which definite figures are available is 1967.

look at the matter as realistically and objectively as possible. In addition to examining the evidence suggesting that the military-industrial complex exerts strong influence in our society, sought or unsought, they should also learn something about the arguments that hold that our fears of this influence are largely unfounded.

There is certainly ample periodical literature for examining both the dangers of militarism and the case for a strong military. As an example of the arguments on one side of the issue, the class might read an article in the

April 1969 issue of *Atlantic Monthly,* written by General David Shoup, former Commandant of the Marine Corps. Shoup points out that over 23 million Americans are veterans of military service, and many of them support what he calls the "creeds and attitudes" of the armed forces: "patriotism, duty and service to country, honor among fellow men, courage in the face of danger, loyalty to organization and leaders, self-sacrifice for comrades, leadership, discipline and physical fitness." Many of these veterans are active in organizations that maintain powerful lobbies in Washington.

In the active military service, Shoup argues, officers are anxious to test their training in combat, to try new tactics and theories in action, and, in the course, to receive promotions. In short, he concludes, "militarism in America is in full bloom."

George Thayer, in *The War Business,* presents the argument that not only is militarism in this country and in the world more widespread than we recognize, but the world actually exists in a state of almost permanent war.

Drawing by Joseph Mirachi.
Copyright © 1966 Saturday Review, Inc.

We consider the multitude of armed clashes that have occurred since 1945 as "small," only because they seem small in comparison to nuclear war. Here is a sample of the evidence he presents:

> Bombing tonnage in the Korean War exceeded all the tonnage dropped by the Allies in the Pacific Theatre of World War II. In the "small" six-day Sinai War of 1967, more tanks were committed to battle than by the Germans, Italians, and Allies together at the crucial twelve-day battle of El Alamein in 1942. And from July 1965 to December 1967, more bomb tonnage was dropped on Vietnam than was dropped by the Allies on Europe during *all* of World War II.
>
> One knowledgeable source estimates that today there are some 750 million operable military rifles and pistols extant in the world. In other words, there is one small arm for every adult male on earth. To this inventory of conventional weapons, one must add hundreds of billions of rounds of ammunition and other explosives; tens of millions of machine guns, mortars and antitank weapons; millions of field artillery pieces and armored tanks; a hundred thousand fighter and bomber aircraft; and tens of thousands of missiles and offensive naval craft. In the twenty-four years of the "Atomic Age," it has been these weapons that have done all the killing in the "small" wars we have experienced.

> George Thayer, *The War Business* (Simon and Schuster, 1969, $6.95), pp. 18–19.

One can carry this argument further by considering the possibility that these "small" wars are actually more divisive than an all-out war would be. Few of these brush-fire conflicts have produced a clear-cut victor; usually some sort of stalemate is reached, a sort of armed truce, constantly threatened by festering resentment. In addition, these wars do not command the full support of a country's population, which frequently results in deep splits within the country.

On the other hand, some observers—as well as those involved in public affairs—feel that the threat posed by militarism is greatly exaggerated, or is, at worst, a necessary evil because powerful military establishments are the insurance we have against another total war. Students could read selections from C. P. Snow's *The State of Siege* (Charles Scribner's Sons, 1969, 44 pages, $2.95) for an elaboration of this point of view. Snow states that "Great countries don't usually commit mass suicide. The military understanding (between the Soviet Union and the United States) has been worked out. The balance of power has remained steady. I believe . . . that both countries will spend increasing sums on armaments. But the balance of power will still remain pretty steady. The risk of major war will be there, but it is small, and probably the least of our worries."

The class can also consider the rationale for a strong military establishment from the vantage point of the decision-makers. A good example of the reasoning was provided by President Nixon in his speech before the Air Force Academy in June, 1969. Recognizing that "it is open season on the armed forces," a time when "military programs are ridiculed as needless if not deliberate waste," the President argued that nevertheless the country had no choice but to maintain a strong military posture:

> We must rule out unilateral disarmament. In the real world that simply will not work. If we pursue arms control as an end in itself, we will not achieve our end. The adversaries in the world today are not in conflict because they are armed. They are armed because they are in conflict, and have not yet learned peaceful ways to resolve their conflicting national interests.
>
> The aggressors of this world are not going to give

the United States a period of grace in which to put our domestic house in order—just as the crises within our society cannot be put on a back burner until we resolve the problem of Vietnam.

Programs solving our domestic problems will be meaningless if we are not around to enjoy them. Nor can we conduct a successful policy of peace abroad if our society is at war with itself at home.

There is no advancement for Americans at home in a retreat from the problems of the world. America has a vital national interest in world stability, and no other nation can uphold that interest for us.

We stand at a crossroad in our history. We shall reaffirm our aspiration to greatness or we shall choose instead to withdraw into ourselves. The choice will affect more than our foreign policy; it will determine the quality of our lives.

In the same vein, it might be well to read to the class other portions of Eisenhower's "military-industrial complex" speech, particularly the following passage:

We face a hostile ideology—global in scope, atheistic in character, ruthless in purpose, and insidious in method. Unhappily the danger it poses promises to be of indefinite duration. . . . A vital element in keeping the peace is our military establishment. Our arms must be mighty, ready for instant action, so that no potential aggressor may be tempted to risk his own destruction. . . . We can no longer risk emergency improvisation of national defense. We have been compelled to create a permanent armaments industry of vast proportions.

To provide a framework for this analysis of the military system, as well as for some useful background information, the class could make use of Topic 6 in the Foreign Policy Association's *Great Decisions—1970*. Here is a sample of the questions raised in the booklet:

What is the proper role of the nation's defense establishment in our government; in American society and in international relations? Has the military machine grown so large that it threatens to undermine our fundamental concept of civilian control? Are basic American values and attitudes in some way threatened? . . .

How much influence—and what kind—does the military-industrial complex wield today in Washington? Are there adequate checks on its power and influence? Are we benefiting as much as we can from the professional military advice available to the nation? Or is this kind of advice already too preponderant in the councils of state?

Foreign Policy Association, *Great Decisions—1970* (Allyn & Bacon, 1970), Topic No. 6 "U.S. Defense Policy: The Pentagon and Its Critics—What Policy Should Prevail," pp. 65, 68.

BIBLIOGRAPHY

Calder, Nigel (ed.), *Unless Peace Comes: A Scientific Forecast of New Weapons* (Viking Press, 1968), 243 pages, $1.95.

Goldwin, Robert A. (ed.), *Armed America: Essays on U.S. Military Policy* (Rand McNally, 1965), 144 pages, $1.50.

Hersh, Seymour, *Chemical and Biological Warfare: America's Hidden Arsenal* (Doubleday, 1969), 307 pages, $1.45.

Knorr, Klaus, *On the Uses of Military Power in the Nuclear Era* (Princeton U. Press, 1966), 185 pages, $5.00.

Ross, Steven (ed.), *CBW: Chemical and Biological Warfare* (Beacon Press, 1969), 209 pages, $1.95.

U.S. Arms Control and Disarmament Agency, *World Military Expenditures* (U.S. Government Printing Office, 1969), 26 pages, $.35.

Waskow, Arthur (ed.), *The Debate Over Thermonuclear Strategy* (D. C. Heath Co., 1964), 114 pages, $2.25.

Kissinger, Henry (ed.), *Problems of National Strategy* (Praeger, 1965), 477 pages, $3.95.

Liska, George, *Imperial America: The International Politics of Primacy* (Johns Hopkins U. Press, 1967), 115 pages, $2.25.

McNamara, Robert, *The Essence of Security* (Harper & Row, 1968), 176 pages, $1.65.

Rostow, Eugene V., *Law, Power and the Pursuit of Peace* (Harper & Row, 1968), 133 pages, $1.60.

3

Is War Useful?

It is sometimes argued that war has been and is too useful to nations for it to be dispensed with. The United States was conceived in war, further integrated through a civil war and two World Wars, and the war system today provides jobs and a convenient enemy to rally against. If we found a way to stop armed conflict, the argument goes, our economy would be in a state of collapse. While this reasoning may seem absurd when speaking of nuclear war, it certainly must be reckoned with in connection with the brush-fire or "safe" wars as well as the arms race itself.

Pro

A useful vehicle for studying the arguments in favor of the war system is provided by *The Report From Iron Mountain on the Possibility and Desirability of Peace,* with an introduction by Leonard Lewin (Dial Press, 1967, 109 pages, $5.00). This book has already found its way into many social studies classrooms. Written in the jargon of the social sciences, the *Report* is offered as a serious American think-tank paper. Actually it is a cleverly disguised satire that examines, tongue-in-cheek, two questions: "What can be expected if peace comes?" and "What should we (the U.S.) be prepared to do about it?" Although most people recognize the satire, the tone is subtle enough that just about everyone who writes about it feels he must explain why he thinks the *Report* is a hoax. The arguments presented are close enough to the way our society seems to operate that they cannot simply be discarded. The basic premise is stated in the foreword, where the anonymous author(s) writes that "lasting peace, while not theoretically impossible, is probably unattainable; even if it could be achieved it would almost certainly not be in the best interests of a stable society to achieve it."

Rather than have students read the entire book, it would be sufficient for some of them to read sections of it and report the arguments developed to the rest of the class. Here is a brief summary of some of the major functions of war as presented in the *Report* (page numbers in parentheses refer to pages of the *Report*):

1. Economic. War-preparation or "defense" is a "dependable system for stabilizing and controlling national economies" (p. 80). More easily than in other parts of the economy, money can be pumped into or withdrawn

from the military to prevent dangerous swings in the economy. In the same way, employment levels can be changed. War-preparation, in fact, is the great "stimulator of the national metabolism."

2. Political. "The permanent possibility of war is the foundation for stable government; it supplies the basis for general acceptance of political authority. It has enabled scientists to maintain necessary class distinctions, and it has ensured the subordination of the citizen to the state, by virtue of the residual powers inherent in the concept of nationhood. No modern political ruling group has successfully controlled its constituency after failing to sustain the continuing credibility of an external threat of war" (p. 81).

3. Social. The military serves to control dangerous youth through conscription. It is the basis of loyalty: "Allegiance requires a cause; a cause requires an enemy" (p. 44). And an enemy requires a war system.

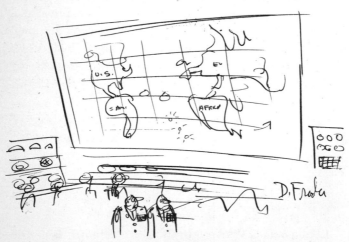

"You know, the war room's no fun when there's no war."

Drawing by Dana Fradon.
Copyright © 1970 by Dana Fradon.

4. Cultural and Scientific. The *Report* points out that much of the great art, music, and literature has been inspired by war, and what is not may usually be described as "sterile," "decadent," etc. War has contributed enormously to the scientific and technological development of nations. "Beginning with the development of iron and steel, and proceeding through the discoveries of the laws of motion and thermodynamics to the age of atomic particles, the synthetic polymer, and the space capsule, all important scientific advances have been at least indirectly attributable to war."

5. Ecological. War has functioned to keep population in ecological balance. But, the *Report* points out, war is not eugenically selective; that is, the superior die as well as the inferior. However, the author(s) hints that the way warfare is developing in the nuclear age, with the killing of masses indiscriminately, "the victims become more genetically representative of their societies" (p. 73).

After examining the functions of the war system, the *Report* then attempts to find possible substitutes, but concludes that "no program or combination of programs . . . has remotely approached meeting the comprehensive functional requirements of a world without war" (p. 87).

Discussion questions should follow the presentation of the major points of the *Report*:

1. Which of the arguments presented strikes you as most persuasive? least persuasive? Explain.

2. What governments or rulers have you studied who might agree with the theories of the *Report?*

3. Can you give examples of cases where war or war-preparation has divided societies rather than providing leaders with a means of maintaining control?

4. Why do you suppose the *Report* is filled with such

language as "the synthetic polymer" and "comprehensive functional requirements"?

5. How would you refute the major arguments presented in the *Report?*

6. Do you believe that war does serve any useful functions? Explain. Is there any way one could consider nuclear war functional?

Con

To provide more detailed analysis of arguments counter to those in the *Report,* the class could use a portion of *Peace and the War Industry* (Aldine, Trans-action Books, 1970, 159 pages, $2.45), which contains a symposium by eight scholars who present brief reactions to the book. For the teacher's use, here is a brief summary of arguments in refutation of the *Report:*

1. Economic. War preparation is not necessary for "stabilizing and controlling national economies." In 1965, a blue-ribbon U.S. Committee on the Economic Impact of Defense and Disarmament concluded that "even general and complete disarmament would pose no insuperable problems; indeed it would mainly afford opportunities for a better life for our citizens." Money can be pumped into and taken out of the economy through such institutions as the Federal Reserve System, education, public works, and a host of other programs. And, of course, war-preparation siphons off funds and resources from important domestic programs. The class could develop an interesting hypothetical national budget using the funds that would come from, say, a 50 percent decrease in annual defense spending.

2. Political. While wars have usually been a time of

heightened patriotism in this country, the teacher can point out that through most of our history the threat of an external enemy was not a major factor in creating loyalty; the same is true of Switzerland and a number of other countries. Far from serving as a means of hardening class lines, it can be argued that war is frequently a great leveller of class and ethnic distinctions. Although loyalty plays a part in war, it is a product of the total political socialization process, of which war is only a part.

3. Social. Military service may "control dangerous youth" for a time, but it can also create difficulties in the individual's re-orientation into civilian life. It may also encourage an acceptance of violence that carries over into domestic society.

4. Cultural and Scientific. Wars frequently seem to cause a dearth of cultural achievement rather than the opposite as argued in the *Report*. The long period of wars during the French Revolution and the Napoleonic era produced strikingly few important works of art. War has inspired or been the subject of much literature and art; but calling peace-time creations "sterile" or "decadent" can hardly be taken seriously. Also, in Nazi Germany, perhaps the most extreme example of war systems, artistic achievement was almost non-existent. War has stimulated scientific and technological achievement, but this does not mean that nations cannot organize such efforts in peacetime; and, of course, one must balance war-time achievements with the costs involved.

5. Ecological. War quite obviously has not functioned as any sort of control on population. A glance at any chart of population growth in the past half-century, will reveal that the long-term result of war is just as likely to be a sharp increase in population.

BIBLIOGRAPHY

Bolton, Roger, *Defense and Disarmament: The Economics of Transition* (Prentice-Hall, 1966), 180 pages, $1.95.

United Nations, *Economic and Social Consequences of Disarmament* (U.N. Publications Office, 1962), 66 pages, $.75.

————, *Economic and Social Consequences of Disarmament: Replies of Governments and Communications of International Organizations* (U.N. Publications Office, 1962), 304 pages, $3.00.

U.S. Arms Control and Disarmament Agency, *Economic Impact of Disarmament* (U.S. Government Printing Office, 1968), 28 pages, $.25.

4

The Possibilities of Large-Scale War

THERE REALLY IS NOT ANY WAY THE TEACHER CAN HELP his students make an accurate appraisal of just how great or how slight the chances of total war might be. As we have seen, some observers, like C. P. Snow, feel that the dangers of nuclear holocaust are very slim; others, like Kenneth Boulding, consider the probability as very great. Although it is obviously impossible to do more than speculate on the subject, a brief examination of some of the ways all-out war might happen will help the students clarify their own thinking and will add to their understanding of the uncertainties of the present world system. In this chapter we will outline some of the approaches that might be used in developing units on *escalation, premeditated attack,* and *accidental war.*

Escalation

Although escalation has already been touched upon in the study of conflict and violence, our purpose here is to examine it as a potential factor in bringing about a third world war.

To paraphrase C. P. Snow, great countries do not *premeditate* their own mass suicide, especially today when the two superpowers know so much about each other's capabilities, and when neither could doubt that any sort of nuclear confrontation would produce "unacceptable damage." There might seem little prospect today of the kind of miscalculation that played such an important role in the outbreak of World War I. But an interesting and valid case study of the events leading to World War I can shed light on the possibilities of war today, especially if the teacher provides readings that make it clear that few people in 1914 seriously considered that war would break out. By tracing the events that followed the relatively unimportant incident of the shooting of the Archduke Francis Ferdinand, the students will gain some idea of how events can spiral into violence even when all the parties involved might want to avoid it.

A more recent case is provided by the series of decisions during the Korean War, when both the U.N. forces and Communist China miscalculated the intentions of the other side. After a brief review of the decisions involved, the teacher can ask the class to project how the crisis might have escalated still further, even to the point of bringing about World War III. The class would also find it profitable to take other situations, such as the current crises in the Middle East, the Russian-Chinese border areas, and Southeast Asia, and develop scenarios indicating how these conflicts might escalate into all-out war.

A number of points should become clear in these exercises. First, it should be seen as at least being conceivable that in a crisis situation, the leaders of a nation might find themselves under such extreme pressure that the risk of mass suicide might be preferable to the surrender of some cherished value—freedom, honor, justice, etc. Second, it should be pointed out that, although Russia and the United States have shown increasing restraint in their direct dealings, it frequently happens that conflicts involving smaller nations drag the superpowers into confrontation. A third point, not unrelated to the other two, is that the personalities of the decision-makers can have an important bearing on the escalation of crisis situations. In connection with this point, the class could read portions of *The Year 2000* (Macmillan, 1968, $9.95), in which the authors, Herman Kahn and Anthony J. Wiener, outline some scenarios on the possible outbreak of nuclear war involving what they call "Hitlerian" behavior. The "Hitler" may have little in common with Adolf Hitler except a willingness to exploit everyone else's desire for peace in order to have his own way.

In the context of escalation, we must also include the arms race itself. Paradoxically, the build-up of arms, while intended to provide security, may exacerbate the underlying conflicts. Today's sophisticated weapons systems make it extremely difficult to know when a nation has enough. And even if a nation would settle for parity, how is it to know when that has been reached?

In practice, nations feel they must err on the side of maximum rather than minimum military power. Both sides of an arms race cannot have an edge on the other.

This being so, the build-up of arms necessarily escalates until one side or the other goes bankrupt, goes to war, or finds some way out of the race. And as the race goes on, especially when it is not certain what constitutes offensive and defensive weapons, the international tensions increase.

Premeditated Attack

A premeditated attack by one of the superpowers upon the other is almost inconceivable, but there are many who would not rule out the possibility of such an attack from Red China. The students might read some of the statements of Lin Piao or other Chinese leaders, statements that seem to indicate that these leaders minimize the dangers of nuclear war. The teacher should point out, however, that China's behavior has been far more circumspect than her language. As Kahn and Wiener point out (*The Year 2000*, p. 317), "Probably the most plausible scenarios involve United States-Chinese wars, but these too would nonetheless be judged by most students in this field to be implausible."

A more likely possibility might be a premeditated war by a lesser power that would act as a catalyst involving the major powers. Again, some of the scenarios developed by Kahn and Wiener would prove useful.

Accidental War

A good way to present the subject of accidental war is through a showing of the film *Fail-Safe,* in which Russia and the United States are brought into nuclear confrontation by a breakdown in the elaborate fail-safe system. Though the class will find the film chillingly realistic, it should be pointed out that the vast majority of experts feel that the safety checks are sufficient to prevent such an occurrence. Students might check on the public reactions to accidents, such as the bombs that fell and broke open in Spain in 1966 and in Greenland

"Oh, for goodness sake, go ahead and push the button!"

Drawing by Herbert Goldberg.
Copyright © 1967 Saturday Review, Inc.

in 1968, to determine how much concern was aroused about similar accidents involving Russia or China.

The purpose of this brief survey of escalation, premeditated attack, and accidental war is not to be overly alarming, but to suggest that the balance of terror is not a foolproof system. Nuclear war can happen, and, as we have seen, small but costly wars are an almost constant part of the current international system. Few would deny that the imperfections in the system must be corrected if we are to secure a more peaceful and stable world. Many proposals have been made for improving the current system. Some people feel that changes within the system are inadequate and that a new system must be devised. Both sets of proposals are outlined in the following chapters.

BIBLIOGRAPHY

Bader, William, *The U.S. and the Spread of Nuclear Weapons* (Pegasus, 1967), 176 pages, $1.95.

Brown, Harrison, and James Real, *Community of Fear* (Santa Barbara, Calif., Center for the Study of Democratic Institutions, 1960), 40 pages, $.25.

Hollins, Elizabeth J. (ed.), *Peace Is Possible: A Reader on World Order* (Grossman, 1967), 350 pages, $2.00.

Kahn, Herman, *On Escalation* (Penguin Books, 1965), $1.65.

Kahn, Herman, *On Thermonuclear War* (Free Press, 1969), $3.95, contains a number of scenarios.

Larson, Arthur, *Questions and Answers Concerning the Spread of Nuclear Weapons* (Duke Rule of Law Research Institute, 1968), 82 pages, $.25.

Larus, Joel, "Nuclear Accidents and the ABM," *Saturday Review*, May 31, 1969.

Stonier, Tom, *Nuclear Disaster* (Peter Smith, 1963), $4.50.

United Nations, *The Threat of Nuclear Weapons* (U.N. Publications Office, 1968), 19 pages, $.10.

FOR TEACHER PREPARATION

Aron, Raymond, *The Century of Total War* (Beacon Press, 1966), 368 pages, $2.25.

Buchan, Alistair, *A World of Nuclear Powers* (Prentice-Hall, 1966), 176 pages, $1.95.

PART III

EXAMINING APPROACHES TO PREVENTING WORLD WAR III

The possibilities for preventing an annihilating war or of eliminating the brush-fire wars depend to some extent upon theories of the underlying causes of war. If war ultimately stems from man's innate aggressiveness—a kind of killer instinct—perhaps it may be argued that war can be avoided only by basic changes in human nature. However, as has been seen, even if man has within his genes the capacity for aggressiveness, the social environment plays a determining role in its expression. No authority in the area of war/peace studies would suggest that there is nothing man can do but resign himself to an endless series of small wars and merely hope that none of them develop into Armaggedon.

The question of war-prevention, then, focuses upon what to do with the environment, both national and international. And the approaches to improving the environment are as numerous as they are varied. Somewhat arbitrarily, we have divided the many proposals into two categories: Gradual Steps, or changes in the current system; and Big Steps, or systems change. Those who favor a gradual approach argue that, although some breaking away from the nation-state system may be a desirable long-term goal, it simply is not feasible now and won't be for some time to come. The nation-state still serves many important functions, and what is needed is improvement in the system rather than a new system. Even many of those who favor some eventual form of international government, feel that gradual changes in the current system, such as strengthening the U.N., are the only wise course.

Those who favor taking big steps away from the current

nation-state structure believe that systems change is possible, at least at the security level. There is consensus in the world on the value of survival, and the present chaotic system cannot guarantee survival; the only answer is a supranational authority, which would not eliminate the nation-state system, but would prevent it from becoming involved in a large-scale war.

It is important for the teacher and the students to understand that the various approaches that will be surveyed are not mutually exclusive. One may advocate, for example, the gradual development of international understanding or improvements in the U.N., and at the same time favor immediate and radical systems change. It is also possible to conclude that the current system offers better chances for peace and stability than do any of the proposed alternatives. Again, limitations of space will make the treatment of these proposals grossly oversimplified; but our purpose is to suggest approaches and at least a sketchy framework for study rather than complete analysis.

1

Examining Proposals for Changes in the Current System

MOST OF THE PROPOSALS MENTIONED IN THIS CHAPTER actually call for placing greater emphasis on trends already underway, rather than developing something entirely new. Although each change or trend is studied as a separate topic, the students should see that they do not exist in isolation; our chances of avoiding World War III within the framework of the current international system can be strengthened by encouraging some mix of these gradual steps. The goal is not the elimination of conflict or of all violence, but rather the discovery of ways to prevent large-scale violence and total war.

Throughought the study, the class should keep certain questions in mind:

1. What possibilities does each step offer for the reduction of tensions that might produce large-scale violence?

2. What are the weaknesses or limitations of each proposal?

3. What combination of steps seems to offer the most promise?

4. What particular gradual step would you most like to see encouraged and why?

5. How are the steps interrelated? Is it possible to encourage something like *deterrence* and *arms control* at the same time?

Increased International Understanding

There was a time when many people felt that international tensions would be reduced if the peoples of the world simply got to know each other better. Although we have since learned that increased contact does not necessarily produce increased understanding, such contacts are still the goal of a great many exchange programs in a variety of fields. Those who feel that improved international understanding is both possible and necessary say that a good deal more is needed than just travel and exchange. International understanding can be improved, it is argued, if we work toward the development of a feeling of community. We must learn to think of all men as being members of the same species, facing common problems that are solvable by common effort.

A brief unit of two or three class periods should be

sufficient for students to grasp what is meant by "building a sense of community," what achievements have been made in this direction, and what proposals are frequently offered to increase this international understanding.

Discussion and research questions might include the following:

1. What are some of the ways commonly advocated for building a sense of community on an international scale?

2. What factors (e.g., ethnocentrism) detract from understanding even when contacts are increased?

3. What is meant by the "global view" of man and man's problems?

4. What specific steps are advocated to increase the sense of community?

Sources for this study can consist of brief selections from the following:

Landmarks in International Cooperation (U.N. Office of Public Information, 1965), 133 pages, $3.00.

Emile Benoit, "Interdependence on a Small Planet," *Columbia Journal of World Business*, 1966, 8 pages, $.15.

Richard Gardner (ed.), *Blueprint For Peace* (Praeger, 1966), 404 pages, $2.95.

Barbara Ward, *The Lopsided World* (Norton, 1968), 124 pages, $1.25.

Improving National Decision-Making

Some authorities believe that improvements in the decision-making process offer the major hope for achieving a reasonably peaceful world. John Burton, Director of the Center for the Analysis of Conflict at University College, London, is one of those who does not believe that there is an "inevitability of doom" in the current nation-state system. In *Systems, States, Diplomacy and Rules* (Cambridge U. Press, 1968, $7.00), he argues that there is no inherent danger in nationalism or other aspects of the system. "What is required," he writes, "is increased wisdom and foresight of State authorities in the pursuit of State interests." If decision-makers would develop greater efficiency in decision-making, they would be able to calculate the risks in particular policies and avoid dysfunctional conflicts, which he defines as those "more costly to States than the worth of values acquired."

While Burton's work is probably too difficult for most high school students, the arguments can be read by the teacher and passed on to the class in digest form. A book that most students can handle, and even have some

"All last night I kept dreaming the whole kit and kaboodle had been beaten into ploughshares."

Drawing by Joseph Mirachi.
Copyright © 1966 Saturday Review, Inc.

fun with, is Roger Fisher's *International Conflict for Beginners*. Developed as a "handbook" for decision-makers, the book emphasizes the pragmatic:

> This book may appear to be a criticism of how officials conduct our foreign policy. It may also appear to be a criticism of how government is set up to pursue international objectives. The real target of my criticism, however, is the critics. In my judgment, the responsible critics of government are drastically falling down on the job. Newspapers, magazines, commentators, and elected public officials regularly demand the wrong kind of performance from the official concerned with foreign affairs. They ask him to play to the grandstand, not to get results. They themselves judge performance not by international results but by the short-term effect on popularity.
>
> Roger Fisher, *International Conflict for Beginners* (Harper & Row, 1969, 231 pages, $5.95) p. 193.

One of Fisher's major theses, in other words, is that more effective decision-making depends in part on a more practically-minded public. As long as decision-makers are unduly hampered by such indices as public-opinion polls, they can't always make the wisest decision. Students will have little difficulty grasping such arguments, and will find that the lucid style and the use of specific examples will increase both their interest and their understanding. In particular, the concluding case study, a hypothetical step designed to ease the Arab-Israeli conflict, will give them important insights into what is involved in making sound foreign-policy decisions.

BIBLIOGRAPHY

Jacobs, Norman, *et al.*, *Making Foreign Policy in a Nuclear Age: 2. Challenges to U.S. Foreign Policy* (Foreign Policy Association, 1965), Headline Series, No. 172, $1.00.

Strausz-Hupé, Robert, *et al.*, *New Directions in U.S. Foreign Policy: A Symposium* (Foreign Policy Association, 1969), Headline Series, No. 193, $1.00.

FOR TEACHER PREPARATION

Ball, George W., *The Discipline of Power* (Little, Brown & Co., 1968), $7.50.

Burton, John, *Systems, States, Diplomacy and Rules* (Cambridge U. Press, 1968), $7.00.

Morgenthau, Hans, *A New Foreign Policy for the U.S.* (Praeger, 1969), $2.75.

Arms Control

Efforts to place limits on the development and deployment of weapons systems should be looked at as something distinct from proposals for disarmament. Although arms limitation is sometimes considered as a step toward disarmament, most authorities in this field feel that it is realistic, at least at the present, to strive only for ways of placing some sort of ceiling on the current arms race, especially in the area of nuclear weapons.

If time permits, it is certainly useful to use an historical approach, surveying some of the past efforts to control the weapons of war. These are some cases that could be developed into "mini-units" on arms control:

1. the "truce of God" efforts by the Church in the Middle Ages;

2. the Rush-Bagot Treaty of 1819, which demilitarized the American-Canadian boundaries;

3. the Hague Conference of 1897 and 1899, so vividly described in Barbara Tuchman's *The Proud Tower* (Bantam, 1966, $1.25);

4. the Washington Naval Conference of 1922.

Discussion and research questions could include the following:

1. In what ways were these efforts successful? For how long?

2. If they failed, why did they fail?

3. What efforts were made to "humanize" war by placing bans on weapons that seemed, at the time, unusually cruel?

4. What efforts were made to prohibit the use of weapons not yet developed?

Parallels can be drawn from these historical cases and then applied to current efforts at arms control. At the Hague Conference, for example, the British, who had a definite superiority in seapower, were quite willing to agree to a freeze on naval construction. The Germans and Japanese, both in the early stages of developing naval power, were opposed. Does the same sort of reasoning apply in arms limitation talks between America and Russia? Does it explain why the newer members of the "nuclear club" (e.g., France and China) are unwilling to take part in such talks?

In considering arms control efforts in the nuclear age, the class might concentrate on the Limited Test Ban Treaty and the Nuclear Non-Proliferation Treaty. Here are some additional questions that might be used:

1. What were the reasons for agreeing to some limitations on testing?

2. Considering the destructive capabilities still maintained by both sides, how can such agreements be considered as hopeful signs?

3. Why are some nuclear powers not involved in the arms limitation talks? Does this render any agreements meaningless? Why or why not?

4. Why do both powers continue to produce nuclear weapons even when limitation talks are taking place?

5. Does the existence and continued development of biological and chemical weapons make nuclear limitations less meaningful? Why or why not?

BIBLIOGRAPHY

Bloomfield, Lincoln, *Disarmament and Arms Control* (Foreign Policy Association, 1968), Headline Series, 73 pages, $.85.

Bull, Hedley, *The Control of the Arms Race* (Praeger, 1965), 235 pages, $1.95.

Dougherty, James (ed.), *The Prospects for Arms Control* (McFadden Books, 1965), 370 pages, $.95.

Rathjens, George W., *The Future of the Strategic Arms Race: Options for the 1970's* (Carnegie Endowment, 1969), 64 pages, $.60.

United Nations Association, *Stopping the Spread of Nuclear Weapons* (U.N.A., 1967), 48 pages, $1.00.

U.S. Arms Control and Disarmament Agency, *Arms Control and National Security* (U.S. Government Printing Office, 1968), 24 pages, $.50.

————, *Ninth Annual Report to Congress* (U.S. Government Printing Office, 1969), 55 pages, $.35.

Wiesner, Jerome, and Herbert York, "National Security and the Nuclear Test Ban," *Scientific American,* 1964, 8 pages, reprint, $.20.

Deterrence

One of the basic reasons for believing in a strong deterrent force as the best guarantee for peace was summed up by Winston Churchill: "When the advance of destructive weapons enables everyone to kill everyone else, nobody will want to kill anybody at all." Of course the matter is made somewhat more complicated by the need to be certain that the other side doesn't develop a first-strike capability. This necessity raises some very difficult questions about how either side can tell when it has achieved sufficient strength to feel secure. How many American nuclear weapons counterbalance Soviet superiority in ground forces in Europe? How does the deterrent value of intermediate-range ballistic missiles compare with intercontinental missiles? How many more missiles should the U.S. have to offset the advantage of the wide dispersal of Soviet industry and population?

Although the students are in no position to answer these questions, they should be aware of the complexity of the situation. By having them read the arguments for and against deterrence, and by keeping pace with current debates in Congress and in the press over the development of ABM's and MIRV's, they will gain some understanding of many issues:

1. why most Americans believe that a strong deterrent force offers the best chance of preventing war;

2. how easily the "balance of terror" can be upset;

3. how difficult it is to reverse the spiral of the nuclear arms race;

4. the problems of knowing and assessing the capabilities of other nations;

5. the question of how civilian control over the military can be maintained in an age of such sophisticated weaponry that only a handful of people can understand what is involved;

6. the growing fear that the greatest nuclear threat comes, not from the Soviet Union, but from Communist China.

BIBLIOGRAPHY

Kinter, William, *Peace and Strategy Conflict* (Praeger, 1967), 264 pages, $6.95.

Schelling, Thomas, *Arms and Influence* (Yale U. Press, 1966), 293 pages, $1.95.

Unilateral Initiatives

Psychologist Charles E. Osgood, in *Alternative to War or Surrender* (University of Illinois Press, 1962, $1.45), presented a strong case for the United States taking step-by-step initiatives in what he called "graduated reciprocation tension-reduction" (GRIT). In the area of "arms management," he suggested that the United States might, for example, reduce weapons and missile sites in certain areas, and invite Soviet reciprocation along with modest inspection procedures. Or the U.S. might deactivate a military base in Pakistan, with inspection, and establish an international university on the site, with all nations participating under U.N. auspices, and, again, invite some Russian reciprocation. Another illustration called for the "denuclearization" of West Germany, with a reduction of NATO forces there, and an equivalent reciprocation requested from Russia.

Students might explore more fully the arguments Osgood presents and then consider some of the steps the United States has taken that can be considered under the heading of unilateral initiatives—the dismantling of some overseas bases, especially Okinawa; the renouncement of further development of germ-warfare weapons except for a limited defense research program; President Nixon's announcement that chemical weapons would not be used by the U.S. except in retaliation.

It is also interesting and rewarding for students to survey some of the more extreme proposals for unilateral steps, especially the arguments offered by proponents of non-violence. *Alternatives to Violence* (Time-Life, 1968, 100 pages, $1.00), edited by Larry Ng, offers a collection of thought-provoking essays on non-violence by Erich Fromm, Arthur Koestler, Harold Lasswell, and others. Students should also become aware of the arguments against such proposals, particularly the question of how practical they are and on what factors (such as restraint by one's opponents) their success would depend.

BIBLIOGRAPHY

Bondurant, Joan V., *Conquest of Violence: The Gandhian Philosophy of Conflict* (U. of California Press, 1965), 261 pages, $1.95.

Carter, April (ed.), *Unilateral Disarmament: Its Theory and Policy from Different International Perspectives* (Housmans, 1965), 68 pages, $.50.

Etzioni, Amitai, *The Hard Way to Peace* (Macmillan, 1963), 294 pages, $.95.

Gregg, Richard B., *The Power of Nonviolence* (Schocken, 1966), 187 pages, $1.75.

Osgood, Charles E., *Perspectives in Foreign Policy* (Pacific Books, 1967), 94 pages, $1.50.

Wright, Quincy, *et al.* (eds.), *Preventing World War III: Some Proposals* (Simon & Schuster, 1962), 460 pages, $6.95.

Functionalism

The "functional" approach looks for the gradual building of the conditions needed for an integrated and peaceful world society by people working together through international and cross-national organizations. Proponents of this approach point out that global problems that can't be solved by individual nations can be attacked in non-political, functional areas—social, economic, technical, and humanitarian. Through such cooperative efforts not only would the underlying causes of war be eradicated, but there would be a growing integration of world society and a shifting of loyalty and sovereignty from the nation-state to legitimized international institutions.

Students should see that functionalism is something that already operates and does not depend on preconceived theories of how various cross-national functions might be in the process of altering the international system. Multinational corporations, for example, which have already managed to "internationalize" one-quarter of the world's production of goods and services, operate across national boundaries simply because it is convenient and profitable to do so. The dimensions and pace of this growth have led some social scientists and journalists to conclude that these operations "threaten the existence of the nation-state system."

International Education for Spaceship Earth, contains a unit on multinational corporations, with special concentration on ways the phenomenon develops a sense of functional loyalty or identity that has little to do with national boundaries. The sudden and dramatic growth of these business activities, which many observers refer to as "the second industrial revolution," is perhaps the most noticeable example of the development of a global society.

In addition to, or in place of, the unit outlined in *International Education for Spaceship Earth,* a highly stimulating exercise can be developed by having students draw a profile of the operations of a single global corporation. A firm in the local area would be useful and quite likely to cooperate; the class can readily identify with a local company and will have the added surprise of discovering how far-reaching its operations are. The public relations departments of many industries and banks are willing to supply free or inexpensive material on the overseas operations of American firms.

BIBLIOGRAPHY

Cordier, Andrew, and Foote, Wilbur (eds.), *The Quest for Peace* (Columbia U. Press, 1965), 390 pages, $2.95.
Gardner, Richard, *In Pursuit of World Order: U.S. For-

eign Policy and International Organizations (Praeger, 1965), 263 pages, $1.95.

Haas, Ernest, *Beyond the Nation State: Functionalism and International Organization* (Stanford U. Press, 1968), 586 pages, $3.85.

Rubinstein, Alvin, *The Soviets in International Organizations* (Princeton U. Press, 1964), 380 pages, $7.50.

United Nations, *Landmarks in International Cooperation* (U.N. Office of Public Information, 1965), 133 pages, $3.00.

Strengthening the United Nations

Functionalism is also a good way to add vitality to the usually dry units on the United Nations and other international organizations. Instead of merely learning about the structure and historical outline of the U.N., students can inquire into the areas in which the organization is successfully working in functional realms that have international significance. As Lincoln Bloomfield said of such activities, "If the member states should find that the U.N. no longer serves their basic national interests in the political realm, they will still have to think long and hard before sacrificing this 'functional' realm, where cooperation has become not an option but a necessity."

Here are some sample questions that could be used to guide this study:

1. What U.N. agencies are engaged in international activities in social, economic, and humanitarian areas? What are the nature and extent of these activities? How many people are affected by this work?

2. For what reasons was the International Labor Organization awarded the 1969 Nobel Prize for Peace?

3. Is national sovereignty affected in any way by the work of these agencies? What other areas (e.g., pollution) do you think could be handled effectively by international agencies?

As in the case of multinational corporations, a good way to approach this study is to have individual students or small groups develop profiles of particular agencies, such as the World Health Organization, the Special Fund for Economic Development, and UNESCO. The same approach may be applied to other organizations— the International Monetary Fund, the European Common Market.

In the political area, study might best concentrate on the peace-keeping functions of the U.N. which, according to the Charter, is the central purpose of the organization. Case studies of various crises are readily available and some are included in many world history texts. These, when matched with some of the conflicts in which the U.N. could do little or nothing—Cuban Missile Crisis, Southeast Asia, Hungary and Czechoslovakia—will give the class an idea of what preconditions are needed for U.N. peace-keeping efforts to be successful.

Many social studies courses deal with proposals for strengthening the U.N. Such proposals should be approached from the question of how practical they might be and what the obstacles are to their enactment. Again, here are some sample questions:

1. What are some of the proposals for: (a) a U.N. Police Force; (b) restriction of the veto power; (c) increased role for the General Assembly; (d) changes in the World Court; (e) universal membership?

2. What are the main arguments for and against each of these proposals?

3. Which proposals seem to you to be the most practical? least practical? Why?

4. What are the major obstacles to these proposals? How might they be overcome?

BIBLIOGRAPHY

Bloomfield, Lincoln, *International Military Forces* (Little, Brown & Co., 1964), 296 pages, $2.50.

——, *The U.N. and World Order* (Foreign Policy Association, 1969), Headline Series, No. 197, 62 pages, $1.00.

——, and Amelia Leiss, *Controlling Small Wars: A Strategy for the 1970's* (Knopf, 1969), 421 pages, $8.95.

Frye, William, *A United Nations Peace Force* (Oceana, 1960), 227 pages, $5.00.

Inis, Claude, Jr., *The United Nations and the Use of Force* (Carnegie Endowment, 1961), 59 pages, $.60.

Sauerwein, Virginia (ed.), *The U.N. at Twenty-Five,* special issue of *Intercom* (N.Y. Center for War/Peace Studies, 1969), 68 pages, $1.50.

Third Conference on the U.N. of the Next Decade, A Report (The Stanley Foundation, 1968), 26 pages, $.10.

United Nations, *Everyman's United Nations* (U.N. Office of Public Information, 1968), 634 pages, $2.50.

United Nations Association, *China, the U.N., and the U.S.* (U.N.A., 1966), 64 pages, $1.00.

——, *Controlling Conflicts in the 1970's* (U.N.A., 1969), 59 pages, $1.00.

2

Examining Proposals for Systems Change

MANY PEOPLE IN THE FIELD OF WAR/PEACE RESEARCH FEEL that the only logical way of achieving a stable international system is to change the current system. As long as competing nation-states possess a monopoly of power, it is argued, the world will constantly exist on the brink of war—until that final war occurs. There must be some way of developing another system that can guarantee security and peaceful methods of conflict resolution.

Because proposals for systems change are unfamiliar to most teachers, an attempt will be made here to summarize some of the major models that have been developed. It seems important to emphasize that these proposals cannot be dismissed as utopian dreams; they are the products of extensive research and study and reveal an attempt to come to terms with the realities of world affairs. The summaries may be reproduced for distribution to the class, although, of course, much more will be achieved if the proposals and the arguments for and against them are explored in greater depth.

The class is likely to feel that none of the models studied is completely practical given the realities of to-day's world. They should understand, however, that the reason for examining these alternative systems is to get at the larger questions of whether or not change is possible, and, if it is, what changes can and should be made.

Disarmament

"Big steps" toward preventing a World War III usually involve disarmament, which may be defined as the reduction of weapons, armed forces, and armament production facilities to levels sufficient for nations to maintain internal order but insufficient for launching war against others. Complete and general disarmament would mean depriving national decision-makers of the means of using war as an instrument of national policy and implies, accordingly, a radical transformation of the international system of nation-states, especially if disarmament has with it the corollary of transferring peacekeeping to an international agency. The arguments for and against disarmament have already been discussed or implied in various contexts above and may be summarized here briefly.

Those who advocate a disarmed world generally believe that warfare, as it can now be conducted, is too dangerous to be left to the decision of a few men in one or more nations. They argue that past experience and research in the social sciences indicate that men cannot be depended upon in all circumstances to act rationally and perceive accurately. Crises can escalate beyond anyone's intentions or madmen can come into power and plunge the world into a war that would destroy civilization.

And, dangerous as the international system is now, it will become even more subject to crises out of which war may result in the future. Among the problems that will be increasingly conducive to international violence are over-population; depletion and pollution of resources; the gap between rich and poor, especially along color lines; and nuclear proliferation. The eventual threat of nuclear war will not deter desperate men. What Communist China's General Hsiao Hua said may increasingly be the attitude of leaders of poor and revolutionary countries: "Imperialist nuclear war threats will only scare those who possess weak nerves or those who have given up their revolutionary will, but can never scare our revolutionary people."

Those who espouse disarmament often argue that arms races are a built-in feature of the international system. Although arms are a result of conflict and mistrust, they also contribute to the intensification of conflict and mistrust, creating a dangerous spiral; arms feed mistrust and mistrust feeds the arms race. To achieve a balance of deterrent weapons or even of conventional weapons is unrealistic; and, even if it could be achieved, the balance could not be expected to last through changing conditions and leadership.

The growth of military systems also results in the preponderant influence of the military in decision-making. Nations are tending to become "war states" in which the military may always be depended upon to base its planning upon the worst possible intentions of a potential enemy and seek a military "solution" to problems.

Disarmament would not mean the collapse of economies. Many studies, including the report of a U.N. committee of economists in 1962, indicate that disarmament could be carried out in stages without serious hardship; in fact, disarmament would mean that countries could finally turn to the eradication of hunger, disease, and ignorance, which underlie so much conflict within and among countries. Also, disarmament would mean neither the end of the nation as the object of identity nor any radical alteration in peoples' way of life. The world would still be a pluralistic one, and no doubt rivalries and conflicts would continue to be a part of world society; however, the means of inflicting massive damage upon others would be denied nations.

Disarmament, its proponents argue, is difficult to achieve but not a utopian impossibility once nations recognize that the present system does not offer security and, in fact, threatens their very existence. The abolition of the means of making war by nation-states is no more utopian than the abolition of slavery might have seemed to a Roman or the peaceful coexistence of religions within a state to Europeans of the 16th century.

On the other hand, some critics of disarmament believe that a disarmed world would not only be undesirable but dangerous. They argue that arms are not the cause but a symptom among peoples of differences. To eliminate arms is to drastically alter power relationships and to invite aggression by the numerically superior states who could overrun neighbors with domestic police-force weapons. Disarmament would make the task of guerrilla insurgents vastly easier. In Southeast Asia, for example, insurgents, with the support of Red China, could easily take over the entire area and then threaten other parts of the world. Because of this likelihood, disarmament would have to include the creation of an international police force, which would have to be under an international organization with legislative, executive, and judicial power. Such a world organization might fall under the control of the numerically superior underdeveloped world and threaten the welfare of the rich nations. However fairly and rationally it acted, it would almost inevitably become deeply involved in the internal affairs of nations.

Other critics of disarmament might agree that it is theoretically desirable at some point in time but impossible for the foreseeable future. Disarmament requires inspection, which cannot be foolproof. Nuclear weapons could be concealed in caves and sealed up. Chemical and biological weapons are even easier to conceal. As Raymond Aron put it in *Peace and War: A Theory of International Relations* (Doubleday, 1966, $10.00), "The resources of concealment are, in the present state of affairs, greater than the resources of inspection." Moreover, even if inspection could become completely effective, advanced nations would not forget how to construct weapons of mass destruction and could do so quickly. Effective disarmament boils down to trust; and if nations trusted each other, it would be unnecessary.

And in any event, such critics maintain, nations are not going to agree to disarmament and its corollary of international organization that would mean the surrender of national prerogatives. Even if a world disarmament conference could be held, few representatives would dare to return having surrendered their national power in the present world system. And many representatives at such a conference would not agree to a disarmament system unless their nation had a relatively improved position in world power relationships.

Is change possible under a world authority with a

monopoly of power? Would not national boundaries and governments be frozen to perpetuate a status quo that is not acceptable to many people? Would, for example, African peoples agree to a system by which South Africa would continue to be controlled by a white minority? And, on the other hand, would South Africa ever agree to join in disarmament unless it had guarantees that its present system would be continued?

Finally, critics of disarmament have argued that most governments and people do not agree that the world is in imminent danger from war. As Alistair Buchan wrote in *War in Modern Society* (Harper & Row, 1968, $1.95), "The fear of war is not sufficiently strong or universal to make all nations willingly relinquish their rights or confront and overcome these inherent difficulties. What might have been possible in the days of a universal church and empire, which might be feasible in the wake of some great future catastrophe, is not possible today" (p. 181).

Despite all the pitfalls in the way of disarmament, it is significant that both the United States and the Soviet Union agreed in 1961 to the desirability of complete and general disarmament, asserting jointly that "war is no longer an instrument for settling international problems." Then in 1962 each country put forward its own draft treaty for a disarmament process that should take place in three stages; that there should be inspection by an International Disarmament Organization; and that threats to peace should be dealt with by a U.N. police-keeping force.

However, the common features are offset by serious differences in the two plans. The Soviets propose that the nuclear deterrent system be drastically reduced in the first stage and all nuclear weapons be eliminated in the second. The U.S. plan would retain a nuclear deterrent force until the final stage. The U.S. plan proposes across-the-board reductions of weapons and armed forces —20 percent at Stage I, 50 percent of what remains in Stage II, and the rest in Stage III. The American plan would let the success of each stage determine the procedures and timetable for the next stage, whereas the Soviets would have a five-year unalterable schedule to achieve complete and general disarmament down to domestic police forces. Thus, the Soviet plan, in the American view, would leave the United States in the early stages without an adequate nuclear deterrent against a possible Russian invasion of Europe by superior land forces. And the American plan, in the Soviet view, would mean that the U.S. would retain vastly superior nuclear forces throughout the early stages, while requiring the Soviets to reduce its conventional forces to a dangerously low level. The proposals would seem to be reminiscent of what Salvadore de Madariaga wrote of an imaginary disarmament conference of animals, "The lion wanted to eliminate all weapons but claws and jaws, the eagle all but talons and beaks, the bear all but an embracing hug."

But the problems of phasing the arms reduction is only part of the difficulty. An even greater obstacle has been inspection. The Soviets would allow inspection only of arms destroyed but not those remaining. Inspection of weapons remaining and continued on-site inspection to see that no one is cheating has been considered essential by the American side. Another obstacle has been the means of policing the disarmed world. The U.S. proposal involves a permanent U.N. force which could be called into action without a veto and strong enough to overcome any state that would threaten the peace. The Soviets envision a peace-keeping force made up of components from the nations that would be called by a vote of the Security Council, where the veto would remain. The American proposal would, in effect, mean the development of a U.N. that would change the international system significantly, while the Soviet plan would mean retention of the present system.

Of course, both plans require universality, which is essential for any disarmament. Thus, even if the two super-powers were to agree to some kind of compromise plan, there would remain the task of persuading the other nations to join. Given Red China's unwillingness to cooperate even with the present U.N., universality seems a difficult and very distant possibility.

Although the process of disarmament may be exceedingly difficult to work out, its ultimate acceptance may depend upon the kind of security system or world order that would replace the present international system. Indeed, the process of disarmament is inseparable from a plan for peace-keeping in a disarmed world. We may now turn to a consideration of "models" for a world operating under law instead of power politics.

Discussion and Research Questions

1. Which of the disarmament proposals, Russian or American, seem to you to be the most practical and realistic? Explain. What are the major obstacles to enactment of either?

2. What do you consider to be the major obstacles to disarmament? Do you think these can be overcome; if so, how?

3. Outline the major arguments for and against disarmament.

4. How might conflicts be resolved in a disarmed world?

5. What effect do you think disarmament might have on the nation-state system? Explain.

The Clark-Sohn Proposal

A monumental plan for keeping the peace in a disarmed world was devised by two distinguished international lawyers and published in a large volume titled
World Peace Through World Law. First published in
1958 and revised in subsequent editions, the proposal
has been translated into many languages and used as a
model for discussion and futuristic thinking by scholars,
government officials, and university and secondary school
students around the world. It is presented as a plan for
revising the United Nations Charter; but, as the authors
indicate, much of the plan could be enacted through
other procedures, such as a world conference to draw
up a disarmament treaty.

Before briefly describing the broad outlines of the
plan, it is important to understand what is meant by
world law in comparison with other kinds of law. As has
been mentioned above, international law refers to a body
of bilateral and multilateral agreements, pacts, and
treaties among nations. It implies the existence of the
nation-state system, since its formation and enforcement
depends upon national governments. International lawyers and others also use the term *supranational law*,
which refers to the law that would be enacted and enforced by a group of nations were they to transfer at
least some of their authority to a supranational authority;
for example, if the Common Market were to develop
into a genuinely political organization with legislative
and enforcement authority, a body of supranational law
would emerge.

World law refers to law under some world order or
system, which would include a universal authority with
some measure of executive, legislative, and judicial

power. Grenville Clark defined it in the introduction to *World Peace Through World Law*: world law refers to "law which would be uniformly applicable to all nations and all individuals in the world and which would definitely forbid violence or the threat of it as a means for dealing with any international dispute. This world law must also be law in the sense of law which is capable of enforcement, as distinguished from a mere set of exhortations or injunctions which it is desirable to observe but for the enforcement of which there is no effective machinery." World law may be conceived of, then, as having the characteristics of domestic law but on a world scale and implies a significant change in the international system of sovereign nation-states.

A fundamental aspect of the Clark-Sohn plan is universal disarmament, which the authors view as "essential for any solid and lasting peace." The disarmament process would include a preliminary period of arms census by an Inspection Service when all nations would be required to present a detailed list of all forces, weapons, arms production facilities and their location; however, the nations would be allowed to keep a small deterrent force in a secret location as security against a breakdown of the disarmament process. Disarmament would proceed in six-month phases during each of which nations would reduce 10 percent of military personnel and destroy, convert, or hand over to the U.N. or World Peace Force 10 percent of all armaments and armament production facilities; thus, after five years there would no longer be any national military forces except those under international control, and what was agreed to as necessary for domestic police. At each phase the Inspection Service would investigate compliance in each nation in a region comprising one-tenth of its territory, which would be selected by the Inspection Service. Nuclear materials from destroyed weapons and all nuclear facilities would be surrendered, with compensation, to the U.N. Nuclear Energy Authority to be used for peaceful purposes.

The international organization would include a World Police Force, which would be built up as national forces are reduced. This force would be made up of between 200,000 and 600,000 full-time professionals from the various nations with a quota limitation of personnel from any one nation. They would possess the most modern and mobile equipment and would be stationed throughout the world in such a way that there would be no fearful concentrations in any one country or region. There would also be a Peace Force Reserve of between 600,000 and 1,200,000 men. Chemical and biological weapons of mass destruction would be completely destroyed; but nuclear weapons would be available, although under civilian control, for use in very special and extremely serious circumstances.

The sole legislative body would be the General Assembly and its direct authority would be confined to overseeing disarmament and peace-keeping. Representation in the Assembly would be proportional to population; however, the largest nations would be limited to thirty members, while the smallest would have one. Through a three-stage process taking twenty-four years, Assembly members would eventually be chosen by the direct vote of the people in their nations.

An Executive Council would be substituted for the present Security Council and would include seventeen members elected by the General Assembly and responsible to it. Large nations would have permanent membership on the Council but no vote. On important matters, such as using peace-keeping forces, at least eight of the larger states and four of the smaller must agree for a measure to be carried. Clark and Sohn envision the

Executive Council functioning in relation to the General Assembly in much the same fashion as the British Cabinet functions in relation to the Parliament.

The judicial system of the present United Nations would be greatly expanded and strengthened. The International Court of Justice would have the right of interpreting the Charter and compulsory jurisdiction in disputes the General Assembly found endangered the peace. Judgments handed down by the court would be enforced under the direction of the General Assembly, with the World Police Force brought in as a last resort. The judicial system would also include regional courts and a World Equity Tribunal.

Functional organizations, such as the Food and Agricultural Organization and the World Health Organization, would continue as under the present U.N. But economic development would be greatly expanded under a World Development Authority with funds from the general revenues collected from the nations.

The General Assembly would adopt annual budgets and assess the members by a complicated formula that would, in effect, require nations to pay in some proportion to their wealth. However, no nation would have to pay more than 2½ percent of its national product. Accordingly, the burden of even the wealthiest nation would be a fraction of the cost of maintaining present military forces; for example, the U.S. now spends about 9 percent of its Gross National Product on defense.

The Clark-Sohn plan also includes a Bill of Rights that provides that "all powers not delegated by express language or clear implication" are reserved to the member nations and their peoples, and that the world organization shall not violate basic rights of any individual, including freedom of speech, press, and assembly, and the right of fair trial and freedom from unreasonable searches and seizures. The Bill of Rights does not protect individuals against deprival of any rights by their own government; for, the authors feel, were the revised Charter to include such protection, it would mean that the revised U.N. might have to become deeply involved in the internal affairs of nations. Further, it would mean that many nations would not even consider joining.

Obviously, membership in such a revised U.N. would have to be universally acceptable. The disarmament aspect of the plan would be impossible to carry out if even one major nation stood outside. The Clark-Sohn proposals stipulate that the revised Charter shall come into force only when ratified by five-sixths of all the nations of the world, the ratifying nations to have a combined population of at least five-sixths of the total world population and to include all the twelve nations that then have the largest populations. When ratified, nations that had not joined would still have to disarm and submit to the "obligations of the disarmament plan."

The Waskow Model

The Clark-Sohn proposal for world order raises the spectre in many minds of a world government with a monopoly of military force that could become uncontrollable and threaten the vital interests of individual nations. Even the U.S. proposal for complete and general disarmament envisions a force "that no state could challenge." Is there a way to police a disarmed world without a frightening concentration of military power in the peace-keeping system? Arthur I. Waskow of the Institute for Policy Studies in Washington, D.C. has developed a plan that is intended to obviate such fears.

Published as a booklet titled *Keeping the World Dis-*

armed by the Center for the Study of Democratic Institutions, the Waskow plan postulates the continuation of a highly pluralistic and conflicted world in which nations had disarmed for self-goals by a variety of means short of full-scale war with weapons of mass destruction —propaganda, subversion, economic aid, economic embargo or boycott, espionage, bribery, etc.

The model would employ a "series of graded deterrent responses to more and more serious violations" of the disarmament agreement. And each step of responses would require more and more consensus among the nations—the more consensus the more force. Also, violations would be treated as the acts of individuals and not of nations in order to "avoid as long as possible the engagement of national prestige."

The fundamental international organization involved in peace-keeping would be a Council made up of permanent representatives from the great powers and non-permanent members from some other nations. (The exact make-up of the organization is not spelled out and is not essential to the concept of the scheme.) When an apparent violation of the disarmament was first discovered, a small force of perhaps less than ten men might be sent to the site by a vote of only two or three members of the Council. If the violator did not cease and desist or refused to cooperate, perhaps a majority of the Council would be required to send a force of several hundred. If the violation still continued, perhaps five thousand men could be sent—but only by the unanimous vote of the Council. Thus, for a "strong" response to a violation to be carried out there would have to be a high level of consensus in the international community and the complete support of the major powers.

It should be emphasized that the largest force that could be sent would still be relatively small, which would mean that a large nation whose people were determined to resist the international body would be able to do so successfully. As Waskow puts it, the great powers would "be granted a legal as well as a physical veto over the use of any international force. . . ."

But resistance would be equivalent to repeal of the disarmament agreement; it would probably mean the rapid rearmament of much of the world and a return to costly and dangerous national defense systems, which Waskow thinks nations would be reluctant to do after having experienced the advantages of a disarmed world.

This system of "graded deterrent responses" is seen in action in *Keeping the World Disarmed* through the device of scenarios of hypothetical but realistic situations. In one scenario, country Zee, a small power, has been accused by country Queue of making bullet-proof tank-like vehicles in an automobile factory. Inspectors from the International Disarmament Organization report the alleged violation to the Disarmament Police Court. The evidence indicated that tanks are indeed being made; and the Court orders the plant to stop. The Enforcement Council, on the vote of two states, sends a single, unarmed policeman to serve the order, who is prevented from carrying out his duty by Zee's police. The situation is brought up in the Council, which votes to send eight armed men, who are violently resisted by Zee's police, and three members of the international force are killed. The Council votes to send a minimal force again but with assurance from a majority of the Council that a larger force would be sent if necessary. Zee realizes that there is increasing opposition to its behavior and decides that it is not worthwhile to continue the violation; so, when the Disarmament Police return to the plant, they are greeted by the plant manager, who tells them that it was all a mistake and offers to show them around.

Other scenarios presented by the author deal with far more complex situations that involve the great powers in direct confrontation. One concerns a pro-Western uprising in East Germany; another, serious black-white violence in South Africa. In the latter, Communist China forces the withdrawal of the peace-keeping force from the area, and the civil war that had broken out rages on. However, despite the bloodshed, rearmament does not take place.

The "graded deterrent response" approach to peace-keeping can be criticized at many points. In the booklet *Keeping the World Disarmed*, Arthur Waskow considers several. One is the argument, already discussed in the context of the Clark-Sohn proposal, that peace-keeping necessarily involves defending the status quo. Waskow states that under his plan nations may move toward establishing a world government with greater power for determining when change is legitimate, or they may abandon international peace-keeping on the modest level he proposes. He says that "the possibility that the police-management institution might become even a temporary world government and the possibility that the disarmament agreement might break down will *both* be so frightening to most states that they will retreat before either choice is made."

The Chicago Constitution

A model that would go far beyond peace-keeping to establish a world government is to be found in the so-called Chicago Constitution, or "A Constitution for the World," which was begun in 1945 and carried out over a two-year period by a group at the University of Chicago under the chairmanship of Robert M. Hutchins, then

Chancellor of the University and now Director of the Center for the Study of Democratic Institutions. It provides for a universal government that would not only keep the peace but would guarantee for all peoples such rights as a decent standard of living; security in old age, sickness, and during unemployment; education up to the age of twelve; "protection . . . against subjugation and tyrannical rule, racial or national, doctrinal or cultural"; freedom of speech, press, assembly, and "any such other freedoms and franchises as are inherent in man's inalienable claims to life, liberty, and the dignity of the human person, and as the legislators and judges of the World Republic shall express and specify."

The government of the Federal Republic of the World would have the power to enact laws and make them "binding upon communities and upon individuals as well." It would have authority to intervene in "intrastate violence and violations of law which affect world peace and justice," and it would have power to settle disputes among "component units." In short, the proposal, if enacted, would radically alter the sovereign nation-state system and create a genuine world government.

The Chicago Constitution provides for a variety of executive, legislative, and judicial institutions, which are described in considerable detail. Only a few of the more interesting features may be mentioned here. The legislative branch includes a Federal Convention elected by the direct vote of the people; however, the Convention would function largely as an electoral college for the selection of the President and the members of the Council, which has the power of initiating and enacting laws. The judicial branch would include a Supreme Court of highest appeal and a Grand Tribunal, which, through its various benches, would decide cases involving not only the states but individuals seeking justice from both the

World Republic and from their own state governments. A unique feature of the system is a Tribune of the People, a sort of ombudsman who would "defend the natural and civil rights of individuals and groups against violation or neglect by the World Government or any of its component units. . . ." Military forces would be under a civilian Chamber of Guardians elected by both the Council and Grand Tribunal, under the chairmanship of the President.

The Constitution also makes provision for world development through a Planning Agency and the establishment of a World Bank that would issue money and create and control credit. Commerce "affected with federal interest" would be regulated by the federal government. It would also grant "federal passports," which symbolizes the extent of change embodied in the plan.

The difficulties in the way of achieving such a plan and the possible dangers from a world government with such extensive power are too obvious to warrant elaboration. However, the Chicago Constitution offers a carefully worked out model of what a true world government, guaranteeing economic welfare, basic human rights, and security from destruction by war, might resemble. In the minds of some who have thought deeply about the problem of war in the nuclear age, such a system is ultimately what is required for a lasting peace.

Discussion and Research Questions

1. What are the major proposals for systems change? What are the major similarities and differences among them?

2. Which model for world order seems to you the most realistic? Explain.

3. What are the major obstacles to each proposal? How might these be overcome?

4. What changes would you make in any of the models to make it more acceptable to the nations and peoples of the world?

5. What effect do you think systems change would have on the nation-state system? Explain.

6. Which do you consider more realistic, systems change or changes in the current system? Explain. What proposals, or combination of proposals, seem to you to offer the best chances for security? Explain.

BIBLIOGRAPHY

Barnet, Richard, and Richard Falk (eds.), *Security in Disarmament* (Princeton U. Press, 1965), 441 pages, $2.65.

Borgese, Elizabeth Mann (ed.), *A Constitution for the World* (Santa Barbara, California, Center for the Study of Democratic Institutions, 1965), 112 pages, $1.00.

Douglas, William O., *Towards a Global Federalism* (N.Y.U. Press, 1968), 177 pages, $7.95.

Fraenkel, Jack R., Margaret Carter, and Betty Reardon, *Peacekeeping: Problems and Possibilities* (World Law Fund); designed for school use—currently available only for testing purposes. For more information on this and other curriculum material being prepared by the World Law Fund, write to WLF (see Resource Organizations listed on page 164).

Hollis, Elizabeth J. (ed.), *Peace Is Possible: A Reader on World Order* (Grossman, 1967), 350 pages, $2.00; useful as a basic text on systems change.

McVitty, Marion H., *Preface to Disarmament: An Appraisal of Recent Proposals* (Washington, D.C., Public Affairs Press, 1970), 73 pages, $1.00.

Noel-Baker, Philip, *The Arms Race* (Oceana, 1958), 603 pages, $2.00.

Reed, Edward (ed.), *Pacem in Terris* (Pocket Books, 1965), 259 pages, $.95.

Seed, Philip, *The Psychological Problem of Disarmament* (Housmans, 1966), 72 pages, $1.00.

United Nations, *The U.N. and Disarmament, 1945–1965* (U.N. Office of Public Information, 1967), 338 pages, $4.50.

U.S. Arms Control and Disarmament Agency, *Documents on Disarmament* (U.S. Government Printing Office, 1967), 820 pages, $2.50; contains the official statements on disarmament of all major powers, including China.

FOR TEACHER PREPARATION

Clark, Grenville, and Louis Sohn, *Introduction to World Peace Through World Law* (World Law Fund, 1966), 52 pages, $.50.

———, *World Peace Through World Law* (Harvard U. Press, 1966), 535 pages, $2.50.

Falk, Richard, and Saul Mendlovitz, (eds.), *The Strategy of World Order* (World Law Fund, 1966), Volumes I–IV, 2,298 pages, $10.00.

Mendlovitz, Saul (ed.), *Legal and Political Problems of World Order* (World Law Fund, 1962), 822 pages, $2.25.

Morgenthau, Hans, *Politics Among Nations* (Knopf, 1967), $8.95.

PART IV

ADDITIONAL APPROACHES TO TEACHING WAR/PEACE CONCEPTS

1

Using History

The Changing Nature of War

WHILE AVOIDING THE "ONE DARNED WAR AFTER ANOTHER" approach and the detailed analysis of strategy in particular wars, the teacher may call attention to the changing nature of war in survey history courses. One of the best relatively short historical treatments of warfare is to be found in the abridged and updated paperback edition of Quincey Wright's *A Study of War* (University of Chicago Press, 1964, $2.95). In a short chapter titled "The History of War," he discusses "The Origin of War," "Animal Warfare," and "Historic Warfare." He devotes a major chapter to "Modern Warfare," in which he discusses the increasing destructiveness of war, presenting useful data; the changing techniques employed in warfare; and some of the functions of war. He concludes the chapter with the following statement: "In the 1960's there appeared some evidence that the very gravity of the situation was convincing man that unless he destroyed war, it would destroy him." Most of this classic study is devoted to an examination of the causes of war and the means of controlling war.

Other books of use to teachers and, at least, the more able students are *Men in Arms: A History of Warfare and its Interrelationship with Western Society* (Praeger, 1964, 402 pages, $1.50) by Richard Preston, *et al.;* Theodore Ropp's *War in the Modern World* (Macmillan, 1966, $1.50); and J. F. C. Fuller's *The Conduct of War, 1789–1961* (Minerva, 1961, $2.95).

The changing nature of warfare, as well as why men fight, can be vividly illustrated by the use of fiction and drama. The fiction shelves of libraries are filled with books on war in different periods, but a few examples may be mentioned here. *The Golden Warrior* by Hope Muntz (Scribners, 1949, $1.65), on William the Conqueror's invasion of England in 1066, has been used in social studies courses and may be used for its descriptions of warfare; more important, it may help teachers in discussing medieval values and war. Bertold Brecht's play, *Mother Courage and Her Children* (Grove Press, 1963, $.95) is set in the Thirty Years' War and is a scathing satire on the aimlessness of war in general. Tolstoy's description of the battle of Borodino in *War and Peace* (Airmont Publishers, 1969, $1.75) can help explain the emergence of mass warfare in the modern period. Other books have been included in history courses: Stephen Crane, *The Red Badge of Courage* (Airmont Publishers, 1964, $.50) (American Civil War); Erich Maria Remarque, *All Quiet on the Western Front* (Crest, 1969, $.75) (World War I); Glenn Gray, *The Warriors* (Harper & Row, $7.00) (World War II); W. F. Irmscher, editor, *Man and Warfare* (Little, Brown & Co., $3.50) (contains a number of accounts of the nature of war, including ones by Machiavelli, George Orwell, Franz Kafka, George Bernard Shaw, Joseph Conrad, and Katherine Anne Porter).

Especially important in studying the changing nature of war is examining how nuclear weapons have signified a kind of mutation in the potential of destructiveness. Students may better grasp the meaning of nuclear war by reading such books as John Hershey's *Hiroshima* (Bantam, 1966, 116 pages, $.50) or Nevil Shute's *On the Beach* (Apollo, 1964, $1.75). Tom Stonier's *Nuclear Disaster* (Peter Smith, 1963, 225 pages, $4.50) is a careful analysis by a scientist of what a nuclear war would be like. A useful exercise for understanding the dimensions of changes in military technology is to have students graph the area of destructiveness of a single weapon from an arrow to an H-Bomb of 50 megatons. (The World Law Fund has prepared a film strip to explain the meaning of megaton.)

Primitive Warfare

The study of conflict among primitive peoples can give students insights into some aspects of war and peace-making. This study provides an opportunity to raise a number of important questions related to war in the modern world. For example, why is it that some peoples are highly warlike and others peaceful? Why is it that African Bushmen know no war? They are described in *The Harmless People* (Knopf, 1959, $4.95) by

Elizabeth Marshall Thomas. Eskimos, although conflict is sometimes violent among them, do not organize to fight other groups. (The EDC materials, *Man: A Course of Study*, includes a novel titled *On Firm Ice* that deals with types of conflict among Eskimos and how they are handled.)

There is a large body of literature on conflict and war among primitive peoples. Useful introductions to the subject appear in *War: Studies from Psychology, Sociology, and Anthropology* (Basic Books, 1968, $4.95) edited by Leon Bramson and George W. Goethals. An article by Andrew P. Vayda, reprinted from the *International Encyclopedia of the Social Sciences,* on "Primitive Warfare" provides an overview. A collection of essays by outstanding anthropologists is found in *War: The Anthropology of Armed Conflict and Aggression* (Natural History Press, 1968, 262 pages, $2.95) edited by Morton Fried and others, which includes an extensive bibliography. Also important is the collection of readings edited by Paul Bohannan, *Law and Warfare: Studies in the Anthropology of Conflict* (Doubleday, 1967, $6.95).

Ancient History

By focusing on questions of war and peace, teachers can bring a relevancy students often feel is lacking in the study of ancient history. A crucial question that can be pursued is the part war has played in the rise and fall of ancient civilizations. How valid was Arnold Toynbee's hypothesis in *War and Civilisation* (Oxford University Press, 1950, $3.00) that war was a major factor in the decline of all major ancient societies? Or, what was the effect of militarism upon the institutions of Rome at the end of the Republic and during the Empire?

Stringfellow Barr has written a booklet for the Center for the Study of Democratic Institutions, *On Consulting the Romans: An Analogy Between Ancient Rome and Present Day America,* that teachers may find suggestive as well as polemical. Are the parallels between Rome's reliance upon military force and contemporary America accurate? Is the U.S. in danger of going the way of Rome? Is there a kind of Pax Americana operating in the world today? These are a few of the questions that the booklet raises.

The study of ancient Greece also offers a number of possibilities for getting at war/peace questions. The relationship of values to warfare may be raised through a study of the *Iliad,* as Simone Weil does in *The Iliad or the Poem of Force* (Pendle Hill, 1956, $.45). The control of war by an "international" organization can be examined through the Achaean League, which is discussed in Tom Galt's *Peace and War: Man-Made* (Beacon Press, 1963, $3.95), a short book for junior high or younger high school students. As Galt puts it, the Achaean League shows us "a method by which states could work together and not fight each other." Also, the Delian League can point up the problem of a league in which one state, Athens, exercised a preponderant and ultimately destructive role.

The study of the Greek city states beginning with the fifth century can provide a model of a bi-polar (Athens and Sparta) international system that raises questions about the bi-polar world that characterizes the international system during most of the period since World War II. (The description of the Greek system during this period, in *International Politics* [Prentice-Hall, 1967, $8.50] by K. J. Holsti, pp. 42–50, is useful to teachers in identifying the important characteristics.) Also, the procedures for resolving disputes by arbitration and conciliation were attempted by the Greek states. Why did they fail? Why was a lasting "balance of power" impossible? Why were the Greeks unable to unite, despite the growing menace of Macedon? (Parts of Thucydides can be read by students seeking answers to such questions.)

The Middle Ages

The long span of time from the "fall" of Rome to the Renaissance can be particularly fruitful for the study of war/peace concepts, of which only a few examples may be discussed here.

The decentralization of authority and the absence of security, which the numerous castles symbolize, deserves close attention. Indeed, the feudal system can be viewed as largely a means of achieving security. Political loyalty was directed to an individual in the hierarchy and not to political institutions.

War was endemic and could be highly destructive, as in the case of the Hundred Years' War. The "international organization" of the medieval church attempted at times to limit warfare through the peace of God and the Truce of God. The church also acted as a mediator of conflicts among political authorities. But in peacekeeping the church could only persuade or, as a last resort, excommunicate; it could not force settlement except through the support of political authorities.

The frequency of violence and the importance of the church raise questions of apparently contradictory values in the Middle Ages. Why was violence so prevalent in a period when Christian ethics were seemingly so pervasive? Violence was not only condoned but honored by the Germanic peoples who became the ruling—and the warmaking—class, as Tacitus pointed out. The warrior fighting for a just cause was a medieval ideal. Medieval epics, such as *Beowulf, El Cid,* and *The Song of Roland,* glorified the military hero; for example, in *The Song of Roland,* "with each blow Roland split a Sarrazin's skull, sectioned his body, and severed the horse's spine. . . . By hundreds, then by thousands, they strewed the field with pagan dead." The teacher may wish to ask students whether they think the glorification of the "warrior" on television, and in films and books, has entirely disappeared in Western culture.

The Crusades can also be used to examine important war/peace concepts. In one sense, they may be considered as an ideological confrontation between Christian and Moslem worlds that may shed some light on the later confrontation between the West and Communism. On the positive side, the Crusades promoted contacts between the two sides and accelerated social, economic, and scientific change within Europe. However, as Robert Lopez has written in *The Birth of Europe* (M. Evans, 1967, $11.50), "Europe learnt a great deal, but it was a school where masters and students hated one another." And the two hundred years of European efforts at expansionism eastward had the result of hastening the decline of the Byzantine Empire and encouraging a narrow orthodoxy in both Moslem and Christian states. In the west, for example, anti-Semitism became virulent, and bloody crusades were launched against religious unorthodoxy, especially against the Albigensians in France. Overseas, what started out as a pious, self-sacrificing movement for the True Faith tended to become selfish, corrupt adventure for ruthless and ambitious men seeking land and booty. The Fourth Crusade, when Constantinople was sacked, more closely resembled a barbarian invasion for plunder than anything else and was vehemently condemned by the Pope himself.

The late Middle Ages were marked by the growth of the power of rulers at the expense of a too often turbulent feudal nobility. In a sense, kings, often with the support of merchants and townsmen, created a larger "security community" (Karl Deutsch's phrase). The king's law and, at least, better order were extended to the boundaries of their states with larger, better trained and equipped forces, which the barons could not match. Arthur Waskow in *Keeping the World Disarmed* writes that "the duchies of France . . . [were] disarmed" and suggests that an examination of the long process by which this "disarmament" took place may be revealing for an understanding of what might be done to create a disarmed world.

Modern History

In addition to the suggestions for using modern history that have already been mentioned in this book, here are a few of numerous other possibilities for study that can further aid the conceptualization of factors in war and peace.

Teachers who devote attention to the Renaissance might wish to look at the "international system" of the Italian city states in the period around 1500, as described by K. J. Holsti in *International Politics* (Prentice-Hall, 1967, $8.50), pp. 50–59, and consider differences and similarities with the present international system. By and large, the conduct of relations among the city states of Italy was "machiavellian"; indeed, Machiavelli's *The Prince* can be read by students as a discussion of values.

The fragile balance of power among the states, however, was short-lived, and Italy became a battleground for the larger, more integrated states like France, Spain, and later the Austrian Empire until Italian achievement of unity in the late nineteenth century, when the peninsula became more secure.

The Thirty Years' War provides an opportunity to discuss conflicting and underlying motives for war. It was also a war that was marked by widespread casualties to civilian populations. The Treaty of Westphalia, ending the war, signifies the formal recognition of the system that continues more or less intact to the present—sovereign states owing no obligations except to themselves. 1648 is often taken as a date after which religion was no longer a major factor in the cause of wars in Europe. The wars of the later seventeenth century and of the eighteenth century broke out from the dynastic ambitions of rulers over territory, succession to thrones, and colonial expansion. Teachers may have students examine the reasons for the decline of religious ideology as a cause of war. Were wars fought less bitterly or more bitterly because of this?

The development of the nation-state and nationalism is a key thread in the context of war and peace. The French Revolution can be studied as an important turning point from the dynastic state to the nation. Important questions to be considered include: How was warfare affected by the Revolution? What was the significance of the *levee en masse* and the Marseillaise? What did the Revolution mean in terms of legitimacy, loyalty, and ideology?

A wealth of teaching materials exists for studying nationalism and the growth of the nation-state. *The Shaping of Western Society: An Inquiry Approach* by John Good contains a chapter on "Nationalism," using primary source material for discussing the differences between loyalty in Tudor England and in nineteenth century Italy and Germany. An "Historical Essay" in the text, suggestions in the accompanying Teachers' Guide, and audio-visual materials help in making the concept of nationalism clear. Also, *Beyond Sovereignty* (Public Affairs Press, 1965) by Max Mark contains a very readable chapter on "Nationalism and the State" that contrasts the medieval period with later ones. A consideration of the development of the nation-state and of loyalty should not omit such questions as the following: What benefits did the more centralized and integrated nation-state bring—both material and psychological? How was war related to the rise of nation-states? (The rise of Germany under Bismarck can make a useful case study.) Why did war become more intensive, albeit less frequent, in the nation-state period? (Quincey Wright's *A Study of War*, especially the unabridged edition, contains an interesting discussion of this question).

"Utopian" Peace Plans in History

Very few history texts written for school devote much attention to efforts to devise plans—or "models"—for organizing the international system for preventing war. One exception is *Modern History* (Silver Burdett, 1964, $6.00) by Carl Becker and Kenneth Cooper. However, the treatment of such plans is very brief. A fuller discussion may be found in *Peace and War: Man-Made*, by Tom Galt. In this short book are plans such as Erasmus' *A Complaint of Peace*, published in 1514, suggesting an international court of arbitration; the Duke of Sully's (or Henry IV's, to whom it was attributed) famous plan of a federal system for Europe; Emeric Cruce's *The New*

Cineas, providing for a Council of Ambassadors who would meet continuously in Venice, hear disputes, and enforce settlement, if need be, by a police force (he also saw the desirability for economic advancement of peoples within the states as a necessary condition for a lasting peace); and William Penn's *Essay Towards the Present and Future Peace of Europe,* which proposed an assembly of representatives from the European States and a peace-keeping force made up of contingents from the members. Immanuel Kant, writing after the French Revolution began, also proposed a plan for a kind of league of nations with the abolition of standing armies under state control. The work of Hugo Grotius in the late sixteenth and early seventeenth centuries in formulating international law is also important; and his influence may be seen in the model proposed by the Abbe St. Pierre in the eighteenth century, which calls for an international congress and world court with the power of enforcement. A much more detailed discussion of these and many other proposals may be found in *International Government* by Clyde Eagleton, and *Plans for World Peace Through Six Centuries,* by S. J. Hemleben.

Functioning Trans-National and International Organizations

Although efforts to prevent war by organizing the international system may go back as far as the Achaean League, the first working organization in modern times may be said to have begun with the Concert System that emerged from the Congress of Vienna of 1814–15. As Innis Claude wrote in *Swords into Plowshares* (Random House, 1964, $9.95), "The Concert system gave Europe . . . something imperfectly resembling an international parliament, which undertook to deal by collective action with current problems ranging from the regulation of international traffic on the great rivers of the Continent (see Tom Galt on the Danube Commission established at the Paris Conference in 1956, pp. 40–41) to the adjustment of relations between belligerent and neutral states, and from the re-division of Balkan territories to carving up Africa." The study of the Vienna Settlement and the Concert system raises the following questions: How successful was the system? What were its limitations? Why did it break down in 1914? Can the Concert properly be called an "international organization"? What role did it play in giving Europe a period of peace lasting nearly a century—the longest interval free of major war that the world has known since the Middle Ages?

The Versailles Conference and the League of Nations are given considerable attention in many school texts. It may suffice here to raise several questions: The League Covenant made aggressive war a crime and provided for collective security, and the peace-makers at Versailles re-drew the map of Europe to correspond more to the principles of self-determination and legitimacy. Why, then, was the peace after World War I so short-lived as compared with the settlement in 1815?

There are also questions on the procedures and instruments for peace-keeping: Why was the League unable to prevent World War II? When we speak of the League "failing," what is meant? Did the League essentially change the international system?

The United Nations has been discussed in several contexts above and is treated even more fully in school texts. There is also a wealth of teaching material available. Again, only a few questions need be raised here: To what extent does the U.N. incorporate and improve upon the League model? The U.N. has been successful in "functional" areas. Have these successes substantially lessened the prospects of World War III? There has been no major war since World War II—a longer period than that following World War I. To what extent has the U.N. been responsible for this? Has the U.N. substantially altered the international system? Can the U.N. be improved to provide for a more secure peace? If so, how? If not, what must be done?

Using United States History

American history offers many opportunities for the study of war/peace concepts, only a few of which can be suggested here. The very formation of the federal system from thirteen independent colonies has often been cited in books on international relations as offering insights into the problems of forming some kind of world federation. The states that emerged from the American Revolution could not effectively provide either security or economic development under the Articles of Confederation where they were virtually sovereign. What was needed was "a more perfect union among the states." The American experience, in devising a constitution at Philadelphia that would be acceptable to all the states, has meaning for some of the difficulties involved in forming an international organization to meet needs of nations today.

The ratification of the United States Constitution by no means meant a perfect union had been formed. The central government was not firmly established in its authority for at least a generation or two after the beginning of the Washington administration. States continued to insist upon the right of interpretation of the Constitution and even withdrawal from the union, until a Civil War was fought; and, even after 1865, the line between states' rights and federal powers was not clear. Also, the authority of the central government in promoting civil rights and economic welfare was only gradually assumed, which may suggest what a non-coercive but effective international organization feasibly may be expected to accomplish in a highly pluralistic world, by comparison with which the American states were relatively homogeneous.

The United States' frequent involvement in conflicts beyond its borders is another topic that can help understanding of war/peace concepts. The Mexican War, like much of America's westward expansion, raises questions about the legitimate extension of national boundaries. Manifest Destiny westward in the American experience can be compared with Russian expansion westward in the same period. (See the New Dimensions book by Stanley Seaberg, *Teaching the Comparative Approach to American Studies.*) The study of the Spanish-American War can be used to examine the conflicting motives and ambivalent values behind a democratic state entering a war that resulted in extensive acquisition of foreign territories.

The American frontier experience has also been used in school classrooms to illustrate the problem of security without law enforcement. The film *High Noon*, with the World Law Fund Study Guide, provides the means for an exciting study of law at the end of a six-shooter instead of in the court room and raises parallels with the contemporary international system.

American history also provides an opportunity to study examples of the peaceful resolution of disputes. Kenneth Boulding, in an article in *Social Education*, November, 1968, suggests that more attention in schools should be given to the process by which the United States achieved a demilitarized border with Canada. The Rush-Bagot Agreement of 1817 and the settlement of the Oregon boundary at the 49th parallel ("we didn't get 54°40′ and we didn't fight," writes Boulding) can be studied to understand "a dynamic process which leads toward stable peace among independent nations. . . ."

World War I: A Case Study

Although at first glance the Great War may seem like ancient history to students who have been reared in the nuclear age, a study of it through the wealth of available materials can help today's generation of students to understand such concepts as misperception, arms race, escalation, militarism, and the functioning of the international system.

Many social studies teachers have used a "problem approach" in which students analyze the various causes of the war, often dividing them up into underlying and immediate. Selections from Sydney Bradshaw Fay's classic, *Origins of the World War* (Free Press, 2 vols., $2.95 each), have frequently been used to consider such underlying causes as entangling alliances, nationalism, militarism, naval arms race, economic imperialism, and the sensationalism of the press. The immediate causes that developed after the shooting of the Archduke Francis Ferdinand have often included such factors as the Blank Check, Austria-Hungary's determination to put an end to Serbian nationalistic activities among the Empire's Slavic peoples and to create a larger Serbia, the Russian mobilization, and the refusal of England to commit herself clearly to the support of Russia and France. A familiar collection of interpretations on the causes of the war and the responsibility for its outbreak is *The Outbreak of the*

First World War: Who Was Responsible? in the Problems in European Civilization Series (D. C. Heath). Other useful books on the causes of the war include Barbara Tuchman's *The Proud Tower* (Bantam, 1966, $1.25), which considers the broad European climate in the generation before the war; *The Guns of August* (Dell, 1962, 575 pages, $.95) by Barbara Tuchman; George Malcolm Thomson's *The Twelve Days: 24 July to August, 1914;* and *The Causes and Nature of World War I* a collection of primary source readings for high school students, edited by William A. Nesbitt and Peter Reinke. An interesting roleplaying exercise, in which students play the part of decision-makers in leading countries on the eve of the war, is found in *The Shaping of Western Society,* by John Good.

But the dust has by no means settled on the reasons why World War I came about. Social scientists, using new techniques of research, in recent years have been taking a new look at causation. One of the most revealing studies has been made by Robert C. North and others at the Stanford University Center for Studies in International Conflict and Integration. They have subjected numerous documents (including diplomatic exchanges, speeches, and press interviews during the crisis period preceding the outbreak of the war) to content analysis, using computers to determine how the parties in the conflict perceived events and communications. They discovered that decision-makers tended to perceive themselves as the object of hostility by "the other side" but not as a source. They found, for example, that the Kaiser believed that the allied powers were preparing, in his words "for a war of extermination against Germany" and acted out of this misperception. (A summary of their findings appears in an article on "The History of Human Conflict," edited by Ole R. Holsti and Robert C. North in *The Nature of Human Conflict,* edited by Elton B. McNeil.)

A broader discussion of misperception and World War I may be found in *Nobody Wanted War* (Doubleday, 346 pages, $5.95) by Ralph K. White. Within the compass of some twenty pages, in prose that is clear and free of social-science jargon, White takes up such topics as "diabolical enemy-image," "virile self-image," "selective inattention," "absence of empathy," and "military over-confidence" as they relate to the causes of the war. He states that "misperception might explain how normally sane human beings can unwittingly, without intending the consequences, involve themselves step by step in actions that lead to war." The remainder of the book is devoted to various distortions of perception that the author feels have been involved in the war in Vietnam.

2

Examples of Units and Courses on War and Peace

WHAT FOLLOWS ARE BRIEF DESCRIPTIONS OF SEVERAL UNITS and courses on war and peace that have been developed for school use and, in most cases, by teachers themselves. What is said about each one is intended to be suggestive of kinds of approaches and teaching materials, and by no means an adequate treatment. Teachers wishing to find out more about a particular course or unit may wish to write to the person or organization mentioned.

"War and Peace"

The Project Social Studies Curriculum Center of the University of Minnesota has prepared a very useful resource unit on "War and Peace" for twelfth graders. It presents students with a great variety of material including suggested readings, films, data, and exercises. The unit begins with the problem of defining war and then provides ways that students can better understand their own attitudes about war and can realize the importance of war to their own lives. The unit employs materials as diverse as data from Quincey Wright and a Bob Dylan recording. The unit then takes up the significance of nuclear weapons to warfare through films and a one-act play. The causes and nature of the war in Vietnam are examined as a case study on war.

An important emphasis in the unit is on understanding the dynamics and instability of the international system. Also emphasized are the extent and limitations of international law. International organizations from the League of Nations to the United Nations receive close attention, and the unit provides an opportunity for critical examination of a range of alternatives to the present system. A final part of the unit suggests procedures for having students develop their own models for world order in which their own value assumptions are to be made explicit; students must also explain how the model will achieve such values. The concluding section contains suggestions for achieving a wider discussion of war/peace matters in the school and community, an "Attitudes Test on War," and a selective bibliography.

"Problems of Peace and War in the Modern World"

Gerald L. Thorpe of the College of Education, Wayne State University, has prepared a twelve-week unit for secondary schools on "Problems of Peace and War in the Modern World." The unit, with detailed lesson plans, employs such materials as case studies, system models, and simulation. Emphasis is placed on getting students "to creatively imagine the future," as the introduction states, "while at the same time being continually reminded of present realities which influence that future."

An important feature of the unit is that it helps students to understand what is meant by a model of an international system and the value of using a "system approach." Part I presents a model of the present nation-state system in action through the Cuban Missile Crisis. Students read about the crisis in Philip Van Slyck's *Peace: The Control of National Power,* which is a basic "text" in the unit. The present system is further examined through readings in *Let Us Examine Our Attitude Toward Peace,* edited by Priscilla Griffith and Betty Reardon.

Part II helps students to develop some understanding of the nature of international law and how it may be compared and contrasted with domestic law, using readings and tape recordings from the World Law Fund. Part III takes up peace-keeping under the United Nations model and presents alternative models, including those of Arthur Waskow and Clark-Sohn. Parts IV, V, and VI involve problems of the U.N., including financing, universality, jurisdiction, and how the U.N. might be strengthened.

Part VII has as its stated objective "To examine the international system models of the 'arms control' type" and "begin the process of building political system models." Along with the regularly assigned readings in Van Slyck, students decide upon the objectives of an arms control system, what characteristics it might have, and what machinery might be necessary. In Part VIII, students turn to a study of general and complete disarmament and begin to develop a model to achieve this purpose. In the course of this section they read McVitty's *A Comparison and Evaluation of Current Disarmament Proposals* and further consider the Clark-Sohn model.

The final Part IX "examines some of the problems and prospects that might present themselves in a disarmed world." The students complete the building of a "security model and test it within the context of hypothetical case studies." Alternative procedures for the model-building are provided in the unit, including a "simulated" conference to draw up agreements on arms control and disarmament. Finally, the students test their model through a simulation of their own design. The unit includes a sample of an arms control model prepared by a group of eleventh grade students, a glossary of terms, and bibliographical suggestions.

"World Order"

A course on "World Order" developed by Priscilla Griffith, a teacher at Melbourne High School in Melbourne, Florida, bears some resemblance to the unit of Gerald Thorpe discussed above; for example, the Van Slyck is used as a basic text, and the Clark-Sohn model is studied. But several different emphases may be pointed out. For one thing, the Melbourne High School course involves the examination of several models suggested by Saul Mendlovitz of the World Law Fund: "The U.N. view," "the protracted conflict theory," "regionalism," "polycentrism," "bi-polarism," and "world law." Students also use a number of case studies to examine the operation of models studied or developed by students. These cases may be historical (Arthur Larson, *When Nations Disagree*, is an important source), contemporary (such as Vietnam), or hypothetical (for example, China invades Taiwan, or Israel and the United Arab Republic have an atomic war).

The Causes and Nature of Human Conflict

Gerald Hardcastle of Nathan Hale High School in Seattle has developed a course on war and peace of importance to other teachers. While much of this course deals with the kind of models for changing the international system already discussed above, an important section provides students with materials on the causes and nature of human conflict. The film *Lord of the Flies* is used at the beginning to raise questions about the roots of conflict and aggression. The students also read selections from Robert Ardrey's *African Genesis* and *Territorial Imperative*, Lorenz' *On Aggression*, and psychiatrist Frederic Wertham's *A Sign for Cain: An Exploration of Human Violence*, which squarely opposes the Lorenz-Ardrey "innate aggression" school. Through class discussions and readings, the students then examine *Men at War—1864, 1917, and 1984* and *War for Fun, Self-Fullfillment, and Satisfaction of Ghosts*, the word "ghosts" being used to refer to wars that were started or perpetuated to avenge "slain comrades or ancestors." The concluding part of the course stresses the alternative possibilities for achieving a more peaceful world, especially using the Griffith-Reardon reader.

"The Resolution of World Conflict Through Political Action in a Democracy"

Paul Biggers and others at the University School of Florida State University in Tallahassee are teaching a course titled "The Resolution of World Conflict Through Political Action in a Democracy." Through readings (such as Lorenz and Ardrey), simulation, and audio-visual aids, the students come to understand something of the nature of conflict. Special attention is given to "systems of conflict, motives and causes of conflict, and the scope and nature of revolution, civil conflict, and war." Then a systems approach and simulation are used to examine conflict resolution and to develop models for world order.

A Unit Based on Data and Simulation

Olin C. Kirkland of San Ramon High School, San Ramon, California, has been preparing a unit on conflict that may be unique in schools for its intensive use of data. He has collected a wide variety of charts, graphs, and tables from such sources as Quincey Wright, Scrokin, and Richardson, and issues of the *Journal of Conflict Resolution* to help students inquire into the nature of war. One particularly relevant exercise has students investigate the possible relationship between national instability and the process of modernization with outbreaks of war. Or, are stable nations less warlike?

The San Ramon High School course employs a number of simulations and games. For example, variations on *Prisoner's Dilemma* (*see* Anatole Rapoport, *Fights, Games and Debates*, University of Michigan Press, 1960, $6.95) and *Arms and Resources* are used to study the dynamics of arms races. Also, a version of the *Inter-Nation Simulation* is played to get at such concepts as threat, misperception, and escalation.

A Unit for College-bound Students

Nathaniel Glidden of the Horace Mann School, the Bronx, New York, has been teaching a one term course on war and peace to college-bound students. One of the principal texts has been *Toward a Theory of War Prevention* (World Law Fund, 1966, $2.50), which is volume I of a four-volume collection of readings, edited by Richard Falk and Saul Mendlovitz, titled *The Strategy of World Order*, that was aimed mainly at university students. Hollin's *Peace Is Possible* is also used. One of the interesting features of this course is the use of a number of outside speakers on such topics as overpopulation, the effects of TV violence, and the military-industrial complex.

A Unit Based on the Evaluation of the Nation-State

A very different kind of course dealing with war/peace concepts has been the product of Mark Emerson and colleagues at Friends Central School in Philadelphia. Inspired by Pierre Teilhard de Chardin's *The Phenomenon of Man* (Torch Books, 1959, $1.95), the course develops the theme that social organization has become gradually integrated "into a smaller and smaller number of larger and larger units"; that is, from the clan and tribe to the large nation-state. In the context of a world history course, such topics as unification, specialization, communications, and values are studied through various media, including readings and graphs.

RESOURCES

Resource Organizations

Ad Hoc Committee for Introducing Peace-Related Material at the Secondary School Level, c/o Nathaniel F. Glidden, 3850 Hudson Manor Terrace, Riverdale, N.Y. 10463. Has collected syllabi and reading lists of school courses. The Committee includes scientists and social studies teachers and aims at bridging the gap between the social studies classroom and scientific peace research.

American Friends Service Committee, Peace Education Division, 160 North 15th Street, Philadelphia 19102. Services and publications available, including *Teaching about Peace Issues* and *In Place of War,* a non-violent approach to national security.

Atlantic Information Centre for Teachers, 23/25 Abbey House, 8 Victoria Street, London, S.W. 1. A number of services and publications available, including "The World and the School," a handbook for teachers of current international affairs that appears three times a year; "Crisis Papers," on important events, and "World Survey," a monthly series on a country or topic; and occasional publications, such as "Interdisciplinary Studies in Secondary Schools."

Canadian Peace Research Institute, Oakville, Ontario, Canada. Publishes "Peace Research Reviews," a series of booklets on various aspects of peace research. See their "Peace Research Around the World," 1969, and others in the series listed below. 514 Chartwell Road, Oakville, Ontario, Canada.

Carnegie Endowment for International Peace, 345 East 46th Street, New York, N.Y. 10017. Publications available, including *International Conciliation,* a periodical issued five times a year.

Center for Teaching International Relations, Graduate School of International Studies, University of Denver, Denver, Colorado 80210. Aids teachers in introducing international materials into the classroom. Publishes a newsletter, runs summer and in-service institutes. An important source of information about effective materials and teaching techniques.

Center for the Study of Democratic Institutions, P. O. Box 4068, Santa Barbara, California. Booklets, papers, and tapes available.

Center for Teaching of Problems of War and Peace, University of Hawaii, Honolulu, Hawaii 96822. A broad-range resource center that includes bibliographies and instructional materials. Teachers may also work with the Center.

Center for Teaching about Peace and War, 784 University Center Building, Wayne State University, Detroit, Michigan 48202. Provides and develops curriculum materials from kindergarten through college. Conducts seminars and conferences for teachers and students. Simulation is an important part of its interest.

Center for War/Peace Studies, 218 East 18th Street, New York, N.Y. 10003. Publishes *War/Peace Report,* a monthly magazine. Maintains a reference library and consultation service.

Committee for World Development and World Disarmament, 218 East 18th Street, New York, N.Y. 10003.

Conference on Peace Research in History, c/o Bernice Carroll, 221 Altgeld Hall, University of Illinois, Urbana, Illinois 61801. A committee of the American Historical Association mainly to help college teachers, this group has available an extensive bibliography, which includes a list of organizations providing materials, and syllabi of peace-related college courses.

Council on Religion and International Affairs, 170 East 64th Street, New York, N.Y. 10021. An inter-denominational organization that publishes a number of pamphlets and paperbacks concerned with religious ethics and international affairs; for example *The Moral Dilemma of Nuclear Weapons,* edited by William Clancy and *Morality and Modern War* by John Murray.

Diablo Valley School Systems Project "Teaching about War and Peace," Center for War/Peace Studies, 1730 Grove Street, Berkeley, California 94709. The Project and the Center have available a wide variety of useful materials for schools, including "To End War," an annotated bibliography; "Key Concepts in the War/Peace Field"; "Criteria for Evaluating Materials in the War/Peace Field"; and "Peace and World Affairs Organization." The Project can also put teachers in touch with other teachers who have had experience in developing peace-oriented materials and courses.

Foreign Policy Association, 345 E. 46th St., New York.

United Nations Association, 833 United Nations Plaza, New York, N.Y. 10017. Numerous publications and materials available to schools for studying the United Nations. Publishes *Vista* magazine, a valuable source of current information on the U.N.

UNESCO Publications Center, 317 East 34th St., N.Y. 10017. Publishes many materials that schools can use. Write for "A List of Free and Inexpensive Materials."

World Law Fund, 11 West 42nd Street, New York, N.Y. 10036. This organization is developing a wide range of materials directly aimed at social studies classrooms, including booklets, film guides, collections of readings, tapes, reprints, film strips, and simulations. Write for the latest catalogue of "Books, Audio-Visual Aids and Other Teaching Materials on War Prevention and World Order."

U.S. State Department, Office of Media Services, Bureau of Public Affairs, Room 5536, Department of State, Washington, D.C. 20520. Many publications and services available. Write for "A Pocket Guide to Foreign Policy Information Materials and Services."

Resource Center for the War/Peace Area in Education, c/o Mrs. Constance L'Aventure, Supervisor of Teacher Training in the Social Studies, School of Education, University of California, Berkeley, California 94707.

United States Arms Control and Disarmament Agency, 2201 C Street, N.W., Washington, D.C. 20451. Publishes a variety of materials, some of which are useful for schools. See especially the latest edition of "World Military Expenditures," which contains useful data on the arms race; also, "Arms Control and National Security," a readable introduction to the subject in booklet form.

Audio-Visual Materials

American Documentary Films, Inc., 336 West 84th Street, New York, N.Y. 10024 is a nonprofit organization specializing in films on social and political issues, including war and foreign policy.

Educational Film Library Association, Inc., 250 West 67th Street, New York, N.Y. 10019 publishes a catalogue of feature-length 16mm films for $7.50.

Messer, John, ed., "Films on War/Peace Issues," 1968, 52 pp., $.75, available from The Center for the Study of Democratic Institutions (see under Resource Organizations), has a variety of tapes available, including "The Warless World."

Weil, Jonathan, "Pictures on Our Mind: Short Films and Peace," *Media and Methods,* October 1969. Reprints available from World Law Fund, 11 West 42nd Street, New York, N.Y. 10036.

The World Law Fund (see under Resource Organizations) has a variety of tapes, films and film guides available.

World Without War Council, 1730 Grove Street, Berkeley, California, 94709 has available a number of useful aids for teachers, including bibliographies on war, civil disobedience, and revolution.

Bibliographies

Cook, Blanche, Bibliography on Peace Research in History, Clio Press, 1969.

Legualt, Albert, 1967, Bibliography on Peace-Keeping. 1967. Available from World Without War Council, 1730 Grove Street, Berkeley, California 94709.

Pickus, Robert and Woito, Robert, To End War: An Introduction to the Ideas, Books, Organizations, Work That Can Help. 1970. World Without War Council, 1730 Grove Street, Berkeley, California 94709. Contains a thoughtfully organized and annotated bibliography with essays introducing each section, as well as a lucid presentation of a conceptual framework for examining war-peace issues and resource organizations and materials. An invaluable aid for the teacher.

Williams, Stillman P., "Toward a Genuine World Security System." 1964. United World Federalists, 1346 Connecticut Avenue, N.W., Washington, D.C. 20036.

Simulation Games of International Conflict

"Conflict," a futuristic simulation based on the disarmament plan developed by Arthur Waskow in *Keeping the World Disarmed*, a booklet published by the Center for the Study of Democratic Institutions. (See Resource Organizations.) This simulation available from the World Law Fund. (See Resource Organizations.)

"Dangerous Parallel," a simulation in which students play ministerial roles for six fictionalized countries facing a situation approximating that of the Korean War. Developed by the Foreign Policy Association. Available from Scott, Foresman & Co., 99 Bauer Drive, Oakland, New Jersey 07436.

"Resources and Arms" and other simple simulations are contained in "Simulating Social Conflict," available from Sociological Resources for the Social Studies, 503 First National Building, Ann Arbor, Michigan 48108.

A number of relevant simulations are listed and described in *Simulation Games for the Social Studies Classroom* by William A. Nesbitt, New Dimensions Series (Thomas Y. Crowell, 1970).

WEST COAST

South African Wild Flower Guide 7

Text by:

John Manning
OF THE NATIONAL BOTANICAL INSTITUTE OF SOUTH AFRICA

Peter Goldblatt
OF THE MISSOURI BOTANICAL GARDEN, USA

Photography by: John Manning

This guide is the 7th in the Botanical Society's series of Wild Flower Guides and is published jointly by the Botanical Society and the Darling Wild Flower Society in association with the National Botanical Institute

The Botanical Society of South Africa was founded in 1913 to support the National Botanic Gardens, to promote the conservation and cultivation of our indigenous flora and to provide environmental education.

One of our projects is the publication of a series of wild flower guides.

Published to date are:

Guide 1: Namaqualand and Clanwilliam	1981 (out of print)
Guide 1: (revised): Namaqualand	1988/1994
Guide 2: Outeniqua, Tsitsikamma &	
Eastern Little Karoo	1982/1996
Guide 3: Cape Peninsula	1983/1996
Guide 4: Transvaal Lowveld & Escarpment	1984
Guide 5: Hottentots Holland to Hermanus	1985
Guide 6: Karoo	1994

On pages 2 and 3: A diversity of species on sandy flats at Hopefield, including *Lachenalia pustulata, Arctotheca calendula, Dimorphotheca pluvialis, Senecio littoreus* and *Trachyandra muricata*

Opposite titlepage: The wet granite soils at Darling are the setting for many floral gems, including *Romulea obscura, Geissorhiza eurystigma* and *Drosera cistiflora.*

First edition, first impression 1996
Botanical Society of South Africa
Kirstenbosch, Claremont 7735 RSA

© Text and photographs
Cape Department of Nature & Environmental Conservation

Design, typesetting and production by Wim Reinders
Reproduction by CMYK pre-press, Cape Town
Printed and bound by CTP Book Printers, Caxton Street, Parow

ISBN 1-874999-11-2

FOREWORD

It is a great honour for me to have been asked by the Botanical Society to write the foreword to the West Coast Wild Flower Guide.

This is the 7th publication in the Botanical Society's Wild Flower Guide series and is a joint publication with the Darling Wild Flower Society, co-authored by two eminent botanists, Drs Manning and Goldblatt.

The Darling Wild Flower Society, still the only conservation body active in Darling, has spearheaded flora conservation efforts since 1917, when it was founded by Mrs Suzanne Malan and my great-grandfather, Frederick Duckitt. They used the annual spring flower shows to promote conservation amongst the district's farmers, who have since maintained the botanical diversity of the region over several generations.

In 1972 the Darling community was involved in the publication of Hilda Mason's Western Cape Sandveld Flowers which has been out of print for some time. In his foreword to Hilda's book, my father, Frederick Duckitt, mentioned the successful contribution that farmers had made to veld conservation. Whilst this success has continued in the ensuing years, the opening of the West Coast to development has placed its most delicate and beautiful part under threat of extinction.

Proceeds from this publication will therefore be used to fund new and continuing flora conservation projects aimed at preserving the flora in our district. We are sure that it will stimulate interest in flora consevation by the public as well as farmers. We have come to realise that the veld is a living entity and have only recently learnt to appreciate the beautiful flowers that appear at different times throughout the year.

The great species richness (less than half are illustrated in this publication) and high level of endemism make the West Coast a very special place to wild flower lovers the world over.

This book honours those who conserve the floral wealth of the West Coast.

John Duckitt
Waylands, Darling
April 1996

CONTENTS

Opposite page: The granite outcrops at Langebaan support several rare and endemic species.

Following pages: Lachenalia aloides, Cheiridopsis rostrata and *Romulea flava* nestling on a granite outcrop at Langebaan.

These guides are made possible through the co-operation of members of
the public and private sector through their dedication to the conservation of
our floral wealth. The Publications Committee that has motivated the
series consists of representatives from the following bodies: the Botanical
Society of South Africa, Cape Nature Conservation and the National
Botanical Institute.

ACKNOWLEDGEMENTS

We thank all those who helped make the publication of this guide possible. The prime instigator of this guide has been the committee of the Darling Wild Flower Society which was lavish with its hospitality, while the farmers on the West Coast made free of their land and shared generously of their time and facilities. This book is a tribute to their vision and dedication to conserving the wild flowers of the West Coast.

Many of the species illustrated in this guide would not have been located without the assistance of those residents in the area whose love of the wildflowers about them encouraged a keen interest in learning more about the diminishing native flora. In particular we would like to thank Kobie Truter of Langebaanweg who first introduced us to the vegetation of the Sandveld many years ago and whose enthusiasm has remained undiminished although her pantry must surely be; Erik & Fiona Kotze of Langrietvlei; Irmgard & Pieter Retief of Aurora; Pixie Littlewort, a lady of unbounded enthusiasm and humour who has done so much to foster a more intelligent interest in the vegetation of the West Coast; and Mark and John Duckitt, energetic successors to generations of a family whose interest in, and dedication to, conserving the native flora of the Darling area is well-known.

The following friends kindly made their photographs available to us: T. Köhler (*Pauridia longituba, Strumaria tenella*); C. Paterson-Jones (*Gethyllis afra, Haemanthus pubescens*); G.D. Duncan (*Lachenalia rubida*)

Finally thanks to our colleagues who assisted in naming species: E. van Jaarsveld, G.D. Duncan, J.P. Rourke, D.A. Snijman, K.E. Steiner, E.G.H. Oliver and E.M. Marais

Following pages: Aloe mitriformis enlivens a rather bleak summer scene south of Langebaan.

13

INTRODUCTION

This field guide covers a strip some 50 km wide along the west coast of Western Cape Province extending from Melkbosstrand in the south to Velddrif and the Berg River in the north. It is an area of mild, wet winters and hot dry summers when temperatures can reach 38°C. The average annual rainfall over the area varies between 125 and 350 mm, virtually all of it falling between April and September.

There are species of plants in flower thoughout the year but the greatest displays are over the short spring during the period from late August to early October. These include a variety of geophytes (plants with underground storage organs) in the families Iridaceae and Hyacinthaceae, numerous annual Asteraceae and Scrophulariaceae as well as various shrubs and shrublets, both deciduous and evergreen. After this the earth dries out rapidly and the annuals and geophytes disappear until the following spring. During summer several species of *Limonium* come into flower and provide a blaze of colour in an increasingly bleak landscape, drawing moisture from their taproots reaching deep into the sands. Another conspicuous species in flower at this time is *Cotyledon orbiculare* which stores water reserves in succulent leaves. In the late summer a number of bulbs send up their inflorescences without their leaves. In so doing they make their flowers available at a time when there is little else in bloom to distract potential pollinators. They are able to do this by drawing on the reserves stored in their underground organs. Their leaves develop later after the first autumn rains when the temperatures are still high enough to permit growth. Plants which have adopted this strategy include many Amaryllidaceae (*Amaryllis*, *Brunsvigia*, *Crossyne*) and a number of Asphodelaceae (*Bulbine cepacea*, *Bulbinella divaginata*). A wealth of species of *Oxalis* take advantage of the warmer weather during the first rains in autumn, their diminutive size enabling them to carpet the ground quickly in flowers. They too are sustained by reserves from underground rootstocks which are replenished following the full development of the leaves. During the wet, winter months the low temperatures inhibit growth but with the lengthening days and rising temperatures in spring the landscape is transformed and a multitude of species burst into bloom, each competing for the attention of pollinating insects and birds with a wide diversity of floral adaptations.

SPECIES RICHNESS

The area covered by this guide is approximately 4400 km² in extent and is home to about 1200 species of flowering plants. Most of these occur elsewhere too but some 80 (6.5%) are endemic to the West Coast and known from nowhere else. The level of endemism on the West Coast compares favourably with that on the Cape Peninsula, which is much more speciose: an area of 470 km² is home to 2285 species of which about 100 (4.4%) are endemic.

The level of endemism on the West Coast is thus high for a region of very limited

---

Geissorhiza eurystigma, G. monanthos, Ixia curta and a lovely magenta form of *Drosera cistiflora* on the damp flats at Kalbaskraal.

topographical diversity. The endemic species occur in sandveld and renosterveld communities and a number are restricted to limestone outcrops. They include the shrubs or shrublets *Agathosma thymifolia, Leucospermum tomentosum, Ruschia tecta*, geophytic species such as *Geissorhiza darlingensis, Gladiolus meliusculus* and *Moraea loubseri*, and the annuals *Cenia duckitii, Diascia collina* and *Steirodiscus speciosus*.

Although the West Coast is limited in topographical variety the modest variation is combined with a diversity of soil types differing substantially from one another in physical and chemical properties and in geological age. The proximity to the sea also results in marked differences in moisture conditions between slopes facing the sea mists and those facing away from them. These steep moisture gradients combined with the juxtaposition of soil types has enabled a wide variety of plant species to occupy the area and stimulated the evolution of new ones.

VEGETATION AND SOILS

The coastal strip from Melkbosstrand to about Elands Bay is known historically as the Sandveld because of the characteristic vegetation type of that name occurring along a narrow belt close to the coast, but two other major types of vegetation are also represented in the area. Each of these occurs on a particular soil and the juxtaposition of different soils and their characteristic vegetation types within the narrow confines of the West Coast is the main factor contributing to the richness of the flora.

Strandveld
Found on low-lying coastal plains with a winter rainfall of 50-300 mm a year and a sandy calcareous soil, this vegetation type extends from near Velddrif all along the southern coast to the Eastern Cape Province. It is an open scrub vegetation in which characteristic woody members include *Chrysanthemoides monilifera, Olea capensis, Euclea racemosa* and *Rhus tomentosa*, sometimes festooned with climbers such as *Cynanchum* and *Dipogon*. The soils are relatively rich in nutrients and many of the shrubs produce fleshy fruits that are readily dispersed by fruit-eating birds. It contains few endemic species and hardly any that are rare.

Sandveld
The most characteristic vegetation type on the West Coast, the sandveld is a type of fynbos in which the dominant plants are restionaceous genera such as *Willdenowia, Chondropetalum* and *Thamnochortus*. It occurs on deep, well drained, coarse sands and gravelly limestones. These soils are relatively recent in origin, deposited in shallow seas during the late Tertiary, 10-2 mya. They are poor in nutrients and support a vegetation lacking in tall shrubs although small shrubs such as *Phylica stipularis, Staavia radiata, Stoebe plumosa* and *Metalasia densa* can be common. In the spring numerous annual Asteraceae and Scrophulariaceae cover the sands and the distinctive rotstert, *Babiana ringens*, with brilliant red flowers is conspicuous.

Renosterveld
This vegetation type occurs on fine-textured soils mostly derived from shales of the

18

Strandveld near Bokbaai

Sandveld near Yzerfontein

Renosterveld on the hills near Darling

Limestone outcrop at Langebaan

Granite hill near Darling

late Precambian Malmesbury System, 800-600 mya, and the Bokkeveld Series of the early Palaeozoic, c. 400 mya. However, a type of renosterveld is well-developed on granite-derived soils, notably around Darling. Renosterveld is not common along the West Coast but covers much of the Swartland slightly further inland. The fine, or granular-leafed shrubs of genera such as *Eriocephalus, Elytropappus* and *Stoebe* are characteristic elements. The soil is fertile and largely given over to agriculture. As a result very little undisturbed renosterveld remains, especially in the lowlands. Over 70% of renosterveld in the Cape flora region has been lost to agriculture and much more than that in the Western Cape coastal plain.The vegetation is very rich in geo-phytic plants which make a fine display in spring when the shrub cover has been heavily grazed or burned.

Limestone
Deposited in shallow seas, the limestones of the West Coast are of Tertiary origin, 10–2 mya. They have a limited distribution and differ in their high alkalinity and nutrient status from the sandy and clay soils that surround them. As a result the veg-etation often supports a number of unusual species although their general aspect is not particularly distinctive. They form a peculiar part of the Strandveld vegetation. *Pteronia divaricata* and *Lycium tetrandrum* are common on the limestones although occurring throughout the Strandveld. A number of species are restricted to the West Coast limestones including *Muraltia harveyana, Agathosma thymifolia* and *Gladiolus caeruleus.*

21

Granite

Granite hills are the dominant landscape feature of the West Coast. These rocks of the early Palaeozoic, 600-520 mya, have largely been worn away to provide some of the richest agricultural land along the West Coast. The hills include extensive areas of exposed rock and shallow soils which provide a substrate for a variety of succulent Mesembryanthemaceae. The soils are of intermediate nutrient status and support a wide range of plant species, mostly part of the Renosterveld communities. The deeper soils have a diverse flora including many of the most beautiful geophytes, among which must be numbered *Ixia monadelpha*, *Gladiolus alatus*, *Romulea eximia* and *Geissorhiza radians*. Particularly characteristic among the shrubs are *Eriocephalus africanus* (kapokbos) and *Lobostemon fruticosus*.

USING THIS GUIDE

This guide illustrates the most common or conspicuous species occurring along the West Coast as well as a number which are rare or very restricted in distribution. It spans the entire year, for although most of the species flower during the spring there are those, some very conspicuous, which flower over the summer months. Species which are endemic or restricted to the West Coast are marked with an asterisk (*).

A total of 572 species are illustrated out of some 1200. Families which have not been well covered are those with inconspicuous flowers unlikely to attract attention. These include the rushes, reeds, sedges and grasses. The characters used to separate the species in these families are not easily visible and often highly specialized.

The species illustrated in this guide are grouped in families, which are in turn arranged approximately in a sequence of increasing specialization. The first group of flowering plants (families Asparagaceae to Iridaceae), including the sedges and rushes (Cyperaceae and Restionaceae), bulbous and cormous families (Hyacinthaceae, Amaryllidaceae and Iridaceae among others), and the orchids (Orchidaceae), are all recognised by having the floral parts in multiples of three and usually have narrow leaves in which the veins are parallel to each other and extend the length of the leaf. These families are collectively known as the Monocotyledons. The second, and larger, part of the book covers the Dicotyledons. These families are characterised by having the floral parts in multiples of four or five and leaves with netted venation, and include the mesembs (Mesembryanthemaceae), buchus (Rutaceae) and daisies (Asteraceae).

Within these two basic divisions the families are broadly arranged from the more generalized to the more specialized. Specializations include fusion of the petals so that the flowers become cup-shaped or tubular and a shift in the ovary from a position above the petals to one below them. The Asteraceae or Daisy family is further specialized in that numerous individual tubular flowers or florets (thus termed because of their diminutive size) are aggregated into flower heads which resemble a single flower, an effect heightened in some species by the extension of the tube in the peripheral florets into a strap-shaped lobe resembling a single petal. Such peripheral florets are termed ray florets while the central or tubular ones are known as disc florets. A similar situation is encountered in the genus *Euphorbia* in which a number of highly reduced flowers are clustered together in false flowers surrounded by petal-like nectar glands. Within the families the species are grouped in smaller units known as genera. In the larger genera we have tried to place similar species together to aid comparison.

Ongoing research has led to some changes in generic circumscriptions, particularly in the Scrophulariaceae and Asteraceae. The scientific names used in this guide are the currently accepted ones and may differ from those used for the same species in earlier parts of this series.

IDENTIFYING THE SPECIES

Plant species are identified technically by using a combination of characters, some of them difficult to see with the naked eye or rather esoteric in nature. The particular characters which are relevant vary tremendously and what is useful for determining species in one genus may be quite useless in another.

In this guide the primary means of identifying the species are the photographs. These have been taken along the West Coast and thus represent forms actually occurring there. Nevertheless, there is still local variation in both floral and vegetative morphology within the area so do not expect the specimen in sight to accord exactly in all details with the one illustrated. Once the plant in question has been related to the illustrations, the accompanying text provides additional information highlighting the most important characteristics of the species which should help to distinguish it from others, as well as information on colour variation, flowering times, habitat and distribution.

Finally it is worthwhile paying attention to the soil type on which the plant is found. In the Western Cape many species show decided preferences for a particular soil type and seldom or never occur on another. The most important to distinguish are sands, clays and limestones. The fourth type common on the West Coast are granite-derived sands which can support both sand and clay loving species, mostly depending on what other soil is most prevalent in the vicinity. Sands, clays and limestones support very distinctive plant communities and soil type can be inferred from the vegetation cover: Restionaceae and *Phylica* spp. on sand; *Elytropappus rhinocerotis* on clay; *Eriocephalus africanus* on granite and various shrublets on limestone.

COMMON NAMES

We have included vernacular names for all of the species. These are derived from common usage where available and unambiguous but we have drawn heavily from the lists developed by the Darling and Hopefield Wildflower Societies. We hope that the names used in this guide will become the standard vernacular names for the species and in order to foster this aim we have avoided using the same common name for more than one species. Slight modifications to some of the names have been necessary to achieve this.

Arctotis hirsuta, Foveolina tenella and *Dimorphotheca pluvialis* contribute to the composite carpet along the road near Velddrif.

DESCRIPTIONS
AND ILLUSTRATIONS
OF PLANTS

SCHIZAEACEAE

Schizaea pectinata Sw. *toothbrush Fern, curly grass Fern*
Tufted fern with slender, twisted, grass-like fronds. Fertile fronds with brown, terminal comb-like pinnae forming a brush. Frequent on sandy flats and slopes from the Western Cape to Malawi, also Madagascar and St Helena.

ASPARAGACEAE

Asparagus asparagoides L. *breëblaar Kransie*
Climber with green stems. Branchlets bearing flattened, leathery "leaves" with a greyish bloom. Flowers scattered, nodding, petals curled back, silvery white, anthers orange, strongly scented. *Flowering* July to September. Widespread among scrub from Gifberg to tropical Africa.

Asparagus capensis L. *Katdoring*
Shrub with widely spreading branches bearing thorns and whorls or clusters of short branchlets closely covered with small "leaves". Flowers one (rarely two) sessile at the tips of the branchlets, petals white with brown midribs, ovary green and anthers yellow, very fragrant (reminiscent of wax polish). *Flowering* April to August. A common species on sandy soils from Lüderitz to Bredasdorp.

Asparagus lignosus Burm.f. *wit Haakdoring*
Rigid, branching shrub bearing thorns and tufts of stiff leathery, needle-like "leaves". Young branches with white, finely grooved bark. Flowers in clusters, petals white with anthers orange and ovary green. *Flowering* October to November and February to April. In rocky and sandy areas from Porterville to Still Bay.

Asparagus rubicundus Bergius *swart Haakdoring*
Shrub with shining brown branches bearing hooked spines with a single branchlet in the axil of each. Branchlets bearing tufts of needle-like "leaves". Flowers scattered on short stalks, petals and ovaries white, anthers brown. *Flowering* January to June. On clay or granite slopes from Clanwilliam to Uitenhage.

ERIOSPERMACEAE

Eriospermum lanceifolium Jacq. *Lanterntjie*
Slender geophyte with irregular pink tuber. Leaf erect, with a grey bloom, sometimes shortly hairy, absent at flowering. Flowers inconspicuous, on short stalks, white with greenish midribs. *Flowering* March to April. On granite outcrops or sandstone slopes from Clanwilliam to Riversdale.

Schizaea pectinata

Asparagus asparagoides

Asparagus capensis

Asparagus lignosus

Asparagus rubicundus

Eriospermum lanceifolium

27

*Pauridia longituba M.F. Thomps.   *pyp Klipsterretjie*
Minute geophyte with bristly corm tunics. Leaves several, grass-like. Flowers solitary per stem but several stems per plant, with a perianth tube much longer than the petal lobes and two small bracts at the base of the ovary. *Flowering* May to June. Rare and restricted to granite outcrops between Vredenburg and Langebaan.
  Pauridia minuta (L.f.) Dur. & Schinz (Klipsterretjie) is smaller and has a perianth tube shorter than the petal lobes and the bracts some distance below the ovary. It grows on granite outcrops and sandy soils and is more widespread than *P. longituba*.

Spiloxene aquatica (L.f.) Fourc.   *water Sterretjie*
Geophyte with softly fibrous corm tunics. Leaves several, rather stiff. Bracts leafy and spreading. Flowers several in a radiating cluster, white. *Flowering* August to October. In pools or wet vleis from Namaqualand to Port Elizabeth.

Spiloxene capensis (L.) Garside   *Poublom*
Geophyte with hard, netted corm fibres. Leaves several, slender with small teeth on the margins. Bracts large and clasping the stem. Flowers solitary, yellow, white or pink, usually with a purple or green centre. Seeds 0-shaped. *Flowering* August to October. On damp flats from Clanwilliam to Humansdorp.

*Spiloxene canaliculata Garside   *geel Poublom*
Similar to *S. capensis* but the flowers with broader tepals, always orange with a brown centre and the seeds J-shaped. *Flowering* August to October. Restricted to damp sandy flats around Malmesbury and Darling.

Spiloxene serrata (Thunb.) Garside   *goue Sterretjie*
Geophyte with corm covered with netted tunics and twisted roots. Leaves several, narrow and channelled with small teeth on the margins. Bracts thread-like. Flowers solitary, yellow, orange or rarely white. *Flowering* June to September. Widespread in the Western Cape on clay or granite slopes.

Spiloxene ovata (L.f.) Garside   *geel Sterretjie*
Geophyte with corm covered with twisted roots. Leaves several, broad and soft, without marginal serrations. Bracts thread-like. Flowers solitary, yellow, often reddish on the reverse. *Flowering* July to October. In damp, rocky places from Gifberg to Caledon.

Pauridia longituba

Spiloxene aquatica

Spiloxene capensis

Spiloxene canaliculata

Spiloxene serrata

Spiloxene ovata

29

HYPOXIDACEAE

Empodium plicatum (L.f.) Salisb. *autumn Star, ploegtyd Sterretjie*
Geophyte with netted corm fibres. Leaves emerging at flowering time, narrow and longitudinally pleated, elongating after flowering. Flowers star-shaped, lemon yellow, with a long solid tube and underground ovary. *Flowering* April to June. In open places on flats and slopes from Langebaan to Kwazulu/Natal

*Empodium veratrifolium (Willd.) M.F. Thomps. *breëblaar Sterretjie*
Geophyte with papery corm tunics. Leaves present at flowering, several, longitudinally pleated. Flowers star-shaped, lemon-yellow, with a long ovary immediately below the flower at the end of a long stalk. *Flowering* May to June. Restricted to granite outcrops along the coast from Lambert's Bay to Saldanha Bay, growing in leaf mould in crevices.

TECOPHILAEACEAE

Cyanella hyacinthoides L. *blou Raaptol*
Deciduous geophyte with deeply buried corms covered with netted tunics. Leaves in a basal tuft, narrow with wavy margins. Flowers on long pedicels in loose racemes, blue to mauve. *Flowering* September to November. On clay or loam flats and slopes from Namaqualand to Riversdale.

Cyanella lutea L.f. *geel Raaptol*
Deciduous geophyte with deeply buried corms covered with netted tunics. Leaves basal, narrow with wavy margins. Flowers on long pedicels in loose racemes, bright yellow. *Flowering* September to October. Widespread on clay soils from Namaqualand to the Eastern Cape.

ASPHODELACEAE

Aloe mitriformis Mill. *krans Aalwyn*
Plants mostly sprawling untidily along the ground with the ends ascending and leafy. Leaves very fleshy, short and broad, mostly without spots or lines, margins prickly. Flowers crowded in dense heads, drooping, tubular, dull scarlet. *Flowering* mostly January to February. On rocky ridges and lower slopes often on granite outcrops, from Nieuwoudtville to Genadendal.

Kniphofia uvaria (L.) Hook.f. *Vuurpyl, Soldaat*
Rhizomatous perennial usually in small groups. Leaves stiff, tough and narrow, keeled, sometimes rough along the margins. Flowers crowded in a dense head on a naked stalk, drooping, narrowly tubular, at first red later orange or yellow. *Flowering* mostly summer and autumn, especially after fires. In seepage areas, marshy places and beside streams at lower altitudes from southern Namaqualand to Barkly East.

Empodium plicatum

Empodium veratrifolium

*Cyanella
hyacinthoides*

Cyanella lutea

Kniphofia uvaria

Aloe mitriformis

31

Bulbine annua (L.) Willd.   *geel Kwassie, Kopieva*
Annual with a tuft of slender, succulent leaves. Flowers crowded on several stems,
star-shaped with woolly stamens, bright yellow. *Flowering* September to
November. On sandy flats and slopes from Saldanha Bay to Riversdale.

Bulbine cepacea (Burm. f.) Wijnands   *herfs Kwassie, herfs Kopieva*
Geophyte with large, flat-based tuber-like rhizome and thick roots. Leaves several,
fleshy or succulent, narrow, often absent at flowering. Flowers crowded on a stout
stem, star-shaped with woolly stamens, bright yellow, scented. *Flowering* March to
April. On lower sandy and stony slopes from Clanwilliam to Riversdale.

Bulbinella divaginata P.L. Perry   *herfs Katstert*
Geophyte with clustered roots. Leaves several, slender and cylindrical, absent at
flowering. Flowers crowded on a slender stem, star-shaped with smooth stamens,
bright yellow. *Flowering* March to June. Common on lower hill slopes or mountains on shale or sandstone from Springbok to Paarl.

Bulbinella triquetra (L.f.) Kunth   *geel Katstert*
Geophyte with clustered roots. Leaves numerous, thread-like, triangular in section.
Flowers crowded on a slender stem, star-shaped with smooth stamens, pale yellow.
Flowering August to October. Common on flats or rocky slopes often on clay from
Clanwilliam to Caledon.

Trachyandra chlamydophylla (Baker) Oberm.   *renoster Kool*
Tufted perennial with leaves like knitting needles. Flowers in a sprawling
unbranched inflorescence, petals spreading, white, scented. Fruits pendulous.
Flowering August to October. Usually on clay soils from Malmesbury to the
Peninsula.

Trachyandra tabularis (Baker) Oberm.   *lang Kool*
Robust herb with few stiff, narrow leaves. Flowers in a tall, branched, willowy
inflorescence, white, scented. Fruit erect. *Flowering* October to November. In
coastal sands from Langebaan to Hermanus.

Bulbine annua

Bulbine cepacea

Bulbinella divaginata

Bulbinella triquetra

Trachyandra chlamydophylla

Trachyandra tabularis

33

Trachyandra filiformis (Aiton) Oberm. *vlei Kool*
Slender herb with few, soft, thread-like leaves usually spotted purple at the base.
Flowers in an unbranched inflorescence, on long spreading pedicels, white, scented. Fruits spreading. *Flowering* August to October. In seasonally waterlogged clay from Hopefield to Stanford.

Trachyandra ciliata (L.f.) Kunth *hotnots Kool, Wildeblomkool*
Sprawling herb with several trailing leaves, flat or keeled and rather spongy, usually hairy. Flowers white or greenish with spreading petals, crowded among hairy bracts at the end of a trailing stalk often with one or two short side branches. Fruits pendulous. *Flowering* August to September. In deep sandy soils, usually near the coast, from southern Namibia to Eastern Cape. The young inflorescences can be used as a vegetable.

Trachyandra falcata (L.f.) Kunth *Namakwa Kool*
Robust herb with curving, flat leathery leaves covered with grey bloom. Flowers densely packed on a few-branched inflorescence, the lowest bract forming a collar, petals spreading, only a few open each afternoon. White or pinkish. Fruits erect. *Flowering* July to October. Common on sandy soils from southern Namibia to Saldanha Bay.

Trachyandra muricata (L.f.) Kunth *rolbos Kool*
Robust perennial with few, flat, smooth or rough leaves. Flowers in a much-branched inflorescence, petals curved back slightly, only a few open each day, white. Fruits dry. *Flowering* July to October. Widespread on clay soils from southern Namibia to the Peninsula.

Trachyandra divaricata (Jacq.) Kunth *duine Kool*
Robust herb forming clumps of several tufts of narrow smooth fleshy leaves. Flowers nodding on a much-branched inflorescence, petals strongly curled back, only a few open each day, scented. Fruits somewhat leathery. *Flowering* June to September. On loose coastal sands and dunes from Hondeklip Bay to Bathurst.

ANTHERICACEAE

Caesia contorta (L.f.) Dur. & Schinz *Sokkiesblom*
Rhizomatous perennial producing tufts of grass-like leaves. Flowers in branched, sprawling inflorescences, nodding, petals curled back, pink to blue with the anther filaments banded in blue and yellow. *Flowering* November to December. In sandy soils from Namaqualand to the Eastern Cape.

Trachyandra filiformis

Trachyandra falcata

Trachyandra ciliata

Trachyandra muricata

Trachyandra divaricata

Caesia contorta

35

Chlorophytum triflorum (Aiton) Kunth *Gifkool*
Geophyte with numerous hard, grey, tapering roots and several narrow leaves. Inflorescence unbranched with several flowers in each bract. Flowers white, star-like, unscented. *Flowering* July to October. In loam or sand from Piketberg to the Peninsula.

Chlorophytum undulatum (Jacq.) Oberm. *Namakwa Gifkool*
Geophyte with numerous slender roots often swollen at the tips and several narrow or broad leaves. Inflorescence unbranched with several flowers in each bract. Flowers white, star-like, unscented. *Flowering* July to October. In clay or loam from Springbok to Prince Albert.

HYACINTHACEAE

Albuca maxima Burm.f. *wit Tamarak*
Robust geophyte with a bulb and several channelled, fleshy leaves. Flowers many, nodding on long pedicels, white with green keels. *Flowering* September to November. Widespread on sandy soils from Namaqualand to Langebaan.

Albuca flaccida Jacq. *slang Tamarak*
Robust geophyte with a bulb and several channelled, fleshy leaves. Flowers many, nodding on long pedicels, yellowish green with green keels. *Flowering* September to November. On stony soils from Vanrhynsdorp to the Peninsula.

Albuca cooperi Baker *Geldbeursie*
Geophyte with a bulb and several channelled leaves, warty below, on drying form-ing a fibrous neck around the base of the stem. Flowers many, nodding on curved pedicals, yellowish green. *Flowering* September to November. In sandy soils from Namaqualand to Swellendam

Albuca juncifolia Baker *klein Tamarak*
Small geophyte with a bulb and several thread-like leaves. Flowers few, nodding on curved pedicels, yellowish green. *Flowering* September to November. On loamy soils from Malmesbury to the Peninsula.

Chlorophytum triflorum   *Chlorophytum undulatum*   *Albuca maxima*

Albuca flaccida   *Albuca cooperi*   *Albuca juncifolia*

37

Veltheimia capensis (L.) DC. *Sandlelie*
Geophyte with several soft leaves with a grey bloom and wavy margins. Flowers clustered at the end of a stout, spotted stalk, drooping, tubular, pink with darker spots, tipped green. *Flowering* May to July. On granite outcrops and gravel flats from Nieuwoudtville to Darling.

Lachenalia rubida Jacq. *sand Viooltjie*
Geophyte with one or two spreading leaves, sometimes spotted below. Flowers drooping, cylindrical, inner petals much longer than the outer, pink to ruby red, sometimes spotted. *Flowering* March to July after the first autumn rains. On sandy flats or slopes, often right on the seashore, from Namaqualand to George.

Lachenalia bulbifera (Cirillo) Engl. *rooi Naeltjie*
Similar to *L. rubida* but the inner petals only slightly longer than the outer, orange or red with the inner tipped purple. *Flowering* April to September. Occurring on dunes and rocky outcrops from near Klawer along the coast to Mossel Bay.

Lachenalia aloides (L.f.) Engl. *klip Viooltjie, Vierkleurtjie*
Geophyte with two spreading leaves, usually heavily spotted. Flowers drooping, cylindrical, the inner petals much longer than the outer, outer petals orange at the base grading to yellow with green tips and inner petals yellow sometimes with purple tips. *Flowering* July to October. On rocky, often granite, outcrops from Lambert's Bay to Bredasdorp.

Lachenalia unicolor Jacq. *pers Viooltjie*
Geophyte with two clasping leaves, pustulate but sometimes withered at flowering. Flowers on short pedicels, petals lilac to purple and darker at the tips. *Flowering* September to October. On damp sandy flats from Nieuwoudtville to Somerset West.

Lachenalia unifolia Jacq. *blou Viooltjie*
Geophyte with one clasping leaf barred with maroon at the base. Flowers spreading on distinct pedicels, outer petals bluish with brown tips, inner petals whitish. *Flowering* August to October. Widespread in sandy soils often on rock outcrops from Namaqualand to the Peninsula.
　　Lachenalia hirta (Thunb.) Thunb. (haarblaar Viooltjie) is similar but the leaf is covered with long erect hairs.

Veltheimia capensis

Lachenalia rubida

Lachenalia bulbifera

Lachenalia aloides

Lachenalia unicolor

Lachenalia unifolia

Lachenalia longibracteata E. Phillips   *renoster Viooltjie*
Geophyte with one or two leaves, sometimes spotted. Flowers sessile with long
slender bracts, outer petals bluish or yellow with brown or green tips, inner petals
cream or yellow. *Flowering* July to September. On moist flats or stony slopes from
Piketberg to Malmesbury.

Lachenalia pallida Aiton   *bleek Viooltjie*
Geophyte with one or two leaves sometimes covered with small pustules. Flowers
shortly stalked in a dense spike, cream to yellow, outer petals brown or green at the
tips. *Flowering* August to October. Common on clay soils from Piketberg to
Stellenbosch.

Lachenalia pustulata Jacq.   *knoppies Viooltjie*
Geophyte with one or two leaves, often covered with pustules. Flowers shortly
stalked, cream, pink or bluish with brownish pink tips, inner petals with brownish
or green tips. *Flowering* August to October. Often in large colonies on sandy flats
or granite outcrops from Saldanha Bay to the Peninsula.

Lachenalia mutabilis Sweet   *bont Viooltjie*
Geophyte with one leaf, sometimes faintly spotted. Flowers in a dense spike with
the upper flowers reduced and stalked, bright blue, the lower urn-shaped, inner
petals protruding, outer petals pale blue to white with brown tips and the inner yellow. *Flowering* July to September. On stony sands and granite from Namaqualand
to Langebaan.

Drimia capensis (Burm. f.) Wijnands   *Maerman*
Geophyte with large bulb, leafless at flowering. Leaves several, strap-shaped, produced before the flowers. Flowers in an elongate spike up to two metres, white, the
petals curled back, scented. *Flowering* December to March. Widespread in sandy
soils throughout much of South Africa.
   Drimia elata Willd. (Brandui) has a reddish bulb, narrower leaves with hairy
margins, and greenish or brownish flowers; *Drimia media* Willd. (Jeukbol) is very
similar to *D. elata* but is smaller and the leaves are like knitting needles and present at flowering.

Tenicroa filifolia (Jacq.) Raf.   *Gifbol*
Deciduous geophyte with numerous very narrow leaves, round in section, surrounded at the base by membranous, ringed sheaths. Flowers crowded on slender
stems, white with brown keels, scented. *Flowering* September to October. On clay
and loam flats and slopes from Nieuwoudtville to Bredasdorp.
   Tenicroa exuviata (Jacq.) Speta (groot Gifbol) is more robust with few stiff
leaves and often occurs on granite outcrops.

Lachenalia longibracteata   *Lachenalia pallida*   *Lachenalia pustulata*

Lachenalia mutabilis   *Drimia capensis*   *Tenicroa filifolia*

Ornithogalum suaveolens Jacq. *bont Tjienk*
Deciduous geophyte with narrow, channelled leaves, sometimes withered at flowering. Flowers slightly cup-shaped, petals green with yellowish margins. *Flowering* September to November. On stony slopes and sandy flats from Namibia to Port Elizabeth.

Ornithogalum thyrsoides Jacq. *Chinkerinchee*
Deciduous geophyte with slender, channelled leaves, often withered at flowering. Flowers in a rounded cluster at the top of the stem, cup-shaped, cream with a green or grey ovary and centre, inner filaments broad and clasping at the base. *Flowering* October to December. In sandy or shale soils, common in pastures and fields from Namaqualand to Caledon.

Ornithogalum conicum Jacq. *somer Tjienk*
Similar to *O. thyrsoides* but with flowers in a cone-shaped cluster and brilliant white in colour. *Flowering* October to December. In seasonally damp loamy or clay washes or slopes from Namaqualand to the Eastern Cape.

Ornithogalum multifolium Bak. *klip Tjienk*
Deciduous geophyte with several narrow, thread-like leaves. Flowers cup-shaped, orange. *Flowering* September to October. In shallow sandy pockets on rock sheets from Namaqualand to Swellendam.

Massonia angustifolia L.f. *Bobbejaanboek, orange Buttonhole flower*
Dwarf geophyte with two spreading, shining dark green, longitudinally grooved leaves. Flowers with inconspicuous pale petals but very prominent orange stamens. *Flowering* May to June. On dry, stony clay flats inland but in damp sandy places near the coast from Namaqualand to Saldanha Bay.

ALLIACEAE

Tulbaghia capensis L. *Wildeknoffel*
Deciduous geophyte with several, narrow, channelled, greyish leaves, smelling of onion when bruised. Flowers several in a cluster at the tip of the stems, tubular, grey and brown. *Flowering* April to September. On clay or loam from Darling to George.

Ornithogalum suaveolens

Ornithogalum thyrsoides

*Ornithogalum
conicum*

Ornithogalum multifolium

Massonia angustifolia

*Tulbaghia
capensis*

Amaryllis belladonna L.   *Belladonna, March lily*
Geophyte with oval or globose bulb. Leaves seven to nine, erect, narrow, channelled, absent at flowering. Flowers large and trumpet-shaped, various shades of pink, strongly scented of narcissus. *Flowering* February to April, particularly after fire. Along the edges of vleis or in small valleys on clay, from near Clanwilliam to George. Poisonous to stock and humans.

Cybistetes longifolia (L.) Milne-Redh. & Schweick.   *Malgaslelie*
Geophyte with large, globose bulb. Leaves many, spreading in a fan, narrow, absent at flowering. Flowers large and showy, trumpet-shaped, cream to pink and darkening with age, strongly and sweetly scented. *Flowering* December to March, mostly after fire. Widespread in open sandy or gravelly soil from the Orange River to the Peninsula.

Brunsvigia orientalis (L.) Eckl.   *Kandelaar*
Geophyte with oval or globose bulb. Leaves two to six, spreading flat on the ground, narrow, velvety, absent at flowering. Flowers strongly upcurved with petals curled back, very irregular, bright red or pink. *Flowering* February to March. On sandy flats, often near the coast, from Saldanha Bay to Riversdale.

Crossyne guttata (L.) D. & U. Müll.-Doblies *Seeroogblom, Sambreelblom, Haarblaar*
Geophyte with globose bulb. Leaves four to six, rather narrow, smooth and leathery but with coarsely bristly maroon margins and maroon spots underneath, absent at flowering. Flowers insignificant, with narrow pink petals curling back and soon turning brown. *Flowering* March to April, rarely except after fire. On clay flats and lower slopes from Piketberg to Swellendam. The bulb is extremely poisonous.

*****Strumaria chaplinii** (W.F. Barker) Snijman   *Saldanha Tolbol*
Small geophyte with globose bulb. Leaves two, prostrate, narrow and hairy above, absent at flowering. Flowers star-like on long stalks radiating from the top of the stem, white with maroon anthers. *Flowering* March to April. Confined to granite outcrops along the coast between St Helena Bay and Saldanha Bay.

Strumaria tenella (L.f.) Snijman   *Tolbol*
Small geophyte with globose bulb. Leaves one to four, erect, narrow and almost cylindrical, present at flowering. Flowers star-like on long stalks radiating from the top of the stem, white to pale pink with red or green anthers, scented. *Flowering* April to July. Often in dense colonies on seasonally moist loam, throughout the Western Cape (also Orange Free State and Lesotho).

Amaryllis belladonna

Brunsvigia orientalis

*Cybistetes
longifolia*

Crossyne guttata

Strumaria chaplinii

Strumaria tenella

Boophane haemanthoides F. M. Leighton   *Kwaslelie*
Geophyte with large, globose bulbs visible above ground. Leaves many, in a
spreading fan, margins wavy, bluish-grey, absent at flowering. Flowers enclosed in
two large reddish bracts, creamy pink, with narrow petals. *Flowering* November to
December. In sandy soils from Namaqualand to Langebaan.

Haemanthus sanguineus Jacq.   *Brandlelie, Velskoenblaar*
Geophyte with large, flattened bulb. Leaves two or three, prostrate, rounded and
leathery with cartilaginous margins, absent at flowering. Flower stalk red,
unmarked, bearing five to eleven red or pink bracts and numerous narrow red or
pink flowers. *Flowering* January to April, especially after fire. On clay or sandy
soils from Clanwilliam to Port Elizabeth.

Haemanthus pubescens L.f.   *Poeierkwas*
Geophyte with large, flattened bulb. Leaves two, rarely three, spreading, narrow,
hairy at least on the margins, absent at flowering. Flower stalk red or pink, sometimes mottled, bearing four or five red bracts slightly longer than the numerous narrow red flowers. *Flowering* March to April. Confined to the sandy coastal plain
from southern Namibia to Cape Town.

Haemanthus coccineus L.   *April fool, Rooikwas*
Geophyte with large, flattened bulb. Leaves two, rarely three, spreading, broad and
leathery without hairs, absent at flowering. Flower stalk cream to light red with
deep red spots, bearing six to nine red or pink bracts usually slightly shorter than
the numerous narrow red or pink flowers. *Flowering* February to April. Widespread
from southern Namibia to Grahamstown. The bulb is poisonous.

Gethyllis afra L.   *Kukumakranka*
Geophyte with globose bulb. Leaves several, narrow and spirally twisted, sometimes hairy, absent at flowering. Flowers at ground level, star-shaped or cupped, on
a slender stiff stalk, white but flushed red outside, with numerous stamens. Fruit
slender and slightly clubbed, yellow to orange, very fragrant, edible. *Flowering*
December to January. In sandy soils from Clanwilliam to Caledon.
  Gethyllis britteniana Baker is very similar in flower but the leaves are enclosed
at the base in a spotted sheath.

Boophane haemanthoides

*Haemanthus
sanguineus*

Haemanthus pubescens

*Haemanthus
coccineus*

Gethyllis afra

All species in this family contain toxic alkaloids and some species of *Ornithoglossum* are suspected of causing livestock poisoning.

Ornithoglossum viride (L.f.) Aiton *groen Spinnekoppie*
Geophyte with two or three greyish leaves. Flowers nodding, star-like, grey or green with white centres. *Flowering* June to October. On lowlands in deep sands from Clanwilliam to Riversdale.

Wurmbea marginata (Desr.) B. Nord. *Swartkoppie*
Geophyte with three narrow, leathery leaves clasping at the base. Flowers sessile, star-shaped with a cup, blackish purple, scented. *Flowering* September to October. On granite soils from Hopefield to Riversdale.

Baeometra uniflora (Jacq.) G.J. Lewis *Slangblom*
Geophyte with several channelled leaves. Flowers sessile, star-shaped with a cup, bright yellow or orange with a black centre. *Flowering* September to November. In sandy soils from Malmesbury to Swellendam.

Onixotis stricta (Burm. f.) Wijnands *Rysblommetjie*
Geophyte with 3 dark green, channelled leaves, the upper 2 inserted immediately below the flowers. Flowers sessile in crowded spikes, star-shaped, pale pink with a maroon centre. *Flowering* August to October. In pools and marshes from Namaqualand to the Peninsula.
   O. punctata (L.) Mabberley (Hanekammetjie) is smaller with the 2 lowermost leaves basal and the uppermost inserted midway up the stem. It occurs on clay or granite slopes.

IRIDACEAE

Aristea africana (L.) Hoffmanns. *Blousuurkanol, Koringblommetjie*
Tufted rhizomatous geophyte. Leaves in a basal cluster, narrow. Flowering stem sparsely branched, bracts membranous and brown, conspicuously fringed. Flowers blue, lasting a few hours. *Flowering* October to February. On sandy flats and slopes from Nieuwoudtville to Riversdale.

Aristea dichotoma (Thunb.) Ker Gawl. *Venstervrug*
Tufted geophyte, often clumped by branching of the rhizome. Leaves in a basal cluster, narrow. Flowering stem slender and much-branched, bracts small with silvery, membranous margins. Flowers blue, lasting a few hours. *Flowering* October to January. On sandy lowland soils from Vanrhynsdorp to Caledon.

Ornithoglossum viride

Wurmbea marginata

Baeometra uniflora

Onixotis stricta

Aristea africana

Aristea dichotoma

49

Melasphaerula ramosa (L.) N.E. Br. *Feëklokkie, Baardmannetjie*
Geophyte with bell-shaped corm and fibrous tunics. Leaves soft. Flowers in delicate, branched inflorescences, creamy-yellow with maroon streaks on the lower lobes, faintly scented. *Flowering* July to September. On rocky clay or granite or sandstone from southern Namibia to Bredasdorp.

Ferraria densepunctulata M.P. de Vos *grys Uiltjie*
Geophyte with short, often purple stem. Lower leaves narrow and upper leaves short and spreading. Flowers olive green at the ends of the petals and pale grey densely spotted with purple in the centre, each petal with a bright green blotch near the base, almost scentless, lasting two days. *Flowering* May to July. In coastal sand and on granite outcrops along the seaboard from Lambert's Bay to Langebaan.

Ferraria ferrariola (Jacq.) Willd. *gespikkelde Spinnekopblom*
Geophyte with slender stem spotted with purple. Lower leaves very narrow, the upper much broader. Flowers not crowded, pale greenish with spots, scented, lasting two or three days. *Flowering* June to September. In sandy or stony soil from Namaqualand to Vredenburg.

Ferraria divaricata Sweet *geel Spinnekopblom*
Geophyte with short stems concealed by the leaves. Leaves short or long, greyish. Flowers yellowish and grey, with a deep cup, scented, lasting a single day. *Flowering* July to November. Sandy flats and rocky slopes from Namibia to Oudtshoorn.

Ferraria crispa Burm. *Spinnekopblom*
Robust geophyte with stem often mottled with red. Lower leaves narrow and ridged. Flowers crowded in inflated bracts, cream with dark brown blotches or completely brown, the petal margins ruffled and greenish or dull yellow, unpleasantly scented, lasting a single day. *Flowering* August to October. In sand or loamy soil from Lambert's Bay to Mossel Bay.

Ferraria uncinata Sweet *blou Spinnekopblom*
Geophyte with short stems concealed by the leaves. Leaves short and diverging, with crisped margins. Flowers with a deep cup, purple with tightly curled, olive green margins, tendril-like at the tips, scented, lasting two or three days. *Flowering* August to October. On shale or clay from Springbok to Kalabaskraal.

Melasphaerula ramosa   *Ferraria densepunctulata*   *Ferraria ferrariola*

Ferraria divaricata   *Ferraria crispa*   *Ferraria uncinata*

Gynandriris setifolia (L.f.) Ker Gawl. *Papieruintjie*
Geophyte with white, fibrous corm tunics. Leaves one or two, narrow and chan-
nelled, long and trailing. Flowers with a long, tubular ovary, enclosed in dry,
papery bracts, greyish blue with orange markings, lasting one day. *Flowering*
August to October. Widespread on sandy soils, often in disturbed places from
Namaqualand to Grahamstown.

Moraea fugax (Delaroche) Jacq. *soet Uintjie*
Robust geophyte with fibrous, netted corm tunics. Leaves one or rarely two, insert-
ed well above the ground immediately beneath the first branch, narrow and chan-
nelled, long and trailing. Flowers large, white, blue or yellow, with orange nectar
guides, strongly scented, lasting a single afternoon. *Flowering* August to October.
Common in deep sands or rocky sandstone or granite, from Namaqualand to
Mossel Bay. The corms were an important food source for early people in the
Western Cape.

Moraea tripetala (L.f.) Ker Gawl. *blou Uintjie*
Slender geophyte with fibrous corm tunics. Leaf solitary, inserted at the base of the
stem, narrow and channelled. Flowers with the inner three petals reduced to
whiskers or absent, blue or purple, rarely pink or yellow, with yellow and white
nectar guides. *Flowering* August to October (December). Common in sand and clay
throughout the Western Cape.

Moraea villosa Ker Gawl. *blou Flappie, Uiltjie*
Geophyte with pale, coarsely netted corm tunics and hairy stems. Leaf solitary,
channelled, softly hairy on the outer side. Flowers mauve to purple with a dark
crescent at the base of the three broadest petals. *Flowering* August to September.
Mostly on clay slopes and flats from Citrusdal to Gordon's Bay.

Moraea tricolor Andrews *spog Uintjie*
Short geophyte with pale, fibrous corm tunics at the base of the three broadest
petals. Leaves three, channelled. Flowers yellow, pink or red with a yellow mark
outlined in brown or maroon, lasting a single afternoon. *Flowering* July to
September. On wet sandy flats from Hopefield to Caledon.

Moraea inconspicua Goldblatt *taai Uintjie*
Slender, branching geophyte with dark brown, coarsely fibrous to woody corm
tunics and sticky reddish stems. Leaves two, channelled, trailing. Flowers pale yel-
low to brown, with the petals folded back, lasting a single afternoon. *Flowering*
September to November. Mostly on shale or granite from Springbok to Port
Elizabeth.

Gynandriris setifolia

Moraea fugax

Moraea tripetala

Moraea villosa

Moraea tricolor

*Moraea
inconspicua*

53

Moraea gawleri Spreng. *renoster Uintjie*
Slender, branching geophyte with pale, hard, ridged corm tunics. Leaves two or three, channelled, often crisped. Flowers white, yellow to brick-red with yellow nectar guides, lasting a single day. *Flowering* August to September. Common and widespread on sandy and clay flats and slopes throughout the Western Cape.

Moraea bituminosa (L.f.) Ker Gawl. *teer Uintjie*
Slender, branching geophyte with coarsely netted corm tunics and sticky, reddish stems. Leaves two, channelled, slender and trailing. Flowers yellow, scented, lasting a single day. *Flowering* October to December. On sandy soils from Porterville to Bredasdorp.

Moraea ramosissima (L.f.) Druce *vlei Uintjie*
Geophyte with the corm enclosed in a basket of spiny roots and bearing many cormels. Leaves several in a fan, channelled. Flowers on branched stems, bright yellow, lasting a single day. *Flowering* October to December. Along streams and in marshy places on sand or granite from Gifberg to Grahamstown.

Moraea neglecta G.J. Lewis *geel Flappie*
Slender geophyte with soft brown corm tunics, the stem with sticky nodes. Leaf one, stiff and resembling a knitting needle. Flowers deep yellow with black streaks on the nectar guides, lasting a single afternoon. *Flowering* September to November. On sandy soils, especially near the coast, from Nieuwoudtville to Hermanus.
   M. angusta (Thunb.) Ker Gawl. (grys Flappie) is similar but has a brownish or blue cast to the flowers which have solid yellow nectar guides and orange, not yellow, pollen.

Moraea bellendenii (Sweet) N.E. Br. *patrys Uintjie*
Tall, slender geophyte with fibrous, netted corm tunics. Leaf solitary, channelled, long, narrow and trailing. Flowers with three large rounded petals and three small trilobed petals, bright yellow with brown speckles in the centre, lasting two or three days. *Flowering* October to November. Common on sandy flats and slopes from Darling to Knysna.

Hexaglottis lewisiae Goldblatt *Volstruisuintjie*
Slender geophyte with brown, coarsely fibrous corm tunics. Leaves two or three, narrow, channelled. Flowers golden yellow, style branches six thread-like and spreading, lasting a single afternoon, scented. *Flowering* October to November. On clay and sandy soils from Springbok to Humansdorp.

Moraea gawleri

Moraea bituminosa

*Moraea
ramosissima*

Moraea neglecta

Moraea bellendenii

*Hexaglottis
lewisiae*

Homeria flaccida Sweet   *groot Tulp*
Geophyte with blackish, coarsely netted corm tunics. Stems branched above. Leaf
solitary, narrow and trailing. Flowers shallowly cupped, salmon-pink with yellow
centre, stamens shortly extended on a central column. *Flowering* August to
October. On damp sandy flats and vleis from Nieuwoudtville to the Peninsula.
Poisonous to stock.

Homeria miniata (Andrews) Sweet   *pronk Tulp*
Geophyte with blackish, coarsely netted corm tunics. Stems much branched above.
Leaves two or three, strap-shaped and channelled. Flowers usually salmon-pink
with a yellow star in the centre, stamens extended on a central column. *Flowering*
August- October. On clay or sand from Namaqualand to Riversdale. Poisonous to
stock.

Homeria minor (Eckl.) Goldblatt   *klein Tulp*
Geophyte with blackish, netted corm tunics. Leaf solitary, long and trailing, chan-
neled. Stems few-branched. Flowers usually salmon-pink, petals forming a deep
cup enclosing the stamens. *Flowering* August-September. On sandy soils from
Citrusdal to the Peninsula.

Galaxia albiflora G.J. Lewis   *wit Horlosieblom*
Dwarf geophyte with narrow, channelled leaves. Flowers funnel-shaped, white with
a yellow centre, lasting a single day from 13h00 to 15h30. *Flowering* July to
September. In seasonally wet, sandy places, often on rocks from Stompneus Bay to
Cape Agulhas.

Galaxia ovata Thunb.   *Horlosieblom*
Dwarf geophyte with small, broad flat leaves. Flowers funnel-shaped, bright yellow, lasting a single day from 10h30 to 16h00. *Flowering* July to September. On
sandy soils from Wuppertal to Elim.

*****Geissorhiza darlingensis** Goldblatt   *geel Kelkiewyn*
Geophyte with overlapping, hard, brown corm tunics spiny above. Leaves three,
broad and ribbed. Flowers few, cup-shaped with the stamens upright, pale yellow
with a black centre. *Flowering* September to October. Restricted to damp granite
soils near Darling.

Homeria flaccida

Homeria miniata

Homeria minor

Galaxia albiflora

Galaxia ovata

*Geissorhiza
darlingensis*

57

Geissorhiza exscapa (Thunb.) Goldblatt *langpyp Sysie*
Geophyte with hard brown corm tunics which fragment irregularly. Leaves three, very narrow and grooved, sticky, often with sand adhering. Flowers large, cream to ivory, with petals 4,5-6 mm wide and a long slender tube, the anthers projecting conspicuously. *Flowering* September to October. In deep sandy soils mostly along the coast and slightly inland from Bloubergstrand to Hondeklip Bay.

Geissorhiza tenella Goldblatt *klein langpyp Sysie*
Similar to *G. exscapa* but the flowers smaller with narrower petals 3-4,5 mm wide. *Flowering* October to November. In seasonally wet sandy soils near the coast from Darling to Bredasdorp.

Geissorhiza aspera Goldblatt *blou Sysie*
Geophyte with overlapping, hard, dark corm tunics notched below and a minutely hairy stem. Leaves three, narrow, flat, sometimes rough. Flowers star-shaped with centrally placed stamens, pale to deep blue or purple. *Flowering* August to September. Mostly on sandy soils but also light clay, common throughout the Western Cape.

Geissorhiza monanthos Eckl. *bleek Sysie*
Geophyte with overlapping, hard, dark corm tunics notched below and a minutely hairy stem. Leaves three or four, narrow. Flowers slightly cupped with the prominent stamens directed downwards, dark blue with a pale yellow centre often ringed in red or black. *Flowering* August to October. In sandy or rocky soils, mostly granitic, from Citrusdal to near Paarl.

Geissorhiza radians (Thunb.) Goldblatt *witring Kelkiewyn*
Geophyte with overlapping, hard, dark corm tunics notched below. Leaves three, very narrow and grooved. Flowers few, cup-shaped with the stamens directed downwards and curled upwards at the tip, deep blue with a red centre ringed in white and a dark notch in the lower part of each petal. *Flowering* September to October. In damp sites in sandy, often granitic soil, on flats between Darling and Gordon's Bay.

*Geissorhiza eurystigma L. Bolus *Kelkiewyn*
Geophyte with overlapping, hard, black corm tunics notched below. Leaves three, broad and ribbed. Flowers few, cup-shaped with the stamens upright and closely clustered in the centre, shorter than the style and plump stigma, dark blue with a red centre. *Flowering* September to October. Local in sandy soil near the coast, between Kalabaskraal and Darling.
    **G. mathewsii* L. Bolus from the same area is very rare and is distinguished by the much shorter style which does not exceed the anthers.

Geissorhiza exscapa

Geissorhiza tenella

*Geissorhiza
aspera*

Geissorhiza monanthos

Geissorhiza radians

*Geissorhiza
eurystigma*

Geissorhiza imbricata (Delaroche) Ker Gawl.   *geel Sysie*
Geophyte with overlapping hard, dark corm tunics notched below. Leaves three, narrow and ribbed. Flowers several, star-shaped with the stamens central, white to pale yellow. *Flowering* September to October. In seasonally waterlogged flats from Clanwilliam to Bredasdorp.

Hesperantha falcata (L.f.) Ker-Gawl.   *bontrok Aandblom*
Geophyte with bell-shaped corms covered with woody, blackish tunics. Leaves sword- to sickle-shaped. Flowers white above, red or brown below, style branches thread-like and spreading, scented and opening in the afternoon. *Flowering* August to September. On granite and clay from Gifberg to Port Elizabeth.
  Hesperantha erecta (Baker) Baker (klein bontrok Aandblom) is similar but the flowers are cream with narrower tepals and the corms are globose.
  Hesperantha pilosa (L.f.) Ker-Gawl. (langkous Aandblom) has similar flowers but the leaves are narrow and densely hairy and the corms are globose.

Hesperantha radiata (Jacq.) Ker-Gawl.   *windhond Aandblom*
Geophyte with bell-shaped corms covered with woody, blackish tunics. Leaves narrow, often withered at flowering. Flowers facing downwards on a curved tube, petals recurving, creamy yellow above, reddish below, style branches thread-like and spreading, usually fragrant, opening in the evening. *Flowering* August to October. On sands and clays from Namaqualand to Swaziland.

Ixia odorata Ker Gawl.   *soet Kalossie*
Geophyte with fibrous corm tunics and slender branched stems. Leaves narrow. Flowers crowded, yellow, sweetly scented. *Flowering* September to November. On sandy flats and slopes from Citrusdal to Hermanus.

Ixia paniculata Delaroche   *pyp Kalossie*
Geophyte with softly fibrous corm tunics and branched stems. Leaves sword-shaped. Flowers with a long tube, flesh-coloured, the stamens included in the tube. *Flowering* October to November. Along streams and marshes from Nieuwoudtville to False Bay.

Ixia scillaris L.   *Agretjie*
Geophyte with coarsely fibrous corm tunics and stiff, erect stems. Leaves sword-shaped. Flowers pink to magenta, fragrant, the bracts small and colourless. *Flowering* August to November. On stony clay or sandy slopes from Namaqualand to Bredasdorp.

Geissorhiza imbricata

Hesperantha falcata

Hesperantha radiata

Ixia odorata

Ixia paniculata

Ixia scillaris

61

Ixia monadelpha Delaroche   *bont Kalossie*
Geophyte with coarsely fibrous corm tunics. Leaves sword-shaped. Flowers with a slender tube, cream, pink or bluish with a dark centre, filaments united and blackish. *Flowering* October. On sandy soils from Malmesbury to the Peninsula.

Ixia lutea Eckl.   *bleek Kalossie*
Geophyte with coarsely fibrous corm tunics. Leaves sword-shaped. Flowers crowded, pale yellow with a brown centre and free filaments. *Flowering* September to October. On clay or granite from Clanwilliam to Paarl.

*Ixia curta Andr.   *bruinoog Kalossie*
Geophyte with finely fibrous corm tunics. Leaves sword-shaped. Flowers crowded, yellow to orange with brown centre edged with red, the bracts pale brownish above and drawn into cusps and the stamen filaments black and completely fused. *Flowering* September to October. On sandy flats and slopes from Hopefield to Kalabaskraal.

Ixia dubia Vent.   *oranje Kalossie*
Similar to *I. curta* but with the bracts membranous and pinkish or colourless and the anther filaments free to the base. *Flowering* October to November. On sandy soils from Piketberg to Caledon.

Ixia maculata L.   *Kalossie*
Similar to *I. curta* but with the bracts large, membranous and rusty coloured and the filaments united below. *Flowering* September to October. On sandy flats and slopes from Clanwilliam to the Peninsula.

*Ixia framesii L. Bolus   *rooi Kalossie*
Geophyte with softly fibrous corm tunics. Leaves linear. Flowers crowded, with a long, slender tube, yellow to orange or salmon-red with a small dark centre, the bracts small and membranous. *Flowering* September to October. On sandy flats from Darling to Kalabaskraal.

Ixia monadelpha

Ixia lutea

Ixia curta

Ixia dubia

Ixia maculata

Ixia framesii

Romulea schlechteri Bég.   *wit Froetang*
Geophyte with woody corm tunics forming a crescent-shaped ridge below. Leaves several, like knitting needles. Flowers pale lilac to cream with a yellow or orange cup, outer tepals blotched or striped on the back. *Flowering* July to September. On damp sandy flats from Doring Bay to Caledon.

Romulea tabularis Bég.   *blou Froetang*
Geophyte with woody corm tunics forming a crescent-shaped ridge below. Leaves several, like knitting needles. Flowers lavender blue with an orange cup, outer tepals marked irregularly on the back. *Flowering* July to October. On damp sand or clay flats from Clanwillam to Bredasdorp.

Romulea obscura Klatt   *kol Froetang*
Stemless geophyte with assymmetrical woody corms rounded below. Leaves several, like knitting needles. Flowers rosy-pink with a dark blotch at the edge of the greenish-yellow cup, outer tepals striped or irregularly marked on the back. *Flowering* August to September. On moist sand or loam from Clanwilliam to Hermanus.

*Romulea eximia M.P. de Vos   *Darling Froetang*
Geophyte with woody corm tunics drawn into a point. Leaves several, like knitting needles. Flowers 40-60 mm long, old rose pink with a dark blotch at the edge of the pale yellow, purple-streaked cup, with outer tepals marked irregularly on the back. *Flowering* August to September. Restricted to seasonally waterlogged silt between Yzerfontein and Kalabaskraal.

Romulea hirsuta (Klatt) Baker   *pienk Froetang*
Similar to *R. eximia* but the corm bell-shaped and the bracteoles with colourless, not brown, membranous margins. *Flowering* August to September. Common and widespread in sandy soils from Clanwilliam to Elim.

Romulea cruciata (Jacq.) Baker   *kruisblaar Froetang*
Similar to *R. eximia* but the flowers smaller (25-35 mm long) and magenta to lilac with golden-yellow cup. *Flowering* July to September. On clay or granite outcrops from Nieuwoudtville to Riversdale.

Romulea schlechteri

Romulea tabularis

Romulea obscura

Romulea eximia

Romulea hirsuta

Romulea cruciata

Romulea flava (Lam.) M.P. de Vos   *geel Froetang, Knikkertjie*
Geophyte with woody corm tunics drawn into a ridge below. Stem short or long,
usually with one long leaf like a knitting needle. Flowers yellow or white, rarely
blue or pink with a yellow cup, outer tepals greenish on the back. *Flowering* June
to September. Widespread from Namaqualand to Humansdorp.

*Romulea elliptica M.P. de Vos   *Vredenburg Froetang*
Geophyte with woody corm tunics drawn into a ridge below. Stem long, with two
leaves like knitting needles. Flowers bright yellow with short dark lines in the cup,
outer tepals green on the back with brown flecks on the margins. *Flowering*
August. Restricted to white sandy soils between Saldanha Bay and Vredenburg.

Sparaxis bulbifera (L.) Ker Gawl.   *Botterblom*
Geophyte with softly fibrous corm tunics. Leaves in a basal fan. Floral bracts
papery, streaked with brown. Flowers cup-shaped, cream to white, often purple outside. *Flowering* September to October. Common on damp sandy flats from
Hopefield to Bredasdorp.

*Sparaxis parviflora (G.J. Lewis) Goldblatt   *klein Kappie*
Low geophyte with finely fibrous corm tunics. Leaves in a basal fan. Floral bracts
papery, streaked with brown. Flowers irregular with the three lower lobes slightly
smaller, cream or the upper tepals pale mauve. *Flowering* August. Restricted to
sandy soils on granite outcrops from Darling to Saldanha Bay.

Sparaxis villosa (Burm.f.) Goldblatt   *blou Kappie*
Geophyte with coarsely fibrous corm tunics. Leaves in a basal fan. Floral bracts
papery, streaked with brown. Flowers irregular, pale yellow with the upper tepals
violet. *Flowering* August to September. On clay slopes from Citrusdal to the
Peninsula.

Freesia viridis (Aiton) Goldblatt & J.C. Manning   *groen Agretjie*
Low geophyte with soft, fibrous corm tunics and angular stems. Leaves several in a
basal fan, narrow. Flowers down-facing with a long tube, green to brown, sweetly
scented at night. *Flowering* August to September. Usually on clay or limestone
soils from southern Namibia to Mamre.

Romulea flava *Romulea elliptica* *Sparaxis bulbifera*

Sparaxis parviflora *Sparaxis villosa* *Freesia viridis*

*Babiana pygmaea (Burm.f.) N.E. Br. *geel Bobbejaantjie*
Geophyte with deeply buried corm covered with netted fibres. Leaves spreading, pleated, very hairy. Flowers large, cup-shaped, sulphur-yellow with a dark brown centre and cream anthers arranged symmetrically, unscented. *Flowering* August to September. Local on sandy flats between Hopefield and Mamre.

Babiana villosula (J. F. Gmel.) Steud. *klein Bobbejaantjie*
Dwarf geophyte with deeply buried corm covered with tough matted fibres. Leaves erect, pleated, hairy. Flowers cup-shaped with a tube 18-25 mm long, pale blue or mauve, rarely pink, with a small white star in the centre and mauve anthers arranged symmetrically, sweetly scented. *Flowering* May to July. Formerly common on sandy flats and lower slopes from Malmesbury to Somerset West.

*Babiana leipoldtii G.J. Lewis *Leipoldt-se-Bobbejaantjie*
Geophyte with deeply buried corm covered with matted fibres. Leaves erect, pleated, hairy. Flowers cup-shaped with a tube 15-20 mm long, mauve to violet with a dark centre and cream anthers arranged symmetrically, sweetly scented. *Flowering* August to September. Local on damp loamy flats between Darling and Klipheuwel.

*Babiana rubrocyanea (Jacq.) Ker Gawl. *kelkiewyn Bobbejaantjie*
Geophyte with deeply buried corm covered with coarse fibres. Leaves pleated, hairy. Flowers cup-shaped with a tube 15-20 mm long, dark blue with a red centre. *Flowering* August to September. Restricted to seasonally damp granite soils near Darling.

Babiana stricta (Aiton) Ker Gawl. *stompstert Bobbejaantjie*
Geophyte with deeply buried corm covered with coarse, matted fibres. Leaves spreading fan-wise, pleated, hairy. Flowers with more or less equal petals, tube 10-12 mm long, dark blue with red marks at the base of the lower petals, anthers broad and purple. *Flowering* August to September. On sandy or granite soils from Piketberg to Caledon.

Babiana angustifolia Sweet *vlei Bobbejaantjie*
Geophyte with deeply buried corm covered in tough matted fibres. Leaves pleated, hairy. Flowers slightly irregular and inverted, dark blue sometimes marked with white, with blackish or red marks in the upper petals. *Flowering* August to September. On clay flats from Piketberg to Paarl.

Babiana pygmaea

Babiana villosula

Babiana leipoldtii

Babiana rubrocyanea

Babiana stricta

Babiana angustifolia

69

Babiana nana (Andrews) Spreng.   *sandveld Bobbejaantjie*
Geophyte with shallow corm covered with netted fibres. Leaves spreading fan-wise, pleated, very hairy, short and broad and abruptly contracted at the tips. Flowers with unequal petals, blue to pink with a small cream area and usually a purple chevron at the base of the lower petals, very fragrant. *Flowering* August to September. Common on sandy coastal flats and dunes from Piketberg to Cape Town.

Babiana ambigua (Roem. & Schult.) G.J. Lewis   *Bobbejaantjie*
Geophyte with shallow corm covered with netted fibres. Leaves spreading fan-wise, pleated, hairy, narrow and tapering. Flowers with unequal petals, blue with a small cream area and usually a purple chevron at the base of the lower petals, very fragrant. *Flowering* July to September. In sandy soil near the coast from Klawer to Riversdale.

Babiana odorata L. Bolus   *soet Bobbejaantjie*
Geophyte with deeply buried corm covered with coarse, matted fibres. Leaves spreading fan-wise, pleated, hairy. Flowers with unequal petals, yellow or creamy with dark yellow on the lower petals, very fragrant. *Flowering* July to September. On clay slopes and flats from Piketberg to Paarl.

Babiana tubulosa (Burm.f.) Ker Gawl.   *wit Bobbejaantjie*
Geophyte with deeply buried corm covered with fibres. Leaves erect, narrow, pleated, hairy. Flowers with unequal petals with a slender tube 65-90 mm long, cream with red chevrons on the lower petals, unscented. *Flowering* September to October. Fairly frequent in white sandy soil on flats and low hills near the coast from Saldanha Bay to Riversdale.

Babiana ringens (L.) Ker Gawl.   *Rotstert*
Geophyte with deeply buried corm covered with matted tunics. Leaves erect, narrow and stiff, pleated, hairless. Flowers strongly two-lipped with the stamens held in the tubular base of the longer upper lip, red with a yellow throat, unscented. *Flowering* July to September, especially after fires. On sandy flats and lower slopes from Clanwilliam to Albertinia.

Micranthus tubulosus (Burm.) N.E. Br.   *holblaar Vleiblommetjie*
Small geophyte with black, coarsely netted corm tunics. Lower leaf tubular and hollow, abruptly pointed. Flowers in a two-ranked spike, pale or dark blue. *Flowering* November to December. On seasonally moist loamy flats from Citrusdal to the Peninsula.
    Micranthus alopecuroides (L.) Rothm. (platblaar Vleiblommetjie) is similar but has flat, sword-shaped leaves.

Babiana nana

Babiana ambigua

Babiana odorata

Babiana tubulosa

Babiana ringens

*Micranthus
tubulosus*

71

Watsonia marginata (L.f.) Ker Gawl. *breëblaar Kanolpypie*
Tall geophyte with coarsely netted corm tunics. Leaves sword-shaped, leathery, greyish green with heavily thickened yellow or purple margins. Flowers many in a spike with side branches, shallowly cupped, pale pink or magenta with a white triangle and callus at the base of each petal. *Flowering* September to November. On sandy soil in temporary seeps or seasonally marshy places from Nieuwoudtville to Caledon.

Watsonia coccinea Baker *klein Kanolpypie*
Geophyte with coarsely netted corm tunics. Leaves leathery. Flowers several in a short spike, trumpet-shaped, red to pink or mauve. *Flowering* August to September. On damp sandy soils from Malmesbury to the Peninsula.

*Watsonia hysterantha J.W. Mathews & L. Bolus *herfs Kanolpypie*
Robust geophyte with coarsely netted corm tunics. Leaves narrow, dry at flowering. Flowers many in a spike, trumpet-shaped, bright red with a whitish throat. *Flowering* March to July. Restricted to granite outcrops between Saldanha Bay and Bokbaai.

Watsonia meriana (L.) Mill. *Lakpypie*
Robust geophyte with coarsely netted corm tunics. Leaves leathery, with thickened margins. Flowers many in a spike with side branches, trumpet-shaped, red but paler outside. *Flowering* October to November. On moist sandy soils often along streams from the Kamiesberg to Cape Agulhas.

Chasmanthe aethiopica (L.) N.E. Br. *klein Piempiempie*
Geophyte with fibrous corm tunics. Leaves several, soft textured. Flowers seven to fifteen arranged on the upper side of the arching stem, the lower part of the tube twisted and abruptly flaring, almost pouched, orange. *Flowering* April to July. In scrub on clay soils often on bottomlands or near watercourses from Darling to the Eastern Cape.

Chasmanthe floribunda (Salisb.) N.E. Br. *Piempiempie*
Geophyte with hard, fibrous corm tunics netted above. Leaves several, rather firm in texture. Flowers usually twenty to forty arranged on both sides of the erect and usually branched stem, the lower part of the tube little twisted and less abruptly flaring above, orange or rarely yellow. *Flowering* July to September. On rock outcrops, especially granite, from Vredendal to Caledon.
    Plants with pale yellow flowers are known as *C. floribunda* var. *duckittii* and occur naturally on a few farms south of Darling.

Watsonia marginata

Watsonia coccinea

Watsonia hysterantha

Watsonia meriana

Chasmanthe aethiopica

Chasmanthe floribunda

73

Lapeirousia jacquinii N.E. Br.   *blou Koringblom*
Geophyte with bell-shaped corm and woody tunics. Stems angled, branched at the base. Leaves ridged. Flowers with long tube, dark purple, lower petals striped with white, bract two-keeled. *Flowering* July to September. Common on sandy soils from Garies to Mamre.

Lapeirousia anceps (L.f.) Ker Gawl.   *pienk Koringblom*
Geophyte with bell-shaped corm and woody tunics. Stems angled and much-branched at the base. Leaves ridged. Flowers with long, slender tube and narrow petals, creamy pink with red markings, bracts small. *Flowering* September to October. In deep sandy soils from Namaqualand to Mossel Bay.

Lapeirousia fabricii (Delaroche) Ker-Gawl.   *katklou Koringblom*
Geophyte with bell-shaped corm and woody tunics. Stems angled and branched. Leaves ridged. Flowers with long, slender tube, cream to pink with red markings, lower petals with hooked processes, bracts large and crisped on the keels. *Flowering* September to November. On sandy or granite slopes from Namaqualand to Darling.

Gladiolus tenellus Jacq.   *Botterlelie*
Delicate geophyte with hard, toothed corm tunics. Leaves three, the lowest like a knitting needle. Flowers funnel-shaped with spreading lobes, creamy yellow, the lower three petals bright yellow at the base with a few maroon lines, extremely fragrant. *Flowering* July to October. In marshy ground or near seasonal pools on sandy or gravel flats from Piketberg to Bredasdorp.

Gladiolus angustus L.   *lang Pypie*
Geophyte with fibrous corm tunics. Leaves rather firm, sword-shaped. Flowers with a very long, slender tube, cream or flesh-coloured with conspicuous red shield-shaped marks on the lower three petals. *Flowering* October to November. On moist sandy flats along streams from the Cedarberg to the Peninsula.

Gladiolus orchidiflorus Andrews   *groen Kalkoentjie*
Geophyte with coarsely fibrous corm tunics. Leaves several, narrow. Flowers greenish or grey, upper petal narrow and arched, the lower three petals narrow and marked with greenish yellow and maroon, very fragrant. *Flowering* August to September. On sandy soils in the western and southwestern parts of South Africa.

Lapeirousia jacquinii

Lapeirousia anceps

Lapeirousia fabricii

Gladiolus tenellus

Gladiolus angustus

Gladiolus orchidiflorus

75

Gladiolus speciosus Thunb. *bont Kalkoentjie*
Short geophyte with soft papery corm tunics and winged stems. Leaves stiff, flowers orange, upper petal hooded and outer petals greenish on the back, the lower three petals greenish-yellow tipped orange, very fragrant. *Flowering* September. In deep sandy soil from Lambert's Bay to Ganzekraal.

Gladiolus alatus L. *Kalkoentjie*
Geophyte with soft, papery corm tunics and winged stems. Leaves stiff with several raised parallel veins. Flowers orange, upper petal usually erect, the lower three petals greenish-yellow tipped orange, very fragrant. *Flowering* August to September. Common on stony flats and from Clanwilliam to Caledon.

*Gladiolus meliusculus (G.J. Lewis) Goldblatt & J.C. Manning *pienk Kalkoentjie*
Short geophyte with soft, papery corm tunics and winged stems. Leaves stiff, with several raised parallel veins. Flowers pink to orange, upper petal usually erect, the lower three petals marked with black and greenish-yellow, fragrant. *Flowering* September. Restricted to moist, sandy soils from Darling to Melkbosstrand.

Gladiolus cunonius (L.) Gaertn. *Lepelblom*
Geophyte with fragile membranous corm tunics. Leaves several, sword-shaped. Flowers irregular, bright red but green below, the upper petal spoon-shaped, flanked by two ear-like petals and the lower three much reduced. *Flowering* September to November. In coastal sands and rocks from Saldanha Bay to Knysna.

Gladiolus priorii (N.E. Br.) Goldblatt & M.P. de Vos *rooi Pypie*
Geophyte with membranous corm tunics. Leaves four, narrow and leathery. Flowers tubular with spreading petals, scarlet with yellow throat. *Flowering* May to July. On granite or sandstone hills from Saldanha Bay to Kleinmond.

Gladiolus watsonius (Thunb.) Goldblatt & M.P. de Vos *rooi Afrikaner*
Geophyte with hard, toothed corm tunics. Leaves three, the lowest narrow and thickened. Flowers tubular with spreading petals, scarlet. *Flowering* August to September. On clay or granite slopes from Piketberg to the Peninsula.

Gladiolus speciosus

Gladiolus alatus

*Gladiolus
meliusculus*

Gladiolus cunonius

Gladiolus priorii

*Gladiolus
watsonius*

IRIDACEAE

Gladiolus gracilis Jacq.   *blou Pypie*
Slender geophyte with woody, strongly toothed corm tunics. Leaves usually four,
the lowest longest, stiff, with prominently flanged margins. Flowers usually blue,
sometimes pink, grey or yellow, the lower three petals with dark streaks, usually
very fragrant. *Flowering* June to September. Common on wet clay flats and lower
slopes from Aurora to Heidelberg.

*Gladiolus caeruleus Goldblatt & J.C. Manning   *Saldanha Pypie*
Similar to *Gladiolus gracilis* but usually more robust with a broader, softer leaf and
the flowers pale blue with dark spotting on the lower three petals. *Flowering*
August. Restricted to limestone outcrops around Saldanha Bay.

Gladiolus carinatus Aiton   *sand Pypie*
Slender geophyte with soft, finely toothed corm tunics and the base of the stem
mottled with white on maroon. Leaves three, the lowest slender with a prominent
midvein. Flowers usually mauve to blue, sometimes pink, the lower three petals
yellow with dark streaks and speckles, very fragrant. *Flowering* July to September.
Common on sandy flats, especially among restios, and in sandy soil on mountain
slopes from Nieuwoudtville to Knysna.

ORCHIDACEAE

Disa draconis (L.f.) Sw.   *wit Disa*
Geophyte with a basal rosette of leaves dry at flowering. Flowers cream with
maroon streaks in the centre, the upper petal with a long, slender spur. *Flowering*
November to December. On sandy soil from Namaqualand to the Swartberg.

Satyrium coriifolium Sw.   *Ewwatrewwa*
Stout geophyte with broad, somewhat soft and fleshy leaves clasping the stem.
Flowers strongly hooded, among down-flexed bracts, orange. *Flowering* August to
October. On sandy flats and slopes from Nieuwoudtville to Humansdorp.

Satyrium carneum (Dryand.) Sims   *rooi Trewwa*
Robust geophyte with broad, somewhat fleshy leaves clasping the stem. Flowers
hooded, with two short spurs, pale pink. *Flowering* September to November. On
sand dunes or lower coastal slopes from Malmesbury to Riversdale.
   Satyrium erectum Sw. (pienk Trewwa) also has pink flowers but is smaller with
the lower petals streaked and spotted with purple. It occurs on clay soils.

Gladiolus gracilis   *Gladiolus caeruleus*   *Gladiolus carinatus*

Disa draconis   *Satyrium coriifolium*   *Satyrium carneum*

Satyrium odorum Sond. *soet Trewwa*
Stout geophyte with broad, somewhat soft and fleshy leaves clasping the stem. Flowers strongly hooded, crowded among broad down-flexed bracts, greenish, strongly scented. *Flowering* August to November. Often among rocks in damp places from Piketberg to Knysna.

Satyrium bicorne (L.) Thunb. *lang Trewwa*
Stout geophyte with broad, somewhat soft and fleshy leaves, the lower two spreading on the ground. Flowers strongly hooded, with two slender spurs, pale yellow or greenish. *Flowering* September to November. On sandy flats and slopes from Namaqualand to Knysna.

Monadenia bracteata (Sw.) Dur. & Schinz *Orgidekie*
Geophyte with tuberous roots and numerous narrow channelled leaves clustered at the base of the stem and grading into the floral bracts. Flowers minute, crowded among large leafy bracts, upper petal hooded and with a spur, brownish and yellow, scented. *Flowering* October to November. Common on sandy flats and slopes, especially in disturbed areas, from Clanwilliam to the Eastern Cape.

Pterygodium volucris (L.f.) Sw. *Groengoggas*
Geophyte with ovate-oblong leaves. Flowers with twisted and cupped petals, pale yellowish-green, the lip with side lobes and a prominent lower lobe. *Flowering* September to October. On clay flats from Clanwilliam to Swellendam.

Pterygodium alatum (Thunb.) Sw. *Vlerkies*
Small geophyte with oblong leaves. Flowers hooded, greenish-yellow, the lip with conspicuous side lobes, pungently scented. *Flowering* August to October. Common on lower slopes usually on clay from Clanwilliam to Humansdorp.

Pterygodium catholicum (L.) Sw. *Moederkappie*
Small geophyte with oblong leaves. Flowers hooded, yellowish-green often flushed with red, the lip without conspicuous side lobes, pungently scented. *Flowering* September to October. Common on damp flats often on clay soils from Nieuwoudtville to Port Elizabeth.

Satyrium odorum

Satyrium bicorne

*Monadenia
bracteata*

Pterygodium volucris

Pterygodium alatum

*Pterygodium
catholicum*

81

ORCHIDACEAE

Corycium orobanchoides (L.f.) Sw. *Bastertrewwa*
Geophyte with numerous narrow leaves. Flowers numerous and crowded, small and tightly hooded, green with reddish-purple tips, pungently scented. *Flowering* August to October. Common on sandy flats and slopes from Gifberg to Caledon.

Corycium crispum (Thunb.) Sw. *geel Bastertrewwa*
Geophyte with tuberous roots and several crisped leaves spotted at the base. Flowers numerous and crowded, small and tightly hooded, bright yellow, scented. *Flowering* September to October. On sandy soils from Namaqualand to the Peninsula.

Disperis villosa (L.f.) Sw. *Babakappie*
Small geophyte with hairy stem and two leaves, the lower stalked. Flowers deeply hooded, with spreading lateral petals, pale greenish, scented. *Flowering* August to September. On clay or sandy soils from the Cedarberg to the Eastern Cape.

Holothrix villosa Lindl. *Wollie*
Minute geophyte with tuberous roots and two round leaves at the base, stem and leaves with long hairs. Flowers minute, green. *Flowering* August to November. On sandy and stony soils from Clanwilliam to Humansdorp.

ARACEAE

Zantedeschia aethiopica (L.) Spreng. *Varkblom, Arum*
Rhizomatous geophyte with stalked, arrow-shaped leaves. Flowers minute, in a narrow column surrounded by a conspicuous white bract. *Flowering* August to January. On damp, often sandy flats from Clanwilliam to Mpumalanga.

APONOGETONACEAE

Aponogeton distachyos L.f. *Waterblommetjie*
Tuberous aquatic perennial with oblong floating leaves carried on long petioles. Flowers white and scented, sessile in forked spikes. *Flowering* July to December. In pools, ditches and vleis from Nieuwoudtville to Knysna.

Corycium orobanchoides

Corycium crispum

Disperis villosa

Holothrix villosa

Zantedeschia aethiopica

Aponogeton distachyos

JUNCAGINACEAE

Triglochin bulbosa L. *Bolletjieblom*
Inconspicuous herb with a tuft of fleshy leaves like knitting needles. Flowers in a spike, small, with conspicuous elongate ovary, greenish. *Flowering* almost throughout the year. Widespread on damp flats and marshy places from Namaqualand to the Eastern Cape.

HAEMODORACEAE

Wachendorfia paniculata L. *rooi Kanol, Koffiepit*
Robust, roughly hairy geophyte with distinctive orange or red rootstock. Leaves pleated. Flowers in a branched inflorescence, orange, the upper three petals with a brown flash at the base, stamens about as long as the petals. *Flowering* August to October. On sandy soils, often rocky, from Clanwilliam to Port Elizabeth.

Wachendorfia brachyandra W.F. Barker *bruin Kanol*
Similar to *W. paniculata* but the stamens half as long as the petals. *Flowering* September to October. On sandy and loam soils from Saldanha Bay to the Peninsula.

Wachendorfia parviflora W.F. Barker *klein rooi Kanol*
Short, roughly hairy geophyte. Leaves narrow and pleated. Flowers in a congested inflorescence, brownish mauve, the upper three petals with a yellow and brown flash at the base, stamens slightly shorter than the petals. *Flowering* August to September. On sandy and loam soils from Namaqualand to the Peninsula.

CYPERACEAE

Ficinia nigrescens (Schrad.) J. Raynal *gras Biesie*
Small tufted perennial. *Flowering* May to October. Widespread from Namibia to the Eastern Cape.

Hellmuthia membranacea (Thunb.) R. Haines & K. Lye *knop Biesie*
Leafless, tufted perennial. *Flowering* July to September. Coastal sands from Jakkalsfontein to Knysna.

Triglochin bulbosa   *Wachendorfia paniculata*   *Wachendorfia*
                                                                  brachyandra

Ficinia nigrescens

Wachendorfia parviflora   *Hellmuthia*
                              membranacea

Willdenowia incurvata (Thunb.) H.P. Linder *sonkwas Riet*
Robust, tufted perennial with branching, minutely grooved stems bearing conspicuous shining tan bracts. Sexes on separate plants. *Flowering* April. Common on sandy flats from Namaqualand to the Peninsula, sometimes forming extensive stands.

Staberoha distachyos (Rottb.) Kunth *Curly cones*
Tufted, reed-like perennial with leafless, unbranched stems. Sexes on separate plants. Male flowers in nodding cone-like clusters, several to a stem; female flowers in erect clusters, solitary. *Flowering* June to August. On clay, sandy or gravel soils but common on sandy coastal forelands from Vanrhynsdorp to Bredasdorp.

Chondropetalum tectorum (L.f.) Raf. *olifant Riet*
Tufted, reed-like perennial with leafless, unbranched stems. Sexes on separate plants, in spike-like branched clusters. *Flowering* August to October. On sandy, marshy coastal forelands from Clanwilliam to Grahamstown.

Thamnochortus spicigerus (Thunb.) Spreng. *duine Riet*
Robust tufted perennial with unbranched stems bearing brown, clasping scale-like leaves. Male flowers in nodding clusters, several to a stem; female flowers in erect clusters, several to a stem. Sexes on separate plants. *Flowering* June to August. On coastal sands from Malmesbury to Knysna.

Willdenowia incurvata

Staberoha distachyos ♂

Staberoha distachyos ♀

Chondropetalum tectorum

Thamnochortus spicigerus ♂

Thamnochortus spicigerus ♀

LAURACEAE

Cassytha ciliolata Nees   *Nooienshaar*
Twining parasite with slender, yellowish stems and leaves reduced to minute scales.
Flowers minute, in tight clusters, usually not opening fully, greenish yellow. Fruits
fleshy, red when ripe. *Flowering* throughout the year with a peak in early summer.
Widespread in the Western and Eastern Cape, attacking a range of plants, especially
woody perennials. The plants may completely overgrow the host and eventually
kill it.

MENISPERMACEAE

Cissampelos capensis L.f.   *Davidjies*
Woody climber or scrambler with the young branches white-hairy. Leaves in pairs
or clusters, blue-green, triangular with rounded angles. Sexes on separate plants.
Flowers inconspicuous, greenish. *Flowering* February to May. Frequent among
bushes on sand or stony slopes from Clanwilliam to Port Elizabeth.

FUMARIACEAE

Cysticapnos vesicarius (L.) Fedde   *Klappertjie*
Twining annual with soft hollow stems. Leaves much divided and forming tendrils.
Flowers in small clusters, two-lipped, pale pink. Fruits forming inflated bladders.
Flowering August to October. On sandy soils from Namaqualand to Riversdale.

MYRICACEAE

Myrica quercifolia L.   *Maagpynbos*
Shrublet. Leaves leathery and deeply lobed with short petioles. Sexes on separate
plants. Flowers inconspicuous, in dense catkins. Fruits round and warty, black.
Flowering July to September. On dry sandy lower slopes or flats from
Namaqualand to Eastern Cape.

Myrica cordifolia L.   *Waxberry, Wasbessie, Glashout*
Densely leafy shrub. Leaves broadly rounded without petioles, closely overlapping.
Sexes on separate plants. Fruits round and warty, usually with a silvery waxy cov-
ering. *Flowering* April-July. Common on sandy flats and dunes from Langebaan to
Eastern Cape. The fat rendered from the plants was formerly used to make candles,
soaps and salves.

POLYGONACEAE

Rumex lativalvis Meisn.   *Veldsuring*
Perennial with tap-root, often flushed reddish. Leaves in a basal cluster, arrow-
shaped on long petioles. Flowers minute, enlarging to form a three-winged cover
for the fruit. *Flowering* September to October. On sand flats or dunes from
Namibia to the Eastern Cape.
   The weedy species *Rumex acetosella* L. (Boksuring) is smaller with much smaller fruits.

Cassytha ciliolata

Cissampelos capensis

Cysticapnos vesicarius

Myrica quercifolia

Myrica cordifolia

Rumex lativalvis

Adenogramma glomerata (L.f.) Druce   *Muggiegras*
Delicate, sprawling annual. Leaves slightly fleshy, needle-like in whorls widely
spaced along the wiry stems. Flowers minute, in tight clusters, white. *Flowering*
August to October. Widespread in sandy soils from Namibia to Humansdorp.

Limeum africanum L.   *Koggelmandervoet*
Creeping greyish annual with slender stems radiating out along the ground. Leaves
slightly fleshy, softly greyish velvety, sharply creased down the middle. Flowers
small, in dense flattened clusters, greyish-green and white. *Flowering* July to
September. On dry sandy soils from Namaqualand to Worcester.

Acrosanthes teretifolia E. & Z.   *wit Spekvygie*
Creeping with reddish, slightly woody stems. Leaves narrow, somewhat fleshy.
Flowers white, with numerous stamens. *Flowering* for most of the year. On sandy
flats from Tulbagh to Bredasdorp.

Pharnaceum lanatum Bartl.   *wolhaar Sneeuwvygie*
Erect perennial, with slightly woody stems, branched in the upper half. Leaves needle-like, crowded, with matted woolly hairs at the base. Flowers in clusters on long
wiry stalks, petals white, green on the back. *Flowering* August to October. In sand
from Namaqualand to Caledon

Pharnaceum incanum L.   *regop Sneeuwvygie*
Similar to *P. lanatum* but the hairs among the leaves not matted. *Flowering* August
to October. On clay or granite from Namaqualand to the Eastern Cape.

Pharnaceum lineare L.f.   *groot Sneeuwvygie*
Sprawling perennial with smooth stems. Leaves needle-like, slightly fleshy, clustered at the nodes, with membranous scales at the base. Flowers in clusters on long
stalks, white, brown on the back. *Flowering* September to November. Sandy
coastal slopes, Namaqualand to Bredasdorp.

Adenogramma glomerata

Limeum africanum

*Acrosanthes
teretifolia*

Pharnaceum lanatum

Pharnaceum incanum

*Pharnaceum
lineare*

91

*Tetragonia chenopodioides Eckl. & Zeyh. *Saldanha Kinkelbossie*
Annual with sprawling, soft, slightly fleshy stems. Flowers crowded among the
upper leaves, small, yellowish-green with prominent styles. *Flowering* August to
September. Restricted to open sand on the coastal plain near Saldanha Bay.

Tetragonia fruticosa L. *Kinkelbossie*
Sprawling shrublet, softly hairy when young, woody below. Leaves soft, slightly
fleshy, narrow with the margins rolled under. Flowers in elongated spikes, dull yellow. *Flowering* September to January. In scrub on sandy soils from Namaqualand
to Port Elizabeth.

Tetragonia namaquensis Schltr. *Namakwa Kinkelbossie*
Sprawling annual with slightly fleshy stems, softly hairy. Leaves soft, slightly
fleshy, narrow with the margins rolled under. Flowers clustered among the leaves,
dull yellow, maroon on the backs. *Flowering* July to October. On clay or granite
from Namaqualand to Langebaan.

Tetragonia nigrescens Eckl. & Zeyh. *geel Klapperbrak*
Tuberous perennial with several sprawling annual stems. Leaves soft, slightly
fleshy and roughly hairy. Flowers clustered at the end of the branches on long
stalks, bright yellow, honey scented and closing at night, the stigmas shorter than
the anthers. *Flowering* June to September. On sandy or granitic flats, often along
roadsides, from Kamiesberg to Struis Bay.

Tetragonia portulacoides Fenzl *wit Kinkelbossie*
Allied to *T. nigrescens* but much smaller and more slender and almost hairless.
Flowers buff or cream with conspicuous green stigmas longer than the anthers.
Flowering June to September. On sandy flats at low altitudes from Calvinia to
Humansdorp.

Aizoon paniculatum L. *pienk Spekvygie*
Sprawling shrublet, softly hairy. Leaves crowded and opposite below, somewhat
fleshy and papillate, hairy. Flowers crowded at the tips of the branches, bright
magenta, hairy below. *Flowering* August to October. On sandy, often disturbed
ground in coastal areas from southern Namaqualand to the Peninsula.

Tetragonia chenopodioides

Tetragonia fruticosa

Tetragonia namaquensis

Tetragonia nigrescens

Tetragonia portulacoides

Aizoon paniculatum

Mesembryanthemum alatum (L. Bol.) L. Bol. *Lizard plant*
Large, mat-forming annual with sprawling, angled or winged stems radiating from
a tuft of broad, fleshy leaves. Stems and leaves covered with shining papillae.
Flowers in flat clusters at the ends of the branches, the petals in several series,
pinkish. *Flowering* September to November. Conspicuous in coastal areas from
Lambert's Bay to Langebaan.

Mesembryanthemum crystallinum L. *Ice plant*
Large, mat-forming biennial with sprawling stems covered with glistening, translucent outgrowths, watery when crushed. Leaves broad and fleshy, covered with shining papillae. Flowers in flat clusters at the ends of the branches, the petals in several series, white to pinkish. *Flowering* November to December. Widespread from
Namibia to the Western Cape, often in coastal areas.

Carpobrotus acinaciformis (L.) L. Bolus *Elandsvy*
Robust succulent with trailing, winged branches, sometimes covering large patches.
Leaves scimitar-shaped, triangular in section. Flowers with numerous narrow
magenta petals and stamens, opening in full sun. *Flowering* August to October. On
coastal sands and rocky outcrops from Saldanha Bay to Mossel Bay.

Carpobrotus edulis (L.) L. Bolus *Suurvy, Hotnotsvy*
Robust succulent with vigorously trailing, winged branches, sometimes covering
large patches. Leaves narrow and slightly curved, triangular in section, slightly
roughened along the keels. Flowers with numerous narrow yellow petals and stamens turning pink with age, opening in full sun. *Flowering* mostly in the spring
and summer. Widely distributed in the Western and Eastern Cape and naturalized in
Britain and California. The fleshy fruits are edible and are used especially for wild
fig "suurvy" preserve.

Cheiridopsis rostrata (L.) N.E. Br. *rots Vygie*
Dwarf tufted perennial, the fleshy leaves triangular in section and covered with
translucent spots on the undersides. Flowers golden yellow. *Flowering* July to
August. Restricted to coastal granite outcrops from southern Namaqualand to
Langebaan.

Ruschia ventricosa (L. Bolus) Schwantes *pers kussing Vygie*
Cushion-forming perennial with boat-shaped leaves triangular in section. Flowers
solitary but massed, petals in numerous series, bright magenta with a white centre.
Flowering August to September. Restricted to limestone outcrops from
Namaqualand to Langebaan.

Mesembryanthemum alatum

Mesembryanthemum crystallinum

Carpobrotus acinaciformis

Carpobrotus edulis

Cheiridopsis rostrata

Ruschia ventricosa

95

Ruschia diversifolia L. Bolus   *rank Vygie*
Trailing perennial with long, blunt leaves. Flowers shining magenta but paler near the centre, each petal with a dark central streak, in a single series, staminodes clustered in the centre around stamens. *Flowering* May to July. On rocky hills from Clanwilliam to Tulbagh.

Ruschia macowanii (L. Bolus) Schwantes   *bos Vygie*
Rounded shrublet with slender, pointed leaves, triangular in section. Flowers clustered at the ends of the branchlets, magenta, petals in a single series with a cone of staminodes in the centre. *Flowering* September to November. On sandy coastal soils in strandveld from Yzerfontein to Bredasdorp.

*Ruschia tecta L. Bolus   *regop Vygie*
Shrublet with stiff, erect, woody branches, often reddish. Leaves long and narrow, recurved at the tips, triangular in section, fused at the base into a long sheath enclosing the stem, the upper leaves with small clear spots. Flowers in flat topped clusters at the ends of the branches, magenta. *Flowering* October to November. In deep coastal sands from Vredenburg to Melkbosstrand.

Ruschia tumidula (Haw.) Schwant.   *pronk Vygie*
Rounded shrublet with stiff, erect, woody branches, often reddish. Leaves long and narrow, recurved at the tips, triangular in section, fused at the base into a sheath. Flowers in flat-topped clusters at the ends of the branches, white to magenta. *Flowering* November to December. In deep coastal sands from Yzerfontein to Riversdale.

Ruschia radicans L. Bolus   *necklace Vygie*
Creeping perennial with slightly woody stems bearing clusters of small, fleshy, triangular leaves. Flowers solitary on lateral branches, bright pinkish, petals in more than one series and staminodes clustered in the centre around stamens. *Flowering* June to July. On rock outcrops from Clanwilliam to Langebaan.

Delosperma asperulum (Salm-Dyck) L. Bolus   *pers bos Vygie*
Twiggy shrublet with woody branchlets. Leaves short with a small recurved point at the tip, joined at the base, succulent, triangular in section. Flowers solitary but clustered at the end of the branchlets, small, the petals in several series, magenta. *Flowering* August to October. On clay slopes from Namaqualand to Riversdale.

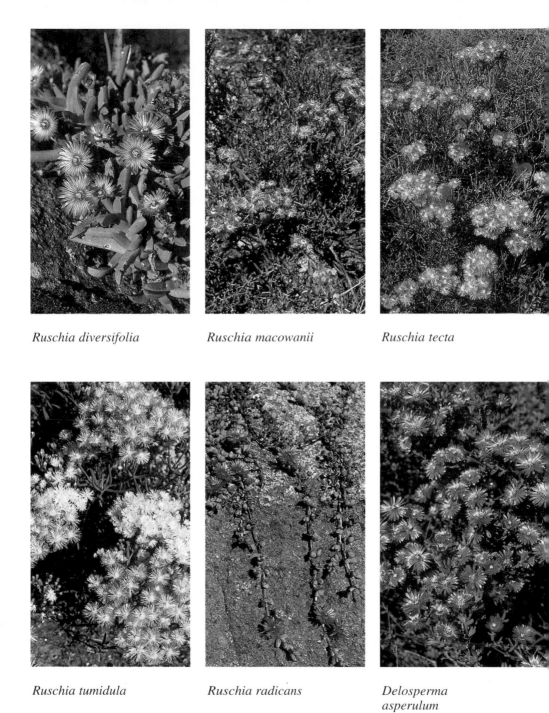

Ruschia diversifolia

Ruschia macowanii

Ruschia tecta

Ruschia tumidula

Ruschia radicans

*Delosperma
asperulum*

Prenia pallens (Aiton) N.E. Br. *bleek kruip Vygie*
Perennial with creeping annual stems radiating from a tuft of slender, pale greyish succulent leaves. Flowers few at the tips of the long, creeping branches, the petals in several series, pale yellow or white to pinkish. *Flowering* September to December. On clay or granite from Namaqualand to the Peninsula.

Sphalmanthus canaliculatus (Haw.) N.E. Br. *kruip Vygie*
Creeping perennial with papillate stems. Leaves small, boat shaped, in tufts along the stems, triangular in section. Flowers in clusters at the tips of the stems, petals in several series, pink or white. *Flowering* November. On sandy soils from Piketberg to Humansdorp.

Drosanthemum calycinum (Haw.) Schwantes *wit Douvygie*
Creeping perennial with stiff slightly woody stems covered in coarse bristles. Leaves slender, covered with glistening papillae, almost circular in section. Flowers solitary at the tips of the branchlets, the petals in several series, white. *Flowering* September to November. On clay or granite from Clanwillam to Darling.

Drosanthemum striatum (Haw.) Schwantes *porselein Douvygie*
Dwarf shrublet with slightly woody stems covered in stiff spreading hairs. Leaves slender, hairy and covered in glistening papillae, almost circular in section. Flowers solitary but clustered at the ends of the branches, the petals in one or two series, glossy shell-pink. *Flowering* August to September. On clay from Nieuwoudtville to Swellendam.

Drosanthemum floribundum (Haw.) Schwantes *pers Douvygie*
Prostrate perennial with the stems covered in spreading hairs. Leaves succulent, almost round in section, blunt, covered in glistening papillae. Flowers solitary, petals in several series, magenta. *Flowering* September to November. On dry clay or brackish sands from Namaqualand to Eastern Cape.

Disphyma crassifolium (L.) L. Bolus *kus kruip Vygie*
Creeping, perennial rooting along the stems. Leaves highly succulent, short and blunt, triangular in section. Flowers solitary, tepals in several series, glistening white, pink or magenta. *Flowering* July to October. On coastal rocks from Lambert's Bay to Port Elizabeth.

Prenia pallens

Sphalmanthus canaliculatus

*Drosanthemum
calycinum*

Drosanthemum striatum

Drosanthemum floribundum

Disphyma crassifolium

*Lampranthus vredenburgensis L. Bolus   *Vredenburg kruip Vygie*
Mat-forming perennial. Leaves short, boat-shaped, succulent and triangular in section. Flowers clustered at the end of the branchlets, the petals stiff and in several series, with a central cone of staminodes, white flushed magenta. *Flowering* July to September. Restricted to granite outcrops from Vredenburg to Stompneus Bay.

Lampranthus reptans (Sol.) N.E. Br.   *sand kruip Vygie*
Creeping perennial with slender stems. Leaves short, succulent, triangular in section. Flowers solitary, erect, the petals in several series, white. *Flowering* August to October. On sandy soils from Clanwilliam to George.

Lampranthus filicaulis (Haw.) N.E. Br.   *langsteel Vygie*
Creeping perennial with slender stems. Leaves short, succulent, triangular in section. Flowers solitary on naked, erect stems, the petals in several series and with a cone of staminodes, white tinged magenta. *Flowering* June to August. In sandy soil from Kalabaskraal to the Peninsula.

Lampranthus aduncus (Haw.) N.E. Br.   *langblaar bos Vygie*
Slightly woody shrublet. Leaves long and narrow with hooked tips. Flowers solitary, the petals in a single series, shining pink with a white central streak, and the stamens in a cone in the centre. *Flowering* May to July. On clay or granite in the Western Cape.

Lampranthus amoenus (Salm-Dyck) N.E. Br.   *pienk bos Vygie*
Slightly woody shrublet. Leaves succulent, long and narrow, triangular in section. Flowers solitary but clustered at the ends of the branchlets, the petals in several series, magenta. *Flowering* July to October. On stony slopes from Namaqualand to Riversdale.

Lampranthus argenteus (L. Bolus) L. Bolus   *silwer bos Vygie*
Slightly woody shrublet. Leaves succulent, triangular in section, joined at the base, the tips pointed and recurved. Flowers massed at the tips of the branches, petals in a single series, glossy white, staminodes in a cone in the center, with purple tips. *Flowering* September to October. On sandy coastal flats from Lambert's Bay to Blouberstrand.

*Lampranthus
vredenburgensis*

Lampranthus reptans

*Lampranthus
filicaulis*

Lampranthus aduncus

Lampranthus amoenus

*Lampranthus
argenteus*

Lampranthus cf. **multiradiatus** (Jacq.) N.E. Br.   *helder sand Vygie*
Sprawling shrublet with slender, woody stems. Leaves slender, succulent, triangular
in section. Flowers solitary on slender stems, the petals in several series, white to
magenta. *Flowering* October to December. On sandy soils from Namaquland to
Humansdorp.

*****Lampranthus aureus** (L.) N.E. Br.   *goue Vygie*
Slightly woody shrublet. Leaves succulent, boat-shaped, triangular in section.
Flowers solitary on the branchlets, the petals in several series, bright orange.
Flowering July to September. On granite outcrops from Vredenburg to Saldanha
Bay.

*****Lampranthus** aff. **aurantiacus** (DC.) Schwantes.   *rooi Vygie*
Sprawling shrublet with slightly woody branchlets. Leaves narrow and pointed,
succulent, triangular in section, joined at the base. Flowers solitary, petals in several series, orange-red, stamens purple. *Flowering* September to October. In deep
sands near Mamre and Jakkalsfontein.

Lampranthus explanatus (L. Bolus) N.E. Br.   *geel sand Vygie*
Perennial with thin, woody stems creeping and looping along the sand, rooting at
the nodes and sending up short erect leafy branches ending in a single bright yellow flower. *Flowering* July to January. On sandy coastal flats between Darling and
the Peninsula.

Jordaaniella dubia (Haw.) H.E.K. Hartmann   *helder kruip Vygie*
Stems creeping, rooting at the nodes. Leaves succulent, in clusters along the stem,
flat above and round below. Flowers solitary, the petals in several series, usually
golden yellow but also salmon, magenta or white. *Flowering* July to September. On
sands or limestone along the coastal belt from Lambert's Bay to Mossel Bay.

Lampranthus multiradiatus   *Lampranthus multiradiatus*   *Lampranthus aureus*

Lampranthus aurantiacus   *Lampranthus explanatus*   *Jordaaniella dubia*

Dorotheanthus bellidiformis (Burm.f.) N.E. Br.   *Bokbaai Vygie*
Low, tufted annual with fleshy leaves covered in glistening papillae. Flowers solitary, various shades of white, pink, orange and yellow, with or without a darker centre. *Flowering* June to September. Sandy soils from Clanwilliam to Bredasdorp. A popular garden plant for drier areas.

Carpanthea pomeridiana (L.) N.E. Br.   *Vetkousie*
Annual with sprawling, somewhat fleshy, coarsely woolly stems. Leaves fleshy, flat and broad, with hairy margins. Flowers solitary on long stalks held above the ground. with numerous pale yellow petals and thread-like staminodes surrounding the stamens, unpleasantly scented. *Flowering* September to November. On deep sandy soil from Lambert's Bay to Bot River.

Apatesia helianthoides (Aiton) N.E. Br.   *Weskus Vetkousie*
Similar to *C. pomeridiana* but stems not hairy. *Flowering* September to October. In sand from Saldanha Bay to the Peninsula

Conicosia pugioniformis (L.) N.E. Br.   *groot Vetkousie*
Large sprawling perennial or biennial with somewhat fleshy stems. Leaves narrow and fleshy, triangular in section. Flowers solitary on stout stalks, large, with numerous thin petals and thread-like staminodes around the stamens, unpleasantly scented. *Flowering* September to October. In deep sands from Namaqualand to Bellville.

Dorotheanthus bellidiformis   *Dorotheanthus bellidiformis*   *Carpanthea pomeridiana*

Apatesia helianthoides   *Conicosia pugioniformis*

CHENOPODIACEAE

Atriplex cinerea Poir. *vaal Brakbossie*
Shrublet with sprawling, woody stems. Leaves silvery grey, trowel-shaped. Flowers minute, sexes separate. *Flowering* September to October. Mostly coastal in saline places from Namibia to the Peninsula.

Atriplex semibaccata R. Br. *rank Brakbossie*
Perennial with softly woody stems. Leaves silvery purple, often slightly toothed. Flowers minute, sexes separate. Bracts in fruit rhombic with blunt angles, joined in the lower part, thick, fleshy and bright red. *Flowering* almost throughout the year. Frequent on roadsides, waste ground and on dry lower slopes near the sea. Introduced as a fodder plant from Australia but now fully naturalized.

CARYOPHYLLACEAE

Spergularia media (L.) C. Presl. *sea Spurry*
Low spreading perennial with many stems from a thick, woody base, glandular hairy. Leaves narrow, opposite or in bundles, somewhat fleshy and with large papery stipules. Flowers white or pale mauve. *Flowering* spring and summer. Typically along the sea shore among rocks or in salt marshes, but also inland, cosmopolitan.

Silene undulata Aiton *Wildetabak*
Sticky perennial, foetid when bruised. Leaves soft, clasping at the base. Flowers in open inflorescences, with deeply notched petals, white or pink, clove scented, open in the evening. *Flowering* July to December. On rocky slopes, often in protected places, from Clanwilliam to tropical Africa.

RAFFLESIACEAE

Cytinus sanguineus (Thunb.) Fourc. *Aardroos*
Dwarf, root parasite without leaves. Flowers cup-shaped, produced at ground level, brilliant crimson, hairy. Sexes on separate plants. *Flowering* July to December. Parasitic on a variety of shrubs throughout the Western Cape.

CRASSULACEAE

Crassula muscosa L. *Akkedisstert, Skoenveterbossie*
Small succulent with densely leafy, somewhat woody, erect or scrambling stems. Leaves small, fleshy, triangular, closely concealing the stem, greyish. Flowers clustered in spikes at the tips of the branches, star-shaped, yellowish green. *Flowering* mainly October to April but almost any time depending on the rains. Usually among rocks in drier vegetation throughout South Africa.

Atriplex cinerea

Atriplex semibaccata

Spergularia media

Silene undulata

Cytinus sanguineus

Crassula muscosa

Crassula natans Thunb. *Watergras*
Minute annual, rarely basal parts perennial. Leaves somewhat succulent, small and fleshy. Flowers solitary among the upper leaves, minute, cup-shaped, white or pinkish. *Flowering* July to October. Growing in moist depressions or floating in shallow standing water, widespread in South Africa.

Crassula expansa Dryand *strepies Crassula*
Dwarf, tufted perennial with jointed stems. Leaves succulent, narrow and boat-shaped, triangular in section, often flushed reddish and with a distinct dark red stripe above. Flowers usually solitary at the tips of the branchlets, on slender stalks which elongate in fruit, usually white. *Flowering* mostly in the summer. Widespread in sandy soils, often near the coast throughout southern and tropical Africa.

Crassula scabra L. *platkop Crassula*
Short, branched perennial with roughly hairy stems often creeping and rooting at the nodes. Leaves at the ends of erect branches, opposite and tapering, succulent with flattened soft papillae. Flowers clustered on slender stems at the ends of the branches, white with red ovaries and stamens. *Flowering* December to February. In low, dry vegetation on granite outcrops and sandy soils from Cape Town to Clanwilliam.
    The similar *C. pustulata* Toelken and *C. pruinosa* L. may hybridise with *C. scabra* and are distinguished from it by their shorter leaves only 5-15 mm long.

Crassula dejecta Jacq. *doiley Crassula*
Shrublet, densely leafy above and hairy on the young branches. Leaves crowded, round, often tinged red, with a row of rounded, bead-like hairs on the margins. Flowers in tight clusters at the ends of the branches, white with red sepals and ovaries, honey-scented. *Flowering* December to February. On large rock outcrops, often granite from Springbok to Stellenbosch.

Crassula dichotoma L. *geel Crassula*
Annual, branched above. Leaves opposite, narrow and succulent, spotted red on the margins. Flowers in flat-topped clusters, star-like, yellow to orange with a red star in the centre. *Flowering* September to October. On sandy flats and slopes from Namaqualand to Caledon.

Crassula natans

Crassula expansa

Crassula scabra

Crassula dejecta

Crassula dichotoma

109

CRASSULACEAE

Tylecodon grandiflorus (Burm.f.) Toelken *rooi Suikerblom*
Succulent perennial with deciduous leaves, the stem covered with old leaf remains.
Leaves in tufts but dry at flowering, fleshy, narrow, often with the margins rolled
upwards. Flowers on long stalks branched near the top, upcurved, tubular, orange
to red. *Flowering* January to February. In sheltered sandy or rocky situations in
scrub from Clanwilliam to the Peninsula.

Tylecodon paniculatus (L.f.) Toelken *Botterboom*
Succulent perennial with stout, fibrous and fleshy stems. Leaves deciduous, fleshy,
broad, present at flowering. Flowers on long stalks branched near the top, nodding
and shortly tubular, greenish to orange. *Flowering* November to December. On
rocky, often granite, outcrops from Namibia to the Eastern Cape.

Tylecodon wallichii (Harv.) Toelken *Kandelaarbos*
Plant similar to *T. grandiflorus*. Flowers on erect stalks with spreading branches,
greenish-yellow. *Flowering* December to January. On sandy or gravelly soils from
Namibia to the Little Karoo

Cotyledon orbiculata L. *Plakkie, Hondeoor*
Brittle perennial shrubs more or less covered with a powdery white bloom. Leaves
opposite, rounded and succulent, grey with a red or pale margin. Flowers on a long
stalk branched at the tip, pendulous, tubular with recurved lobes, red or orange.
Flowering December to January. Widespread in coastal scrub thoughout South
Africa and Namibia.

FRANKENIACEAE

Frankenia pulverulata L. *klein Sandangelier*
Flat, spreading perennial with velvety stems. Leaves small, rounded, in whorls of
four. Flowers in clusters on the branchlets, pale mauve or pink. *Flowering*
September to January. On salt pans or seashore from Clanwilliam to Port Elizabeth.
Frankenia repens L. (Sandangelier) is similar but has narrow, sessile leaves and
larger flowers in clusters.

PLUMBAGINACEAE

*****Limonium acuminatum** L. Bol. *Saldanha Seelaventel*
Tufted perennial. Leaves spoon-shaped in a small basal tuft, dry at flowering.
Flowering stems sprawling, densely and shortly hairy, flowers on short zig-zag
branchlets at the ends of the stems which bear sterile branchlets along the lower
portion, small and pale pink. *Flowering* November to January. Restricted to limestone outcrops at Saldanha Bay.
Limonium equisetinum (Boiss.) R. A. Dyer (Seelaventel) is very similar but less
hairy and occurs on coastal sands from Namaqualand to Saldanha Bay.

Tylecodon grandiflorus

Tylecodon paniculatus

*Tylecodon
wallichii*

Cotyledon orbiculata

Frankenia pulverulata

*Limonium
acuminatum*

111

PLUMBAGINACEAE

Limonium longifolium (Thunb.) R.A. Dyer *wit Papierblom*
Tufted perennial. Leaves long, clustered at the base. Flowers in loosely branched, flat-topped inflorescences, white with the calyx dull orange, papery when dry. *Flowering* October to January. In deep sandy soil from Clanwilliam to Riversdale.

*****Limonium purpuratum** (L.) L. H. Bailey *Papierblom*
Shrublet with the leaves mostly at the base. Leaves long, tapering below, smooth. Flowers in flattened, branched clusters at the tips of the branches, magenta with the calyx dull pink, papery when dry. *Flowering* November. In deep coastal sands from Yzerfontein to Milnerton.

Limonium peregrinum (Bergius) R.A. Dyer *Strandroos*
Shrub with the branches leafy towards the tips. Leaves long, tapering below and clasping the stem, rough. Flowers more or less congested in flattened clusters at the tips of the branches, magenta with the calyx dull pink, papery when dry. *Flowering* November to January. On dunes and sandy coastal forelands from Clanwilliam to Melkbosstrand.

*****Limonium capense** (L. Bol.) L. Bol. *Saldanha Strandroos*
Rounded shrublet with rough, grey bark. Stems densely leafy to the top. Leaves short, overlapping, twisted, greyish and minutely pitted. Flowers in small clusters at the tips of the branches, magenta with the calyx dull pink, papery when dry. *Flowering* November. Restricted to coastal limestone flats near Langebaan.

MALVACEAE

Anisodontea scabrosa (L.) D.M. Bates *kus Sandroos*
Erect shrub, often glandular. Leaves irregularly toothed and sometimes lobed, roughly hairy, very variable in size. Flowers shallowly cupped with the stamens in a central tuft, pale to deep pink. *Flowering* mostly in the spring and summer. Typically in more disturbed and transitional situations near the coast on a variety of substrates, widely distributed in coastal regions from Saldanha Bay to Kwazulu/Natal.

Limonium longifolium

Limonium purpuratum

Limonium peregrinum

Limonium capense

Anisodontea scabrosa

113

Hermannia althaeifolia L.   *wolhaar Poproos*
Shrublet with softly hairy branches. Leaves wrinkled and roughly toothed, softly
hairy. Stipules large and leaf-like. Flowers in axillary clusters, bright orange-yellow
with swollen, hairy calyx. *Flowering* August to March. On clay flats and slopes or
along sandy watercourses from Namaqualand to Uniondale.

Hermannia alnifolia L.   *bos Poproos*
Shrublet with rough, maroon branches. Leaves round and wrinkled, paler below.
Stipules heart-shaped. Flowers crowded at the tips of the branchlets, bright yellow
with a rough calyx. *Flowering* August to October. On stony hills and shale slopes
from Clanwilliam to George.

Hermannia scabra Cav.   *gewone Poproos*
Low, spreading shrublet with rough stems. Leaves shortly petiolate, coarsely lobed,
thinly woolly below. Stipules heart-shaped. Flowers nodding, solitary or in sparse-
ly-branched clusters arranged along a long, leafless branch, yellow turning orange.
Flowering June to September. On stony plains and slopes from Clanwilliam to
Bellville.

Hermannia linifolia Burm.f.   *geel kruip Poproos*
Creeping shrublet with sparsely hairy stems. Leaves shortly petiolate, narrow,
coarsely lobed. Stipules long and narrow. Flowers nodding, in ascending branched
clusters arranged along the creeping stems, yellow fading cream, scented.
Flowering August to September. Restricted to sandy flats from Aurora to the
Peninsula.

Hermannia myrrhifolia Thunb.   *fynblaar kruip Poproos*
Creeping shrublet with smooth stems. Leaves petiolate, deeply divided, hairless.
Stipules heart-shaped. Flowers nodding, very narrow at the mouth, on ascending
branchlets, yellow turning orange. *Flowering* August to September. Restricted to
coastal sands or granite from Lambert's Bay to the Peninsula.

Hermannia ternifolia Harv.   *soet Poproos*
Sprawling shrublet with soft, roughly velvety stems. Leaves petiolate, wedge-
shaped and toothed at the apex. Stipules large and leaf-like. Flowers nodding, solitary in the axils of the upper leaves, yellow with orange margins and red on the
underside, with a very small mouth, strongly scented of narcissus. *Flowering* June
to October. In coastal scrub, often on limestone, from Saldanha Bay to Bredasdorp.

Hermannia althaeifolia

Hermannia alnifolia

Hermannia scabra

Hermannia linifolia

Hermannia myrrhifolia

Hermannia ternifolia

115

STERCULIACEAE

*Hermannia pinnata L. *kwasblaar kruip Poproos*
Spreading, mat-forming perennial with creeping branches, roughly hairy. Leaves narrow, apparently in whorls. Stipules divided into narrow, leafy segments. Flowers on short erect branches, nodding, creamy orange, strongly sweetly-scented. *Flowering* September to November. Restricted to sandy flats from Langebaan to the Peninsula.

*Hermannia humifusa Hochr. *pers Poproos*
Sprawling shrublet with roughly hairy branches. Leaves narrow, irregularly lobed, roughly hairy. Stipules leaf-like. Flowers nodding, mauve, sweetly scented. *Flowering* September to October. On sandy coastal flats from Saldanha Bay to the Peninsula.

DROSERACEAE

Drosera trinervia Spreng. *klein Snotrosie, small Sundew*
Glandular herb with naked, unbranched stem. Leaves in a basal rosette, narrow, reddish. Flowers several, clustered at the tip of the stem, white or rarely violet. *Flowering* August to November. On damp sandy flats from Calvinia to Swellendam.

Drosera cistiflora L. *Snotrosie, Sundew*
Glandular herb with unbranched, sparsely leafy stem. Leaves sessile, narrow, reddish. Flowers one to several, clustered at the tip of the stem, white, yellow, mauve or dark red, with a dark green centre. *Flowering* August to September. Widespread in moist, sandy places throughout the Western Cape.
   Drosera pauciflora DC. has large flowers like those of *D. cistiflora* but a basal rosette of leaves like *D. trinervia*.

CUCURBITACEAE

Kedrostis nana (Lam.) Cogn. *Ystervarkpatat*
Tuberous climber with annual stems climbing by tendrils, strongly aromatic. Leaves alternate, lobed, shining dark green. Flowers unisexual, on separate plants, greenish-yellow, males in short clusters, females solitary. Fruit fleshy, yellow-orange. *Flowering* February to March. Frequent among bushes at low altitude, especially near the sea from the Western Cape to Natal. All parts are poisonous.

Hermannia pinnata

Hermannia humifusa

Drosera trinervia

Drosera cistiflora

Drosera cistiflora

Kedrostis nana

117

Heliophila africana (L.) Marais   *sand Flaks*
Erect, coarsely hairy annual, sometimes branching from the base. Leaves simple or
with a few lobes, flat and roughly hairy. Flowers with hairy sepals, blue or mauve.
Fruits thread-like. *Flowering* August to October. In wet, sandy places from
Namaqualand to Swellendam.

Heliophila digitata L.f.   *kleinblom Flaks*
Erect, slender annual, sometimes hairy. Leaves shortly or much-divided, sometimes
hairy. Flowers with hairy sepals, rather small, blue or pink. Fruits thread-like, erect
on stalks less than 1 cm long. *Flowering* August to October. On sandy soils from
Clanwilliam to Riversdale.

Heliophila refracta Sond.   *draadblaar Flaks*
Erect annual sometimes branched from the base, hairless. Leaves thread-like or
divided into thread-like segments. Flowers with hairless sepals, blue. Fruits thread-
like, pendulous on stalks 1-2 cm long. *Flowering* August to September. On sandy
soils from Clanwilliam to Riversdale.

Heliophila coronopifolia L.   *blou Flaks*
Robust, erect annual, branching above, hairless, base of the branches purple.
Leaves simple or with a few lobes, flat and leathery with a greyish bloom. Flowers
with reddish sepals, blue with white or yellow centre. Fruits constricted between
the seeds. *Flowering* August to October. On loamy soils from Vanrhynsdorp to
Caledon.

ERICACEAE

Salaxis axillaris (Thunb.) G. Don   *bruin Basterheide*
Twiggy shrublet with fine branchlets. Leaves minute, in whorls of four. Flowers
minute, nodding in clusters at the tips of the branchlets, pinkish brown with a flat-
topped stigma. *Flowering* May to December. On sandy soils from Langebaan to the
Peninsula.

Erica lasciva Salisb.   *bruin Heide*
Small, erect shrub with short, leafy side branches bearing small clusters of nodding
flowers. Leaves small, the margins rolled under, closely appressed to the branches.
Flowers inconspicuous, pale brown with prominent brown anthers and protruding
stigma. *Flowering* February to July. Sandy flats from Ganzekraal to Riversdale.

Heliophila africana   *Heliophila digitata*   *Heliophila refracta*

Heliophila coronopifolia   *Salaxis axillaris*   *Erica lasciva*

Erica decora Andrews   *klokkies Heide*
Loose, erect shrub. Flowers slightly drooping in loose, untidy clusters, bell-shaped
and slightly sticky, pink. *Flowering* January to July. On clay slopes from
Malmesbury to the Peninsula.

Erica mammosa L.   *rooiklossie Heide*
Loose, erect shrub with narrow leaves. Flowers drooping in tight or loose clusters,
tubular with four dents or grooves at the base, red, pink or creamy white.
Flowering December to April. Common on sandy flats near the sea and also on
higher mountain slopes, from Clanwilliam to Caledon.

Erica parviflora L.   *berg Heide*
Diffuse, sprawling shrublet with hairy branches and tufts of minute, hairy leaves.
Flowers nodding on radiating shoots arranged in tiers up the stems, hairy, bell-
shaped, pink. *Flowering* May to September. In moist seepage areas or next to
streams from Darling to Bredasdorp.

Grisebachia incana (Bartl.) Klotzsch   *silwer Basterheide*
Compact, much-branched shrublet with delicate, greyish velvety branchlets. Leaves
small, clasping the stems in whorls of four. Flowers nodding in small silvery hairy
clusters at the tips of the branchlets, pink with four brown anthers. *Flowering*
March to June. In sandy places on the flats from Mamre to Gordon's Bay.

EBENACEAE

Euclea racemosa Murray   *Kersbos*
Low shrub or small tree with thick, leathery leaves, the margins thickened and
rolled under. Flowers small, in short clusters, bell-shaped, creamy-white with a
fruity scent. Fruits globose, thinly fleshy, shiny black when ripe. *Flowering*
December to March. In coastal dune scrubland and low coastal forest all along the
western and southern seaboard.

VAHLIACEAE

Vahlia capensis (L.f.) Thunb.   *Verkleurmannetjiekruid*
Glandular-hairy, branched herb. Leaves opposite, narrow. Flowers in pairs among
the leaves, yellow, turning reddish brown, with the sepals larger than the petals and
bent back. *Flowering* August to December. On sandy soils from the Westen Cape to
tropical Africa.

Erica decora

Erica mammosa

Erica parviflora

Grisebachia incana

Euclea racemosa

Vahlia capensis

Staavia radiata (L.) Dahl *Altydbos*
Tufted shrublet with erect branches, coppicing from rootstock. Leaves minute, needle-like, pressed against the stems. Flowers minute, pink, in compact heads surrounded by radiating white bracts. *Flowering* throughout the year. On sandy flats and slopes near the coast from Malmesbury to Riversdale.

Berzelia abrotanoides (L.) Brongn. *Rooibeentjies*
Erect shrublet with wiry branchlets. Leaves minute, closely overlapping. Flowers in tight, round heads borne on swollen red stalks, clustered at the tips of the branchlets, creamy white. *Flowering* April to October. On seasonally damp, sandy flats from Clanwilliam to Bredasdorp.

Berzelia lanuginosa (L.) Brongn. *vlei Kolkol*
Shrub with erect willowy branches. Leaves minute, needle-like, rather soft. Flowers in tight round heads in branched clusters at the end of the stems, creamy white, honey-scented. *Flowering* July to November. Along watercourses from the Cedarberg to Bredasdorp.

MONTINIACEAE

Montinia caryophyllacea Thunb. *Peperbos*
Erect shrub with alternate, leathery, blue-green leaves. Sexes on separate plants. Flowers with four or five white petals. Fruits dry, woody capsules with winged, papery seeds. *Flowering* July to October. On clay or sandy soils from Angola to the Eastern Cape.

ROSACEAE

Grielum grandiflorum (L.) Druce *Duikerwortel*
Sprawling perennial with cobwebby stems. Leaves finely divided, gray, cobwebby. Flowers opening in bright sunshine, shining yellow with a green centre. *Flowering* September to October. On sandy coastal flats from Port Nolloth to the Peninsula.

Grielum humifusum Thunb. *Pietsnot*
Prostrate herb with creeping stems. Leaves divided into blunt segments, thinly woolly. Flowers opening in bright sunshine, shining sulphur yellow with a white ring in the centre. *Flowering* August to September. Common in sandy places, often in disturbed areas and along roadsides throughout Namaqualand and the drier parts of the Western Cape.

Staavia radiata

Berzelia abrotanoides

*Berzelia
lanuginosa*

Montinia caryophyllacea

Grielum grandiflorum

*Grielum
humifusum*

123

Aspalathus hispida Thunb.   *wit Ertjiebos*
Twiggy shrub with pale, grey-streaked bark, velvety on the young parts. Leaves minute, in clusters on short lateral branchlets. Flowers at the ends of the short branchlets, creamy white with the keel tipped violet, honey-scented. *Flowering* June-December. Widespread on clay and sandy soils in the Western and Eastern Cape.

Aspalathus albens L.   *duine Ertjiebos*
Twiggy shrub with brown, streaky bark, not velvety on the young parts. Leaves needle-like, in clusters. Flowers clustered at the tips of the branchlets, pale yellow, scented. *Flowering* August to November. On sandy flats and hills from Nardouwsberg to the Peninsula.

Aspalathus ternata (Thunb.) Druce   *bolblom Ertjiebos*
Twiggy shrub, silky on the young parts. Leaves with three leaflets, silvery and silky-hairy. Flowers in sessile clusters, the calyx swollen and softly hairy, petals yellow, silky and silvery on the backs, honey-scented. *Flowering* September to December. On marine sands from Lambert's Bay to the Peninsula.

Aspalathus quinquefolia L.   *knoppies Ertjiebos*
Slender, erect shrublet with pale, grey-streaked bark, velvety on the young parts. Leaves small, overlapping on the young branchlets, silvery grey and velvety. Flowers in round clusters at the tips of the branchlets, yellow, honey-scented. *Flowering* August to November. On coastal sands and limestones from Lambert's Bay to Mossel Bay.

Aspalathus cordata (L.) Dahlgr.   *steek Ertjiebos*
Stiff shrublet, branches with silky tufts when young. Leaves bright green, spreading, broad and spine-tipped. Flowers clustered at the tips of the branches, yellow. *Flowering* October to December. On sandstone or clay from Piketberg to Hangklip.

Aspalathus pinguis Thunb.   *jakkalsstert Ertjiebos*
Erect shrublet with the young branches shortly white-woolly. Leaves extremely variable from short and broad to long and needle-like, in tufts along the branches. Flowers among the leaves, yellow. *Flowering* May to December. On clay soils or clay-sandstone transitions from Piketberg to Uniondale.

Aspalathus hispida

Aspalathus albens

Aspalathus ternata

Aspalathus quinquefolia

Aspalathus cordata

Aspalathus pinguis

Aspalathus spinescens Thunb. *Wolfdoring*
Rigid, twiggy shrub with pale, grey-streaked bark, velvety on the young parts.
Leaves minute, fleshy, in clusters on short lateral branchlets which become stiff and
spine-like. Flowers solitary along the short branchlets, yellow, honey-scented.
Flowering August to October. On deep sands from Vanrhynsdorp to Mamre.

Aspalathus spinosa L. *Dansdoring*
Shrub with rigid, spreading branches bearing many thin, stiff pale thorns. Leaves
small, in clusters. Flowers single or paired, pale yellow, sometimes partly reddish.
Flowering August to April. Widespread in a variety of habitats but often on clay at
low altitudes, from near Clanwilliam to Kwazulu/Natal.

Wiborgia mucronata (L.f.) Druce *steek Korrelertjie*
Rigid shrublet with branches more or less at right angles, smooth and yellowish
when young, becoming stiff and spiny. Leaves with three leaflets, leathery with a
pale bloom, notched at the tips. Flowers in spikes, yellow, with a sour scent. Fruits
flat and rounded. *Flowering* August to October. Mainly on sandy soil or granite
from Namaqualand to Swellendam.

Wiborgia obcordata (Bergius) Thunb. *skraal Korrelertjie*
Willowy shrub with the young branches velvety and the old branches with streaky,
pale grey bark. Leaves small, with three leaflets, rounded or minutely notched at
the tips, thinly hairy. Flowers in slender spikes, yellow, sweetly scented. Fruits flat
and rounded. *Flowering* August to October. On sandy, often coastal soils from
Calvinia to Mossel Bay.

Wiborgia fusca Thunb. *Korrelertjie*
Shrub with the old branches pale grey and more or less spiny. Leaves with three
leaflets, minutely pointed at the tips. Flowers in spikes, pale creamy yellow. Fruits
flat and rounded. *Flowering* June to September. On clay and granitic soils from
Namaqualand to Mamre.

Rafnia angulata Thunb. *soet Houtbossie*
Shrublet with branches spreading from the base. Leaves simple, pale green with a
grey bloom. Flowers crowded among the leaves, pea-like, yellow, honey-scented.
Flowering September to December. On stony slopes from Yzerfontein to
Swellendam.

Aspalathus spinescens

Aspalathus spinosa

Wiborgia mucronata

Wiborgia obcordata

Wiborgia fusca

Rafnia angulata

127

Cyclopia genistoides (L.) R. Br. *Heuningtee*
Rounded shrub, leafy at the ends of the branches. Leaves divided to the base into three narrow leaflets. Flowers clustered at the ends of the branchlets, pea-like, golden-yellow, honey scented. *Flowering* July to October. Along drainage lines in sandy soil from Darling to Uniondale.

Lebeckia spinescens Harv. *sand Ganna*
Rigid shrub with spiny branches at right angles. Leaves with three small, folded leaflets on a long petiole, silvery-hairy. Flowers in clusters on short branches, bright yellow. *Flowering* March to May (to September). On dry clay or granite slopes from Namibia to Malmesbury and in drier Karoo areas to the Eastern Cape.

Lebeckia simsiana Eckl. & Zeyh. *jakkalsstert Ganna*
Tufted perennial with trailing branches. Leaves thread-like and jointed. Flowers in long, erect spikes, bright yellow, lightly scented. *Flowering* September to November. On sandy flats and lower slopes from Clanwilliam to Swellendam.

Lebeckia plukenetiana E. Mey. *klein Ganna*
Spreading perennial with short, erect, unbranched stems. Leaves thread-like and jointed. Flowers in short, erect spikes, bright yellow. *Flowering* November to December. On sandy soils from Langebaan to the Peninsula.

Crotalaria excisa (Thunb.) Baker f. *Wildeklawer*
Creeping perennial with leaves divided into three narrow leaflets, silky below. Flowers one or two on erect stalks, bright yellow. *Flowering* August to October. On clay or granite from Kamiesberg to Montagu.

Lotononis prostrata (L.) Benth. *kruip Wildeklawer*
Creeping perennial with silky leaves divided into three leaflets. Flowers solitary, erect on long stalks, slightly wrinkled, yellow with darker veining. *Flowering* August to September. On clay or granite from Clanwilliam to Riversdale.

Cyclopia genistoides

Lebeckia spinescens

Lebeckia simsiana

Lebeckia plukenetiana

Crotalaria excisa

Lotononis prostrata

Dipogon lignosus (L.) Verdc. *Bosklimop*
Twining perennial with annual branches, sparsely hairy on the young parts. Leaves divided into three trowel-shaped leaflets, greyish below. Flowers clustered at the ends of long naked stalks, pea-like, lilac and magenta. *Flowering* mostly September to December. In coastal bush or forest from Yzerfontein to the Eastern Cape.

Indigofera complicata Eckl. & Zeyh. *silwer Lewertjie*
Shrublet with thinly hairy, grey, slightly fleshy stems and leaves. Leaves divided into three narrow, channelled leaflets on long, fleshy petioles. Flowers in erect spikes, dark pink. *Flowering* June to November. On coastal limestones from Saldanha Bay to Mossel Bay.

Indigofera incana Thunb. *pienk Lewertjie*
Dwarf shrublet with numerous straggling stems from a woody base, erect at the ends. Leaves divided into three oval leaflets, densely covered with hairs pressed to the surface. Flowers in erect spikes, pea-like, bright rose-pink. *Flowering* August to October. On clay soils from Piketberg to Caledon.
  Indigofera procumbens L. (Lewertjie) is similar but the leaflets are almost hairless and the flowers are salmon-pink to orange.

Amphithalea ericifolia (L.) Eckl. & Zeyh. *Persbossie*
Shrublet with slender, sometimes wand-like branches. Leaves silvery-hairy, held against the stem. Flowers clustered at the tips of the branches, dark pink with a purple keel, scented like sweet peas. *Flowering* April to November. Widespread on sandy soils in the Western Cape.

Otholobium hirtum (L.) C.H. Stirton *grys Keurtjie*
Rigid, much-branched shrub with diverging branchlets, whitish velvety when young. Leaves divided into three leaflets, thinly hairy and with the tips hooked. Flowers two or three in clusters at the tips of the branchlets, mauve and purple. *Flowering* October to January. On clay or granite from Piketberg to Caledon.

Lessertia rigida E. Mey. *Blaasertjie*
Shrublet with erect branches. Leaves divided into numerous narrow leaflets. Flowers loosely clustered on stalks among the upper leaves, magenta. Fruits bladder-like. *Flowering* August to September. On sandy soils or granite outcrops from Clanwilliam to Darling.

Dipogon lignosus

Indigofera complicata

Indigofera incana

Otholobium hirtum

Amphithalea ericifolia

Lessertia rigida

131

Sutherlandia frutescens (L.) R. Br. *Kankerbos*
Shrublet branching from the base, stems covered with grey hairs. Leaves divided
into numerous narrow leaflets, paler below. Flowers large, pea-like, red. Fruits
inflated and bladder-like. *Flowering* July to December. Widespread in the Western
Cape on stony slopes and flats.

PROTEACEAE

Serruria fasciflora Knight *fyn Spinnekopbos*
Shrublet with slightly hairy stems and finely divided hairy leaves, the segments
needle-like. Flower heads several, in loose clusters at the ends of the branches, silvery pink. *Flowering* October to December. On sandy slopes from the Cold
Bokkeveld to George.

*Serruria decipiens R. Br. *Weskus Spinnekopbos*
Shrublet with hairy stems and finely divided leaves, the segments needle-like.
Flower heads several, in tight clusters at the ends of the branches, pink or white.
Flowering August to November. On sandy coastal flats from Piketberg to
Melkbosstrand.

Serruria fucifolia Knight *klein Spinnekopbos*
Shrublet with hairy stems and finely divided leaves, the segments needle-like.
Flower heads solitary, silvery. *Flowering* August to December. On coastal sands
from Clanwilliam to Hopefield.

*Serruria trilopha Knight *rooi Spinnekopbos*
Shrublet with hairy stems closely covered with short, divided leaves. Flower heads
solitary at the end of the branches, strawberry pink with silvery hairs. *Flowering*
August to December. Restricted to coastal sands from Mamre to Ysterplaat.

Leucospermum calligerum (Knight) Rourke *pienk Luisiebos*
Erect to spreading shrub, much-branched from a short trunk. Leaves elliptic, pointed, covered with fine grey crisped hairs. Flower heads in clusters, creamy-green
turning carmine with age, sweetly scented. *Flowering* August to November.
Widespread on dry mountain slopes from Lokenburg to Riversdale.

Sutherlandia frutescens   *Serruria fasciflora*   *Serruria decipiens*

Serruria fucifolia   *Serruria trilopha*   *Leucospermum
calligerum*

Leucospermum rodolentum (Knight) Rourke   *sandveld Luisiebos*
Erect to spreading shrub, much-branched from a short trunk. Leaves elliptic with
three to six apical teeth, covered with fine grey crisped hairs. Flower heads in clusters, bright yellow and sweetly scented. *Flowering* August to November. Frequent
on sandy coastal forelands from near Graafwater to Darling (with an isolated population near Worcester).

***Leucospermum tomentosum** (Thunb.) R. Br.   *vaal Luisiebos*
Suberect shrub with somewhat sprawling branches. Leaves erect, very narrow with
two to four apical teeth, covered with fine grey crisped hairs. Flower heads in clusters, bright yellow and sweetly scented. *Flowering* July to November. Restricted to
coastal sands between Langebaan and Silverstroomstrand.

Leucospermum hypophyllocarpodendron (L.) Druce   *kruip Luisiebos*
Sprawling or trailing shrub forming mats, stems mostly creeping. Leaves erect,
along the upperside of the stems only, narrow with two to four red apical teeth,
covered with fine grey crisped hairs. Flower heads in clusters of one to four, bright
yellow and sweetly scented. *Flowering* July to January. On sandy coastal flats from
Piketberg to Bredasdorp.

Protea scolymocephala (L.) Reichardt   *Skollie*
Erect, rounded shrub with a single trunk. Leaves narrow, hairless. Flower heads
with the bracts spreading, hairy on the margins, greenish with pink tips. *Flowering*
September to November. In deep white sandy soils near the coast from Clanwilliam
to Hermanus.

Protea burchellii Stapf   *Suikerbos*
Erect shrub with a single trunk. Leaves narrow, at first hairy, with hard margins and
midrib. Flower heads with the bracts shining and only the inner hairy on the margins and bearded at the tips, cream, greenish or pink. *Flowering* June to August. On
a variety of soils, essentially lowland, from Redelinghuys to Sir Lowry's Pass.

Protea repens (L.) L.   *Sugarbush, Suikerkan*
Erect shrub or tree with a short trunk. Leaves narrow, greyish-green with pale margins and midrib. Flower heads rather narrow, with the bracts quite hairless but
sticky and glutinous, variously coloured pink or red or creamy-white. *Flowering*
mainly April to October. The commonest Western Cape protea, widespread mainly
on flats, coastal forelands and lower mountain slopes from Nieuwoudtville to
Grahamstown.

Leucospermum rodolentum   *Leucospermum tomentosum*   *Leucospermum*
                                                                    hypophyllocarpodendron

Protea scolymocephala   *Protea burchellii*   *Protea repens*

135

Leucadendron cinereum (Aiton) R. Br. *vaal Tolbos*
Erect shrublet with slender, closely leafy stems. Leaves long, narrow and tapering below, overlapping, bluish grey. Sexes on separate plants, heads not surrounded by conspicuous bracts. Seed body not winged. *Flowering* October. On sandy flats from Piketberg to Tygerberg.

***Leucadendron thymifolium** (Knight) I. Williams *katstert Tolbos*
Erect shrublet with slender, closely leafy stems. Leaves short, oblong, overlapping. Sexes on separate plants, heads not surrounded by conspicuous bracts. Seed body not winged. *Flowering* August to September. On sandy coastal flats around Malmesbury.

Leucadendron lanigerum Meisn. *rooikop Tolbos*
Erect shrublet with slender stems. Leaves narrow, parallel-sided. Sexes on separate plants, heads surrounded by narrow yellow bracts. Seed body winged. *Flowering* August to September. On clay or granitic soils from Darling to Faure.

Leucadendron cinereum ♂

Leucadendron thymifolium ♂

Leucadendron lanigerum ♂

Leucadendron cinereum ♀

Leucadendron thymifolium ♀

Leucadendron lanigerum ♀

PROTEACEAE

Leucadendron salignum Bergius *geel Tolbos*
Erect shrub, resprouting after fire. Leaves narrow, especially numerous round the flower heads, yellowish. Sexes on separate plants. Male heads globose, yellow; female heads larger, enclosed by enlarged bracts. *Flowering* August to September. Common on hills and mountain slopes on sand and clay from Nieuwoudtville to Port Elizabeth.

THYMELAEACEAE

Passerina vulgaris Thoday *sand Gannabos*
Shrublet with erect branchlets and bark which strips in tough strings. Leaves needle-like. Flowers inconspicuous, reddish or yellow, clustered at the branch tips, with protruding stamens. *Flowering* August to September. Widespread on sandy flats from Hopefield to Natal.

Gnidia geminiflora Meisn. *geel Koorsbossie*
Shrublet with leaves 4-ranked, rounded below and sparsely hairy. Flowers in pairs at the tips of the branchlets, creamy, with conspicuous fleshy petals. *Flowering* June to December. On sandy flats and slopes from Namaqualand to Malmesbury.

Gnidia pinifolia L. *wit Koorsbossie*
Shrublet with slender branches and narrow, keeled leaves. Flowers in heads at the ends of the branches, cream, sometimes flushed pink, with a long hairy tube, honey-scented. *Flowering* June to November. Widespread in the Western Cape and extending to the Transvaal.

Struthiola leptantha Bolus *Roemenaggie, Veertjie*
Slender shrublet with opposite leaves closely appressed to the stem. Flowers solitary in the axils of the upper leaves, with a long slender tube, white and scented at night. *Flowering* June to December. In sandy or stony soils from Namaqualand to Worcester.

Lachnaea capitata Meisn. *Vleiblom*
Shrublet with slender, willowy branches. Leaves narrow, alternate and held close to the stem. Flowers small, in terminal heads which often elongate into spikes, densely silky, white. *Flowering* July to January. On sandy coastal forelands from Namaqualand to Caledon.

Leucadendron salignum

Passerina vulgaris

Gnidia geminiflora

Gnidia pinifolia

Struthiola leptantha

Lachnaea capitata

139

Lachnaea grandiflora (L.f.) J. Beyers   *groot Letjiesbos*
Slightly hairy shrublet. Leaves narrow and boat-shaped, appressed to the stem,
opposite. Flowers solitary and mostly terminal, silky outside, pale to dark pink.
Flowering August to November, often sporadically throughout the year. On sandy
soils from Piketberg to Caledon, frequent on the Cape Flats.

Lachnaea uniflora (Meisn.) J. Beyers   *Letjiesbos*
Shrublet with wiry branchlets. Leaves narrow, needle-like and appressed to the
stem, opposite. Flowers solitary and mostly terminal, silky outside, pale to dark
pink. *Flowering* October to February. On sandy flats or lower slopes from
Piketberg to the Peninsula.

SANTALACEAE

Osyris compressa (Bergius) A. DC.   *Pruimbas*
Shrub or small tree with flattened twigs. Leaves opposite, crowded, tough with
thickened margins, bluish-green with a grey bloom. Flowers small, in clusters, yellowish-green. Fruit oval, fleshy, red turning purplish-black. *Flowering* almost
throughout the year. Particularly common on coastal sand dunes but also among
rocks and on lower mountain slopes along the seaboard from near Lambert's Bay
to southern Mozambique.

Thesium capitatum L.   *Groenbasbossie*
Shrublet with erect, densely leafy branchlets. Leaves triangular, closely overlapping, with the margins membranous and wing-like especially the upper ones.
Flowers clustered in heads, white. *Flowering* for most of the year. On sandy flats
and slopes from Malmesbury to Humansdorp.

Thesium spinosum L.f.   *steek Groenbasbossie*
Intricately branched shrublet, pale green or yellowish. Leaves small, triangular and
spine-tipped. Flowers in the axils of the upper leaves, greenish. *Flowering* July-
September. On sandy soils from Namaqualand to Saldanha Bay.

Thesidium fragile (Thunb.) Sond.   *breek Groenbasbossie*
Yellowish shrublet with crowded erect, stiff branchlets. Leaf scales keeled. Sexes
separate, flowers greenish. Fruit white and fleshy tipped with the scarlet remains of
the sepals. *Flowering* throughout the year. On sandy flats and dunes along the coast
from Saldanha Bay to Riversdale.

Lachnaea grandiflora   *Lachnaea uniflora*   *Osyris compressa*

Thesium capitatum   *Thesium spinosum*   *Thesidium fragile*

141

LORANTHACEAE

Septulina glauca (Thunb.) Tiegh.   *Candles, Kersies*
Parasite with woody branches, often growing on species of *Lycium*. Leaves rounded, slightly fleshy, grey and roughly powdery. Flowers two or three in the leaf axils, narrowly tubular with four narrow lobes, splitting shortly down one side, roughly powdery, dull orange-red but green at the tip. *Flowering* February to May. Scattered thoughout the Western and Northern Cape.

VISCACEAE

Viscum rotundifolium L.   *rooi Voëlent*
Parasite with brittle, jointed stems, attached to the branches of the host tree, leafy only on new growth. Leaves opposite, broad, greyish. Flowers in threes, small and greenish-yellow. Fruits usually in pairs in the axils of older, often fallen leaves, fleshy and pale green turning red. *Fruits* ripening February to March. Widespread throughout South Africa.

Viscum capense L.f.   *Voëlent, Cape Mistletoe*
Parasite with brittle, jointed stems, attached to the branches of the host tree, leafless. Flowers often in clusters of three to five, inconspicuous. Fruits fleshy, watery, white and almost translucent. *Fruits* ripening April to November. Widespread in the southern half of the country.

CELASTRACEAE

Maurocenia frangularia (L.) Mill.   *Hotnotskersie*
Shrub or small rigid tree with purplish branchlets. Leaves opposite, round, tough and leathery with the margins hard and rolled under. Flowers small, in compact clusters, whitish, honey-scented. Fruit thinly fleshy, red when mature. *Flowering* February to April or June. In coastal bush, often among rocks or along mountain streams from Velddrif to Caledon.

Maytenus heterophylla (Eckl. & Zeyh.) N. Robson   *stink Pendoring*
Thorny shrub with grey bark, lateral branches spike-like. Leaves leathery, widest near the tip, blunt, dull green. Flowers in dense clusters among the leaves, white, foul-scented. *Flowering* October to December. Widespread in southern Africa.

Putterlickia pyracantha (L.) Szyszyl.   *Pendoring*
Thorny shrub with red-brown bark, lateral branches spine-like. Leaves widest near the tip, blunt, glossy dark green. Flowers in loose clusters on slender stalks, cream. Fruit woody, pinkish-red when mature. *Flowering* November to January.
Widespread in scrub and dune forest over much of the drier parts of South Africa.

Septulina glauca *Viscum rotundifolium* *Viscum capense*

Maurocenia frangularia *Maytenus heterophylla* *Putterlickia pyracantha*

143

Clutia daphnoides Lam. *Vaalblaar*
Rounded shrublet with erect branches, mealy when young. Leaves spreading, leathery, dull and covered with a powdery meal when young. Flowers small, cup-shaped, greenish. *Flowering* June to October. On sands or limestone near the coast from Malmesbury to the Eastern Cape.

Clutia ericoides Thunb. *klein Vaalblaar*
Rounded shrublet with smooth brown or grey branchlets. Leaves slightly spreading, brittle and somewhat fleshy, smooth and shiny. Flowers small, cup-shaped, greenish. *Flowering* May to July. On sandy soils from Piketberg to Port Elizabeth.

Euphorbia mauritanica L. *geel Melkbos*
Deciduous shrublet with cylindrical, fleshy branches exuding milky latex when damaged. Leaves crowded on the new growth. False flowers in clusters at the tips of the branches, each with five glistening, dull yellow lobes. *Flowering* July to September. On dry stony slopes throughout southern Africa.

Euphorbia burmannii Boiss. *Steenbokbos*
Intricately branched shrublet with jointed branches exuding a milky latex when wounded. Leaves reduced to tiny scales, with conspicuous glands at the base. False flowers minute, in clusters at the tips of the branchlets, with five green lobes. *Flowering* July to August. On drier slopes from Namaqualand to Port Elizabeth.

Euphorbia arceuthobioides Boiss. *klein Steenbokbos*
Similar to E. burmannii but smaller and false flowers solitary at the tips of the branchlets, with five to seven greenish lobes. *Flowering* September to February. On dry slopes in clay or sand from Stellenbosch to Namaqualand.

144

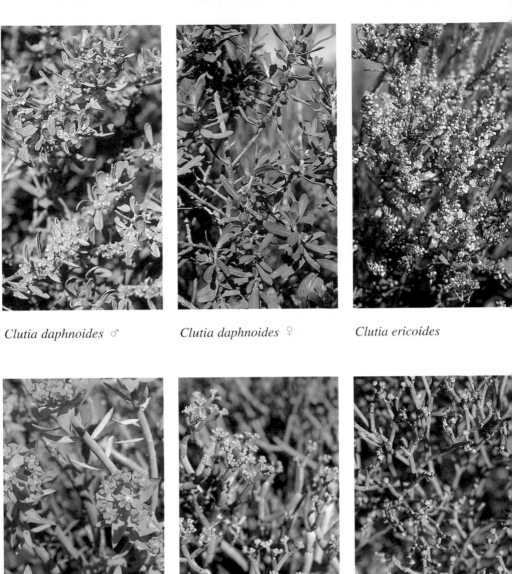

Clutia daphnoides ♂ *Clutia daphnoides* ♀ *Clutia ericoides*

Euphorbia mauritanica *Euphorbia burmannii* *Euphorbia*
arceuthobioides

Euphorbia tuberosa L. _Melkbol_

Dwarf plant with tuberous roots and a cluster of wavy, greyish leaves borne at ground level, exuding a milky latex when damaged. False flowers in clusters at the tips of trailing shoots, with five yellowish or green lobes. _Flowering_ April to September. On sandy flats from Vanrhynsdorp to the Peninsula.

Euphorbia caput-medusae L. _Vingerpol_

Succulent with thick, sprawling stems and reduced leaves soon falling, exuding a milky latex when damaged. False flowers in clusters at the tips of the branches, with five fringed lobes white at the ends. _Flowering_ June to September. On coastal sands from Hopefield to the Peninsula.

RHAMNACEAE

Phylica parviflora Bergius _klein Hardeblaar_

Compact shrublet with thinly hairy, slender branches. Leaves usually closely set, narrow with the margins rolled under. Flower heads very numerous at the ends of short branchlets, containing five to eight greenish, woolly florets. _Flowering_ January to May. On sandy soil near the coast from Saldanha Bay to Mossel Bay.

Phylica cephalantha Sond. _tol Hardeblaar_

Shrublet with more or less erect, greyish-yellow, velvety branches. Leaves narrow, leathery with the margins rolled under, white and velvety below. Flowers minute, in tight, rounded, white-woolly heads at the ends of the branches, scented. _Flowering_ April to September. On sandy flats and lower slopes from near Clanwilliam to the Peninsula.

Phylica stipularis L. _Hondegesiggie_

Small shrublet with more or less erect, velvety, greyish branches. Leaves narrow, leathery with the margins rolled under, white and velvety below, with paired dry stipules at the base. Flowers crowded in woolly heads at the ends of the branches, with five narrow pink lobes and a strong, spicy scent. _Flowering_ March to June. Common on flats, hills and lower mountain slopes in the Western Cape.

Phylica plumosa L. _Veerkoppie_

Sparsely branched shrublet with velvety, rusty brown branches. Leaves narrow, roughly hairy with the margins rolled under, greyish and velvety below. Flowers minute, clustered at the ends of the branches in loose heads among conspicuous, narrow, feathery golden bracts. _Flowering_ May to August. On clay slopes from Clanwilliam to Montagu.

Euphorbia tuberosa

Euphorbia caput-medusae

Phylica parviflora

Phylica cephalantha

Phylica stipularis

Phylica plumosa

147

Nylandtia scoparia (Eckl. & Zeyh.) Goldblatt & J. Manning   *Duinebessie*
Shrub or small tree with stiff, erect branches, leafless at flowering, blunt or spiny.
Flowers scattered, small, pea-like with a fringed crest on the lower, keeled petal,
pink. Conspicuous when in flower. *Flowering* August to September. On deep sandy
soil from Namaqualand to Darling.

Nylandtia spinosa (L.) Dumort.   *Skilpadbessie*
Rigid, low shrublet with spine-tipped branchlets. Leaves scattered, small and thick.
Flowers small, pea-like with a fringed crest on the lower, keeled petal, lilac and
purple. Fruit globose, fleshy, shining red when ripe, edible but astringent.
Flowering May to October. Common in sandy places from Namaqualand to the
Eastern Cape.

Muraltia macropetala Harv.   *Skilpadbos*
Rigid shrublet with velvety branches at right angles. Leaves in clusters, with a
hard, downcurved tip. Flowers magenta, two conspicuous narrow upper petals
longer than the lower keel which bears a prominent four-lobed crest, heavily
honey-scented. *Flowering* in the July to November. Usually social and providing
brilliant splashes of colour on clay or loam soils from Malmesbury to the
Peninsula.

*****Muraltia harveyana** Levyns   *Saldanha Skilpadbos*
Stiff shrublet with branches often at right angles. Leaves leathery, broadest near the
tip which has a small downcurved point. Flowers scattered on the branchlets, pink
fading to white, with two minute upper teeth and a lower keel bearing a prominent
four-lobed crest. *Flowering* October to January. Restricted to shallow sands on
limestone ridges between Yzerfontein and Saldanha Bay.

Muraltia filiformis (Thunb.) DC.   *Skilpadblom*
Slender shrublet with flexible branches, shortly hairy when young. Leaves leathery,
very narrow with a small curved tip. Flowers aggregated at the tips of the branches,
pink with the tip of the lower keel dark purple. *Flowering* for most of the year. On
sandy flats, often in damp places, from Mamre to Bredasdorp.

Nylandtia scoparia

Nylandtia spinosa

Nylandtia spinosa (fruit)

Muraltia macropetala

Muraltia harveyana

Muraltia filiformis

Polygala myrtifolia L. *Septemberbos*
Shrub with broad, alternate leaves. Flowers showy, mauve or purple with two large petaloid sepals and the lower keel bearing a fringed crest at the end. Fruits flattened. *Flowering* mostly May to September. Widespread in a variety of habitats, in dune bush or sand dunes and on hillsides from the Western Cape to KwaZulu/Natal.

Polygala umbellata L. *skoenlapper Skaapertjie*
Shrublet with slender, wiry branches. Leaves narrow and needle-like, clasping the stems in the upper part. Flowers clustered at the tips of the branchlets, the outer petals spreading, magenta, green on the backs, the keel with a fringed purple crest tipped with white. *Flowering* August to October. On dry lower slopes from Ceres to Riversdale.

ANACARDIACEAE

Rhus glauca Thunb. *Taaiblaar*
Much-branched evergreen shrub. Leaves divided into three blunt, paddle-shaped segments, greyish green. Flowers bisexual, very small in open, branched clusters, greenish. Fruits round and shining, chestnut-brown. *Flowering* May to September. A coastal species on clay or granite soils from Velddrif to the Eastern Cape.

Rhus laevigata Thunb. var. **laevigata** *Taaibos*
Rhus laevigata var. **villosa** (L.f.) R. Fernandes *Koerentebos*
Multi-stemmed deciduous shrub often forming thickets. Leaves divided into three egg-shaped segments, hairless or more or less covered with long, straight hairs. Flowers usually unisexual, very small in branched clusters, greenish. Fruits round and shiny, dull yellow to reddish, drying brown. Flowering October to December. Common on sand on the coastal forelands from Lambert's Bay to East London.

Rhus dissecta Thunb. *Rosyntjiebos*
Dwarf deciduous shrublet with reddish branches. Leaves divided into three triangular segments toothed at the ends, bright green. Flowers bisexual, small in fewbranched clusters, greenish. Fruits rough, yellow to red. *Flowering* June and July. On mountains and coastal forelands from near Vanrhynsdorp to MacGregor.

Polygala myrtifolia

Polygala umbellata

Rhus glauca

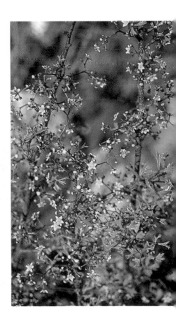

Rhus laevigata var. *laevigata*

Rhus laevigata var. *villosa*

Rhus dissecta

Melianthus elongatus Wijnands   *Truitjie*
Shrub with smooth, grey branches, foetid when bruised. Leaves clustered at the
branch tips, with winged axis and toothed leaflets. Flowers in fours in spikes, the
buds with bright red petals fading as they mature. *Flowering* July to September. On
sandy soils among rocks, often granite from Kamiesberg to Malmesbury.

RUTACEAE

*Agathosma thymifolia Schlechtd.   *kalk Buchu*
Weakly aromatic shrublet with dense, erect branchlets. Leaves alternate, rounded.
Flowers pinkish to deep mauve, in clusters at the tips of the branches, the staminodes thread-like. *Flowering* July to September. Rare and restricted to coastal sands
overlying limestone from Velddrif to Geelbek.

Agathosma imbricata (L.) Willd.   *sand Buchu*
Aromatic shrublet with dense, erect branchlets, smelling strongly of citrus. Leaves
alternate, heart-shaped, more or less erect, with scattered fine hairs on the margins.
Flowers white, in clusters at the tips of the branchlets, the petals with a slender
claw twice as long as the blade, the staminodes narrow and hairy. *Flowering*
August to February. On coastal sands, limestones and granite from Saldanha Bay to
Mossel Bay.

Agathosma latipetala Sond.   *Swartland Buchu*
Weakly aromatic shrublet with dense, erect branchlets. Leaves alternate, pointed,
spreading or deflexed, with scattered fine hairs on the margins. Flowers white, in
clusters at the tips of the branchlets, often on maroon pedicels, the staminodes
erect, narrow and hairy. *Flowering* August to October. On shale or granite flats and
slopes from Malmesbury to Joostenberg.

Agathosma bisulca (Thunb.)Bartl. & Wendl.   *denneblaar Buchu*
Low, somewhat spreading shrublet smelling of citrus. Leaves alternate, needle-like,
hairless. Flowers white, in clusters at the tips of the branchlets, the petals with a
slender claw a little longer than the blade, the staminodes spathula-shaped and
hairy below. *Flowering* July to December. In deep sands from Nieuwoudtville to
Yzerfontein.

Macrostylis villosa (Thunb.) Sond.   *kousie Buchu*
Shrubs with many slender stems. Leaves narrow, greyish. Flowers crowded in
heads at the tips of the branches, with hairy white petals, strongly smelling of olive
oil. *Flowering* mostly in summer and autumn. On sandy coastal flats from Mamre
to Gordon's Bay.

Melianthus elongatus

Agathosma thymifolia

Agathosma imbricata

Agathosma latipetala

Agathosma bisulca

Macrostylis villosa

Diosma hirsuta L.　　　　　　　　　　　　　　　　　　*rooi Buchu*
Slender resprouting shrublet with smooth brown stems, aromatic when crushed.
Leaves narrow and needle-like, slightly channelled above, erect, gland-dotted and
resinous. Flowers in small clusters at the branch tips, white. *Flowering* almost
throughout the year, mostly in spring. On sandy, often gravelly soils from
Clanwilliam to Riversdale.

*****Diosma aspalathoides** Lam.　　　　　　　　　　　　　　　*haas Buchu*
Much-branched shrublet. Leaves needle-like, smelling of citrus when crushed.
Flowers in clusters at the tips of the branchlets, white with a lobed green disc in the
centre. *Flowering* September to October. On sandy coastal flats from Langebaan to
Milnerton.

Diosma oppositifolia L.　　　　　　　　　　　　　　　　*bitter Buchu*
Aromatic shrubs with slender stems, aromatic when crushed. Leaves mostly opposite, with sparse hairs on the margin. Flowers white, cup-shaped. *Flowering* almost
throughout the year, mostly during late summer. On sandy flats and mountain
slopes from near Darling to Napier.

Adenandra villosa (Berg.) Roem. & Schult
　　　　　　　　　　　Porseleinblom, China flower, Kommetjietee
Slender shrublet with velvety stems. Leaves minute, the margins rolled under.
Flowers in clusters at the tips of the branches, glistening white with maroon streaks
in the centre, pinkish underneath. *Flowering* July to November. On sandy soils
from Malmesbury to Caledon.

OXALIDACEAE

Flower colour is of limited use in distinguishing the species of *Oxalis* as many of
them come in a variety of colours. Flowering time is useful in excluding some possibilities, while many of the species have very decided preferences for soil type.

Oxalis livida Jacq.　　　　　　　　　　　　　　　　　*steentjie Suring*
Stem often branched, hairless, with a few scales below the flower stalk, leafy
above. Bulb horizontal, ridged, producing long runners. Leaves with three deeply
divided leaflets. Sepals broad and blunt with two orange warts at the tips. Flowers
in clusters nodding in bud, lilac or white with a funnel-shaped, hairless greenish-
yellow tube shorter than the squared lobes. *Flowering* April to June. On stony clay
flats and low slopes from Piketberg to Stellenbosch.

Oxalis polyphylla Jacq.　　　　　　　　　　　　　　　*fynblaar Suring*
Stem hairless or shortly hairy with a few scales, terminating in a cluster of leaves
and flowers. Leaves with three very narrow leaflets, these and the narrow sepals
tipped with two conspicuous orange warts. Flowers pink or white with a narrowly
funnel-shaped, hairy yellow tube about as long as the lobes. *Flowering* March to
June. On sandy flats from Wellington to Port Elizabeth.

154

Diosma hirsuta

Diosma aspalathoides

Diosma oppositifolia

Adenandra villosa

Oxalis livida

Oxalis polyphylla

Oxalis hirta L.
Oxalis hirta var. **tubiflora** (Jacq.) T.M. Salter   *stam Suring*
Stem softly hairy with the upper part leafy, sometimes very short. Leaves with three narrow or broad hairy leaflets and short broad petioles. Sepals broad, hairy. Flowers purple, white, yellow or coppery with a narrowly funnel-shaped, hairy yellow tube as long as or much longer than the lobes. *Flowering* April to June. On clay or granite hillslopes from Clanwilliam to Swellendam.

Oxalis pusilla Jacq.   *klein Suring*
Very similar to *O. polyphylla* and *O. glabra* but distinguished from the former by the smaller bulb (1 cm long with smooth dark tunics) and from the latter by not producing underground runners. It also tends to have fewer leaves (six to ten) than *O. polyphylla* (ten to thirty) and favours clay soils rather than sand. *Flowering* May to July. On lower stony clay slopes from Langebaan to Stellenbosch.

Oxalis glabra Thunb.   *tapyt Suring*
Stem shortly hairy or hairless, terminating in a cluster of leaves and flowers, producing underground stolons and runners. Leaves with three narrow leaflets, hairless above. Sepals narrow and pointed. Flowers reddish, rose, orange or white with a rather narrow funnel-shaped, hairless yellow tube about as long as the lobes. *Flowering* April to November. On sandy flats and lower slopes from Clanwilliam to Caledon. The characteristic stolons and runners enable it to form large carpets and it is common and prolific near the Peninsula.

Oxalis purpurea L.   *groot Suring*
Stemless, somewhat robust. Bulb with gummy dark brown tunics. Leaves with three broad leaflets with hairy margins, sprinkled with transparent dots and streaks. Sepals broad, similarly dotted. Flowers rose, mauve, salmon, yellow, cream or white, with a cup-shaped, hairless tube shorter than the lobes. *Flowering* April to September. On lower stony clay or granite slopes from Namaqualand to Humansdorp.

Oxalis obtusa Jacq.   *geeloog Suring*
Stemless or with a softly hairy stem. Leaves with three broad, hairy or hairless leaflets. Sepals broad, hairy. Flower stalks with two minute opposite scales at an articulation. Flowers pink, brick-red or pale yellow, often red-veined, with a funnel-shaped, hairless tube shorter than the lobes. *Flowering* June to October. Common and widespread on sandy soils from Namaqualand to Knysna.

Oxalis hirta   *Oxalis hirta* var. *tubiflora*   *Oxalis pusilla*

Oxalis glabra   *Oxalis purpurea*   *Oxalis obtusa*

Oxalis pes-caprae L. *Suring, Sorrel*
Stemless or with naked stem. Leaves with three heart-shaped, more or less hairy leaflets, often purple-zoned. Sepals often with orange warts at the tip. Flowers in clusters, nodding in bud, yellow with a broadly funnel-shaped, hairless tube. *Flowering* May to October. Very common on clay or sandy soils from Kamieskroon to Knysna.

Oxalis compressa L.f. *baster Suring*
Similar to *Oxalis pes-caprae* but distinguished by the flattened petioles. The flowers are also a lighter yellow. *Flowering* July to September. On sandy soils, often on granite from Kamiesberg to Caledon.

*Oxalis burtoniae T.M. Salter *Saldanha Suring*
Stem shortly hairy, red below, terminating in a cluster of leaves. Leaves with five to seven very narrow leaflets each with small warts at the tips. Sepals narrow, reddish, hairy, with small warts at the tips. Flowers yellow, with a narrowly funnel-shaped tube as long as the lobes. *Flowering* June-July. Restricted to granite outcrops at Saldanha Bay and Paternoster.

Oxalis luteola Jacq. *geel Suring*
Stemless. Bulb with gummy dark brown tunics. Leaves with three broad hairy leaflets, often with hard margins. Sepals broad, hairy, often with warts at the tip. Flower stalks with two, minute, opposite scales at an articulation. Flowers yellow, with a funnel-shaped, hairless tube rather shorter than the lobes. *Flowering* May to July. On sandy flats from Clanwilliam to Albertinia.

Oxalis flava L. *dikvinger Suring*
Stemless. Leaves thick and jointed with two to twelve narrow, folded leaflets. Sepals broad, usually with orange warts near the tips. Flowers yellow (also white or mauve elsewhere) with a funnel-shaped, hairless tube slightly shorter than the lobes. *Flowering* May to June. On sandy flats from Namaqualand to Riversdale.

Oxalis tomentosa L.f. *wolhaar Suring*
Stemless or almost so, densely and softly hairy. Leaves with ten to twenty hairy leaflets in a tuft at the tip of a stout, woolly stalk. Sepals hairy. Flowers white with a rather narrow, hairy greenish tube slightly longer than the lobes. *Flowering* April to June. Common on stony slopes, particularly granite from Clanwilliam to the Peninsula.

Oxalis pes-caprae

Oxalis compressa

Oxalis burtoniae

Oxalis luteola

Oxalis flava

Oxalis tomentosa

159

Oxalis argyrophylla T.M. Salter   *silwer Suring*
Stem silky hairy, terminating in a cluster of leaves. Leaves with three oblong hairy leaflets, each with a pair of warts at the tip. Sepals narrow, with small warts at the tips. Flowers pink or white with the petal margins streaked violet, with a hairy, funnel-shaped tube longer than the lobes. *Flowering* May to July. Locally common on sandy soils from Aurora to Stellenbosch.

Oxalis versicolor L.   *candystick Suring*
Stem almost hairless with leaves in an apical tuft. Bulbs often massed together, with hard, black and often gummy tunics. Leaves with three narrow leaflets, broadest at the tips, with a pair of warts at the tips. Sepals hairy with apical warts. Flowers white with a conspicuous reddish margin, especially evident in buds and a widely funnel-shaped yellow tube about as long as the lobes. *Flowering* May to November. Common on sandy or granitic flats and lower slopes from Gouda to Hermanus.

ZYGOPHYLLACEAE

Zygophyllum sessilifolium L.   *wit Spekbos*
Dwarf shrublet with spreading branchlets. Leaflets broad, sessile, greyish, often held together, the stipules small and curved. Flowers cup-shaped, nodding, white with red streaks in the throat. *Flowering* July to September. On sandy flats and slopes from Vanrhynsdorp to the Peninsula.

Zygophyllum spinosum L.   *smalblaar Spekbos*
Shrublet with brown, rounded stems. Leaflets narrow, sessile, the dry and hard stipules sharp and persistent after the leaves have fallen. Flowers solitary between the leaves, nodding, pale yellow, darker in the centre. Fruit round. *Flowering* June to November. On sandy soils from Clanwilliam to Caledon.

Zygophyllum flexuosum Eckl. & Zeyh.   *Spekbos*
Shrublet with pale, angled stems. Leaflets ovoid, sessile, the dry and hard stipules recurved and persistent after the leaves have fallen. Flowers solitary between the leaves, yellow with a reddish blotch at the base of each petal. *Flowering* June to October. On stony ground from Vredendal to Riversdale.

Zygophyllum morgsana L.   *Slaaibos*
Shrub with grey, rounded stems. Leaflets broad, shortly stalked, with an unpleasant smell, the stipules green and fleshy. Flowers in pairs between the leaves, with petals abruptly rounded at the base, pale yellow with a purple blotch. *Flowering* June to November. On sandy flats from Namaqualand to Plettenberg Bay. The green plant is toxic to man and animal and the seeds are also poisonous.

Oxalis argyrophylla

Oxalis versicolor

Zygophyllum
sessilifolium

Zygophyllum spinosum

Zygophyllum flexuosum

Zygophyllum
morgsana

161

Monsonia speciosa L.f.   *Sambreeltjie*
Tufted perennial. Leaves finely divided and parsley-like, hairy. Flowers solitary on long, naked stalks, cream to pink, darker toward the centre, greenish on the outside, closing in the evening and in cool weather. *Flowering* August to October. On granite and clay flats from Clanwilliam to Caledon.

Geranium incanum Burm.f.   *Horlosies*
Soft, much-branched, spreading perennial forming thick mats. Leaves finely divided, greyish below. Flowers in pairs on slender naked stalks, whitish to pale pink or mauve. *Flowering* August to November. On coastal sands from Malmesbury to tropical Africa.

Pelargonium myrrhifolium (L.) L'Hér.   *fynblaar Malva*
Small shrublet with coarsely hairy branches. Leaves much-divided and similarly hairy. Flowers in clusters, white to pink with red veins in the upper two petals. *Flowering* sporadically throughout the year with a peak in spring. Widespread in the Western Cape, usually on clay soils.

Pelargonium senecioides L'Hér.   *teer Malva*
Annual with smooth, somewhat fleshy, widely-branched stems. Leaves much-divided, slightly fleshy. Flowers in small clusters on short stalks, small, white with maroon flecks at the base of the upper petals. *Flowering* September to November. In sandy soils from Calvinia to the Peninsula.

Pelargonium carnosum (L.) L'Hér.   *rots Malva*
Succulent shrublet with a thick short stem. Leaves absent at flowering, deeply divided, somewhat fleshy. Flowers in clusters, white, cream or pale pink, with reddish streaks on the upper petals, anthers orange. *Flowering* January to April. In drier habitats among rocks in sandy soil from southern Namibia to Eastern Cape.

Pelargonium longicaule Jacq.   *rank Malva*
Scrambling shrublet with shortly hairy stems. Leaves much-divided, leathery. Flowers few on long stalks, white or cream with maroon streaks on the upper petals. *Flowering* October to January. On coastal sands from Yzerfontein to Still Bay.

Monsonia speciosa *Geranium incanum* *Pelargonium myrrhifolium*

Pelargonium senecioides *Pelargonium carnosum* *Pelargonium longicaule*

Pelargonium longifolium (Burm.f.) Jacq. *strepies Malva*
Deciduous geophyte with a tuft of narrow or much-divided, sparsely hairy leaves. Flowers in several radiating clusters at the end of erect stalks, white with maroon streaks. *Flowering* November to January. On sandy soils from Calvinia to Port Elizabeth.

Pelargonium longiflorum Jacq. *spookasem Malva*
Deciduous geophyte with a tuft of narrow, leathery leaves. Flowers in several radiating clusters at the end of erect stalks, with slender, curled petals, cream with the upper two glossy maroon at the base. *Flowering* November to January. On granite or clay from Namaqualand to Paarl.

Pelargonium triste (L.) L'Hér. *Kaneeltjie*
Deciduous geophyte with a cluster of finely-divided, more or less hairy, carrot-like leaves. Flowers in radiating clusters at the end of long, erect stalks, yellowish green to dull purple with paler margins, scented of cloves at night. *Flowering* August to February. Usually in sandy soil from Steinkopf to Albertinia.

Pelargonium lobatum (Burm.f.) L'Hér. *Kaneelbol*
Very like *P. triste* but the leaves broadly lobed. *Flowering* August to November. On granite or other rocky outcrops from Piketberg to George.

Pelargonium gibbosum (L.) L'Hér. *dikbeen Malva*
Scrambling or sprawling shrub, the stems succulent when young but becoming woody with conspicuously swollen nodes. Leaves deciduous in summer, variable in shape but usually divided into three to five leaflets, smooth with a fine bloom. Flowers in radiating clusters, greenish or yellow, scented at night. *Flowering* November to April. Frequent in sandy and rocky places near the sea from Hondeklip Bay to the Peninsula.

Pelargonium fulgidum (L.) Aiton *rooi Malva*
Small shrub with somewhat succulent stems becoming woody. Leaves variously lobed, covered in soft, often silvery hairs. Flowers in radiating clusters of four to nine blooms on dark purplish stems, bright red. *Flowering* June to November. Growing on granite or other rocky outcrops from the Orange River to Yzerfontein.

Pelargonium longifolium   *Pelargonium longiflorum*   *Pelargonium triste*

Pelargonium lobatum   *Pelargonium gibbosum*   *Pelargonium fulgidum*

165

Pelargonium hirtum (Burm.f.) Jacq.   *wortelblaar Malva*
Shrublet with somewhat fleshy stems. Leaves crowded at the ends of the branches, finely divided and carrot-like, softly hairy. Flowers clustered at the tips of hairy stalks, pink with red marks on the upper petals. *Flowering* July to November. On sandy soil or granite outcrops from Velddrif to Stellenbosch.

Pelargonium capitatum (L.) L'Hér.   *kus Malva*
Low-growing, somewhat sprawling shrublet with softly woody and hairy stems, sweetly scented when bruised. Leaves velvety, variably lobed with toothed margins. Flowers in compact heads on naked stems, pink. *Flowering* almost throughout the year but mostly in the spring and summer. Abundant on sand dunes or low hillsides near the sea and commonly found on disturbed ground from Lambert's Bay to Kwazulu/Natal.

Pelargonium cucullatum (L.) L'Hér.   *wilde Malva*
Shrub with the main stem woody at the base. Leaves rather tough, kidney-shaped and sparsely hairy with a resinous smell. Flowers in radiating clusters, pink to dark purple with bright orange anthers, faintly scented. *Flowering* mostly in the spring. Common near the coast from Saldanha Bay to Elim.

GENTIANACEAE

Sebaea aurea (L.f.) Roem. & Schult.   *klein geel Naeltjiesblom*
Erect annual, usually unbranched below. Flowers usually many in a flat-topped cluster at the end of the stem but sometimes reduced to a single one in small plants, with four petals and a short tube, white or yellow, the sepals keeled or winged on the back. *Flowering* October- December. In damp sandy places, often along streams from Clanwilliam to Humansdorp.

Sebaea albens (L.f.) Roem. & Schult.   *klein wit Naeltjiesblom*
Similar to *S. aurea* but distinguished by the sepals which are rounded on the back and not keeled or winged. *Flowering* October to December. In marshy places from Piketberg to Riversdale.

Sebaea exacoides (L.) Schinz   *Naeltjiesblom*
Erect annual, unbranched below. Leaves broad. Flowers usually many in a flat-topped cluster at the end of the stem but sometimes reduced to one, with five petals and a long tube, cream or yellow with orange flecks in the throat. *Flowering* August to October. On sandy soils from Nieuwoudtville to Riversdale.

Pelargonium hirtum

Pelargonium capitatum

Pelargonium cucullatum

Sebaea aurea

Sebaea albens

Sebaea exacoides

GENTIANACEAE

Chironia baccifera L.   *bitter Bessiebos, Perdebossie*
Intricately branched shrublet. Leaves narrow and sharply spreading. Flowers one to three at the ends of the branchlets, small and shining pink. Fruit berry-like, red when mature and drying black, very bitter. *Flowering* in the summer. On dry sandy soil and on sand dunes in the shade of shrubs from Namaqualand to Natal.

Chironia linoides L.   *vlei Bessiebos*
Shrublet with stout or slender, erect or radiating branches. Leaves narrow and spreading. Flowers one to three at the ends of the branchlets, medium-sized, shining rose-pink or with a violet tint. Fruit small and dry, black and shining at first. *Flowering* November to January. In sandy or marshy places in valleys or on mountains from Calvinia to Bredasdorp.

Orphium frutescens (L.) E. Mey.   *Teeringbos*
Erect shrublet with more or less velvety branches. Leaves narrow or broad and more or less velvety. Flowers borne loosely at the end of the branches, large and glistening, deep pink with conspicuous, twisted, yellow anthers. *Flowering* November to February. Common on sandy flats and vleis along the coastal belt from near Graafwater to George.

OLEACEAE

Olea capensis L.   *Ysterhout*
Bushy shrub or small to medium tree, exuding characteristic blackish gum from bark wounds. Leaves broad with a thickened, often wavy margin, often paler below. Flowers many in branched clusters, small, white or cream. Fruit fleshy and purple when ripe, edible but bitter. *Flowering* August to February (or later). In bush, littoral scrub and evergreen forest along the southern and eastern seaboard to Mozambique, extending inland to eastern Zimbabwe.

Olea europaea subsp. **africana** (Mill.) P.S. Green   *wild Olive, Olienhout*
Shrub or small to medium-sized tree. Leaves narrow with the margins rolled under, grey-green above, densely covered below with silvery or golden scales. Flowers in branched clusters, small, whitish and scented. Fruit ovoid, thinly fleshy, black when ripe, edible but bitter. *Flowering* October to February. Usually near water on stream banks or riverine fringes but also in open woodlands and among rocks throughout South Africa, extending to Ethiopia.

Olea exasperata Jacq. (baster Olienhout) is similar but usually smaller and with the leaves broadest in the upper two-thirds. It is restricted to coastal sands in the Strandveld.

ASCLEPIADACEAE

Orbea variegata (L.) Haw.   *Aasblom*
Somewhat sprawling succulent with short, four-sided, tubercled or toothed stems. Leaves absent. Flowers large, fleshy, mottled cream and brown with a fleshy ring in the centre, unpleasantly scented. *Flowering* December to September. Coastal, often on granite outcrops from Lambert's Bay to Humansdorp.

Chironia baccifera

Chironia linoides

Orphium frutescens

Olea capensis

Olea europaea subsp. *africana*

Orbea variegata

169

Some species of *Asclepias* and *Gomphocarpus* are more or less toxic, especially if consumed in quantity.

Gomphocarpus cancellatus (Burm.f.) Bruyns   *Katoenbos*
Stiff, roughly hairy shrub, densely leafy and exuding milky sap when damaged. Leaves opposite, broad. Flowers in tight clusters among the upper leaves, pale purplish, with five boat-shaped ivory-coloured corona lobes. Fruits inflated and covered with fleshy spines. *Flowering* March to December. Widespread in the Western and Eastern Cape on rocky and clay soils.

Asclepias crispa Bergius   *Bitterwortel*
Perennial with short, spreading stems, densely hairy and exuding milky sap when damaged. Leaves opposite, narrow, crisped. Flowers in radiating clusters, brownish. *Flowering* November to January. On sandy soils from Nieuwoudtville to Transkei.

Cynanchum africanum R. Br.   *Bobbejaantou*
Climber with opposite leaves, exuding a milky latex when damaged. Leaves oblong, blunt below. Flowers in stalked clusters, with narrow, twisted chocolate brown or green petals and a cup-shaped white corona. *Flowering* June to November. On sandy soils from Namaqualand to Humansdorp.

Microloma sagittatum (L.) R. Br.   *Bokmaellie*
A greyish, shortly hairy climber with opposite leaves, not exuding a milky latex. Leaves pointing down, narrowly arrow-shaped. Flowers in stalked clusters, ridged and tubular with the tips twisted together, bright pinkish red with green tips. *Flowering* May to September. On sandy flats and lower slopes from Hondeklip Bay to Riversdale.

SOLANACEAE

All Solanaceae contain toxic and potentially deadly alkaloids and should be avoided.

Solanum guineense L.   *Melkellie*
Straggling shrub with smooth, softly woody branches. Leaves broad, wavy, dull green. Flowers in clusters, nodding on long stalks, ruffled, mauve with conspicuous yellow anthers. Fruits globose, shining and yellow when ripe. *Flowering* irregularly. Widespread in the Western Cape.

Solanum linnaeanum Hepper & Jaeger   *Gifappel*
Spiny shrub with softly woody branches, velvety when young. Leaves deeply lobed and spiny on the veins. Flowers one or more together, pleated, mauve with conspicuous yellow anthers. Fruits globose, shining and yellow when ripe. *Flowering* July to December. Common in disturbed areas, especially along roadsides, apparently native from the Western Cape to KwaZulu/Natal.

Gomphocarpus cancellatus   *Asclepias crispa*   *Cynanchum africanum*

Microloma sagittatum   *Solanum guineense*   *Solanum linnaeanum*

SOLANACEAE

Lycium afrum L. *Bokdoring*
Twiggy shrub, the branchlets stiff and becoming spiny at the ends. Leaves slightly succulent, with a greyish bloom. Flowers scattered among the leaves, with tubes three to four times as long as the five lobes, deep purple. *Flowering* June to November. In dry habitats on stony ground from Clanwilliam to Port Elizabeth.

Lycium ferocissimum Miers *Slangbessie*
Much-branched shrub, the greyish branches often horizontal and ending in stout thorns. Leaves broadest near the tip, somewhat fleshy and bright green. Flowers solitary or in pairs, cup-shaped with the tube slightly longer than the five lobes, pale lilac. Fruit a round berry, shiny red when ripe, possibly edible but also reported to be poisonous. *Flowering* May to December. Widespread in southern South Africa.

Lycium tetrandrum Thunb. *Kraaldoring*
Intricately branched shrub with short often horizontal branches ending in sharp thorns. Leaves in tight clusters, small and succulent, bright green and paler below. Flowers solitary, small, shortly tubular with the tube twice as long as the four lobes, white. Fruit an ovoid berry, orange-red when ripe, edible but small. *Flowering* throughout the year. Widespread in the drier parts of southern South Africa.

CONVOLVULACEAE

Convolvulus capensis Burm.f. *Morning glory*
Scrambling vine with sparsely hairy stems and leaves. Leaves deeply divided into narrow, folded lobes with wavy margins. Flowers funnel-shaped, fragile, pale pink or white with five green ribs on the underside, lightly scented, lasting only a day. *Flowering* May to September. Widespread in the Western Cape.

BORAGINACEAE

Anchusa capensis Thunb. *Forget-me-not, Ystergras*
Perennial branching from the base with roughly hairy stems. Leaves very narrow and tapering, roughly hairy. Flowers in branched clusters at the ends of the stems, dark blue with five small white lobes in the centre. *Flowering* August to November. On sandy flats or lower slopes from Namibia to the Eastern Cape.

Echiostachys incanus (Thunb.) Levyns *Bottelborsel*
Perennial branching from the base, roughly hairy. Leaves mostly basal, narrow and tapering, roughly hairy. Flowers crowded in spike-like inflorescences, white. *Flowering* August to October. On sandy soils from Clanwilliam to Swellendam.

Lycium afrum

Lycium ferocissimum

Lycium tetrandrum

Convolvulus capensis

Anchusa capensis

Echiostachys incanus

173

Lobostemon argenteus (Bergius) Buek   *disselblaar Luibos*
Rounded shrublet with erect branches, pink when young and roughly hairy. Leaves along the branches, softly hairy with stiff bristles along the margins. Flowers in long spikes, dark blue. *Flowering* October to January. On stony slopes from Namaqualand to the Eastern Cape.

Lobostemon hispidus (Thunb.) DC.   *growweblaar Luibos*
Shrublet with young branches coarsely bristly. Leaves leathery, erect, rounded at the tips, the undersides with scattered bristles. Flowers small, clustered at the ends of the branches, funnel-shaped, blue, pink or white. *Flowering* August to October. On clay slopes from Ceres to Worcester.

Lobostemon fruticosus (L.) Buek   *Luibos, Pyjama bush*
Shrub with hairy branches, mottled pink when young. Leaves leathery, softly hairy. Flowers clustered at the ends of the branches, funnel-shaped, pink or blue suffused with pink. *Flowering* July to October. On clay soils from Ceres to Worcester.

Lobostemon glaucophyllus (Jacq.) Buek   *blosblaar Luibos*
Loose shrub with reddish branches. Leaves leathery with rough white margins and a dull bloom, curved upwards. Flowers in loose clusters at the ends of the branches, funnel-shaped, pale blue suffused with pink. *Flowering* July to November. On sandy soils from Namaqualand to Robertson.

Lobostemon capitatus (L.) Buek   *Borselbos*
Shrublet with hairy branches. Leaves leathery, glossy, roughly hairy on the margins. Flowers in tight clusters at the ends of the branchlets, petals minute, white with brown midrib, but stamens prominent. *Flowering* August to September. Rare on clay soils from Piketberg to the Peninsula.

STILBACEAE

Stilbe ericoides L.   *Borselblom*
Rounded shrublet branching from the base, with slender, erect stems. Leaves small, clasping the stem and closely overlapping. Flowers in tight oblong heads at the tips of the branches, pink. *Flowering* June to December. Sandy coastal flats and limestone outcrops from Hopefield to Uitenhage.

Lobostemon argenteus   *Lobostemon hispidus*   *Lobostemon fruticosus*

Lobostemon glaucophyllus   *Lobostemon capitatus*   *Stilbe ericoides*

Ballota africana (L.) Benth. *Kattekruie*
Soft greyish, aromatic perennial. Leaves densely hairy, broad and irregularly
toothed. Flowers crowded in whorls, two-lipped, hairy, purple or pinkish. Calyx
densely hairy, cup-shaped with ten to twenty spreading teeth. *Flowering* in spring.
Found most commonly along water courses in the shelter of rocks and bushes and
also as a semi-weed of disturbed places, mainly from the more arid areas of the
Western and Eastern Cape.

Stachys aethiopica L. *klein Kattekruie*
Hairy, aromatic herb. Leaves opposite, broad with toothed margins, more or less
hairy. Flowers in whorls at the ends of the branches, two-lipped with the upper
hooded and the lower larger, white or pink to mauve, usually with purple flecks on
the lower lip. *Flowering* mostly May to December. In a variety of habitats but usually on sandstone, often among rocks, from Clanwilliam to Swaziland.

Salvia africana-coerulea L. *bloublom Salie*
Greyish, hairy shrub. Leaves broad, green with grey hairs, mostly without teeth.
Flowers at the tips of the stems, equally two-lipped, blue or pinkish with the lower
usually white in the centre. Bracts persistent. Calyx with long hairs. *Flowering* August
to December. In coastal fynbos and rocky slopes from Vanrhynsdorp to Montagu.
  Can be confused with *S. chamelaeagnea* Bergius but this species has deciduous
bracts and short, coarsely glandular hairs on the leaves and calyx.

Salvia africana-lutea L. *strand Salie*
Grey, hairy shrub with densely leafy stems. Leaves broad, grey and minutely hairy,
sometimes coarsely toothed, aromatic. Flowers crowded at the tips of the stems, the
upper lip hooded and almost twice as long as the lower, velvety, golden to reddish
brown. Bracts large and persistent. *Flowering* June to December. Common on
coastal sand dunes and in arid fynbos on rocky slopes from Namaqualand to Port
Alfred. The leaves smell of lemon pepper and can be used in cooking, particularly
with fish.

Salvia lanceolata Lam. *rooi Salie*
Grey shrub. Leaves narrow or broad, grey and hairy, sometimes coarsely toothed.
Flowers crowded at the tips of side branches, the upper lip hooded and only slightly longer than the lower, velvety, dull rose to brownish crimson or grey blue.
Bracts soon deciduous. *Flowering* November to March. Common on coastal sands
and limestone and on drier rocky slopes from Namaqualand to Montagu. The
leaves smell of lemon pepper and can be used in cooking, particularly with fish.

Leonotis leonurus (L.) R. Br. *Wildedagga*
Roughly hairy, somewhat woody shrub. Leaves rather narrow and toothed, shortly
hairy. Flowers in dense whorls up the stem, with a large hooded upper lip and
minute lower lip, densely hairy, orange. *Flowering* November to January. Locally
common in scrub and on rocky hillsides from Clanwilliam to Mpumalanga.

Ballota africana

Stachys aethiopica

*Salvia africana-
coerulea*

Salvia africana-lutea

Salvia lanceolata

Leonotis leonurus

Hebenstreitia repens Jarosz   *wit Slakblom*
Annual, branching from the base with the branches more or less sprawling. Leaves narrow with a few teeth in the upper part. Flowers in spikes, the corolla tube slit underneath and flaring at the tip, white and scented. *Flowering* July to November. On clay or sandy flats from Namaqualand to Bredasdorp.

Hebenstreitia dentata L.   *Slakblom*
Distinguished from *H. repens* by the more or less erect habit. Flowers usually with an orange throat, scented. *Flowering* July to October. On sandy soils from Namaqualand to the Peninsula.

Hebenstreitia robusta E. Mey.   *bos Slakblom*
Shrublet with more or less erect, dark purple branches. Leaves in clusters, narrow, channelled, minutely toothed on the margins. Flowers in spikes, corolla tube slit underneath and flaring at the tip, white with a red throat, scented. *Flowering* August to October. On sandy soils from Namaqualand to the Eastern Cape.

Microdon capitatus (Bergius) Levyns   *Knoppiesbos*
Rounded shrublet with closely leafy branches, velvety when young. Leaves narrow and leathery in overlapping clusters along the branches. Flowers in cone-like heads at the tip of the branches, subtended by large heart-shaped bracts, white with an orange throat, honey-scented. *Flowering* October to December. On stony, sandy slopes from Clanwilliam to the Peninsula.

Manulea corymbosa L.f.   *stomp Witkoppie*
Similar to *M. altissima* but calyx markedly two-lipped and white-woolly, and stigma shortly protruding from the flower tube which has a round mouth. The flowers unpleasantly scented.

Manulea altissima L.f.   *Witkoppie*
Shortly hairy annual or perennial, foetid when bruised. Leaves mostly in a basal rosette, narrow and often with scattered teeth. Flowers clustered in round heads at the tips of stout, naked stems, flaring from a narrow tube, white with a yellow or green centre, stigma deeply included in the flower tube which has a keyhole-shaped mouth, vanilla scented. *Flowering* June to October. Common on sandy flats from Namaqualand to Malmesbury.

Hebenstreitia repens

Hebenstreitia dentata

Hebenstreitia robusta

Microdon capitatus

Manulea corymbosa

Manulea altissima

Manulea tomentosa (L.) L.   *duine Vingertjies*
Perennial branching from the base and becoming a shrublet, stems densely covered
with short, matted hairs. Leaves opposite, grading into the bracts, slightly toothed,
densely hairy. Flowers densely crowded at the ends of the stems, narrowly tubular
below with five narrow, spreading lobes, brownish-yellow to dull orange.
Flowering August-December (-March). Common on sand dunes along the coast
from Stompneus Bay to Pearly Beach near Bredasdorp.

Manulea rubra (Bergius) L.f.   *rooi Vingertjies*
Similar to *M. tomentosa* but typically with the leaves crowded in a rosette at the
base of the unbranched stem which is more or less bare of leaves and hairless.
Where the two species grow together intermediates may occur. *Flowering*
September to December. On sandy soil from near Hopefield to Somerset West but
not along the foreshore.

Lyperia lychnidea (L.) Druce   *soet Traanblommetjie*
Spreading perennial, branching from the base, young stems velvety. Leaves scat-
tered, leathery, narrow and toothed near the tips. Flowers clustered at the ends of
the branches, pale greenish yellow, with a slender hairy tube, sweetly scented.
Flowering September to December On sandy coastal flats from Saldanha Bay to
Caledon.

Lyperia triste (L.f.) Benth.   *Traanblommetjie*
Erect, glandular-hairy annual, usually branching from the base. Leaves mostly clustered at the base, broad and toothed. Flowers clustered at the top of the stem, tubular with down-flexed lobes, yellowish to brown, strongly scented of cloves at night.
Flowering August to October. In sandy soil from Namibia to Mossel Bay.

*Zaluzianskya parviflora Hilliard   *mini Drumsticks*
Hairy annual, usually branching from below. Leaves lightly toothed. Flowers
crowded at the ends of leafy branches, minute, with bilobed petals flaring from a
narrow tube, cream with a yellow centre. *Flowering* September. Restricted to granite outcrops from St. Helena Bay to Darling.

Zaluzianskya villosa F.W. Schmidt   *Drumsticks*
Hairy, branched annual. Leaves narrow with scattered teeth. Flowers at the ends of
leafy branches, with deeply bilobed petals flaring from a long, narrow tube, lilac or
white with an orange centre. *Flowering* June to November. Widespread in the
Western Cape on sandy or clay flats and lower slopes.

Manulea tomentosa   *Manulea rubra*   *Lyperia lychnidea*

Lyperia triste   *Zaluzianskya parviflora*   *Zaluzianskya*
villosa

181

Phyllopodium capillare Hilliard *wit Opslag*
Annual, branching from the base. Leaves ovate, toothed. Flowers in small heads at
the ends of the branchlets, the heads elongating in fruit, white. *Flowering* August to
September. On sandy soils from Velddrif to Bredasdorp.

Phyllopodium cephalophorum (Thunb.) Hilliard *perskop Opslag*
Roughly hairy annual, branching from the base and at the tips of the stems. Leaves
narrow, toothed in the upper part, hairy. Flowers in round heads at the tips of the
branchlets, lilac. *Flowering* September to November. On sandy coastal flats from
Vanrhynsdorp to the Peninsula.

Phyllopodium phyllopodioides (Schltr.) Hilliard *pers Opslag*
Roughly hairy annual, branching from the base and at the tips of the stems. Leaves
narrow, toothed in the upper part, hairy. Flowers in heads at the tips of the branchlets, arranged in flat-topped inflorescences, lilac. *Flowering* July to September. On
sandy coastal flats from Lambert's Bay to Langebaan.

Polycarena lilacina Hilliard *lila Opslag*
Annual, branching in the upper part of the stem, shortly hairy and slightly foetid-
smelling, . Leaves narrow and toothed. Flowers in small clusters at the tips of the
branches, with slender tubes, white or pale lilac. *Flowering* September to October.
On the sandy coastal plain from Graafwater to Bokbaai.
    P. capensis (L.) Benth. (geel Opslag) is very similar but the flowers are cream to
yellow.

Sutera uncinata (Desr.) Hilliard *bos Opslag*
Small shrublet with the branches narrowly winged or ridged and with short shoots
in the leaf axils. Leaves elliptic, coarsely hairy, with the base running down the
stem as a wing. Flowers loosely aggregated at the end of the branches, mauve with
an orange tube. *Flowering* mostly June to October. In scrub on flats or rocky
slopes, often near the coast from Gifberg to Somerset East.

Oftia africana (L.) Bocq. *Sukkelbossie*
Sprawling, semi-creeping shrub with roughly hairy branchlets. Leaves heart-shaped
and closely overlapping, with sharply toothed margins, roughly hairy. Flowers clustered at the ends of the branchlets, shortly tubular with spreading lobes, white,
sweetly fragrant. *Flowers* throughout the year. Frequent on flats and slopes, usually
among rocks from Gifberg to Riversdale.

Phyllopodium capillare

*Phyllopodium
cephalophorum*

*Phyllopodium
phyllopodioides*

Polycarena lilacina

Sutera uncinata

Oftia africana

Nemesia bicornis (L.) Pers. *wit Leeubekkie*
Sparsely hairy annual, often branched. Leaves usually opposite, narrow or broad, toothed. Flowers white, striped with coloured lines outside, lower lip hairy at the base with two warty outgrowths and a straight, blunt spur somewhat swollen at the tip. *Flowering* July to October. Common on sandy soils from southern Namaqualand to Riversdale.

*Nemesia strumosa Benth. *Nemesia, Balsa mienie*
Annual, usually branched from the base, glandular-hairy above. Leaves opposite, narrow and somewhat toothed. Flowers in a compact cluster, two-lipped and pouched at the base, variously coloured yellow, orange, pink, mauve or white, with dark marks in the throat. *Flowering* September to October. Confined to sandy flats from Bokbaai to Hopefield.

Nemesia barbata Benth. *blou Bekkie, Fluweeltjie*
Annual, often branched and leafy below. Leaves opposite, broad and usually coarsely toothed. Flowers few at the ends of the stems, two-lipped with the upper lobes white or lilac streaked with purple and the lower lip folded and deep velvety blue or purple with a short, blunt spur at the base. *Flowering* August to September. Common in sandy places from the Kamiesberg to Bredasdorp.

Nemesia ligulata Benth. *wit Bekkie*
Annual, often branched from the base. Leaves opposite, narrow and usually toothed. Flowers clustered at the tips of the branches, white and yellow, the lower lip with paired orange mounds at the base and a hanging spur thickened at the tip. *Flowering* July to September. On sandy flats from Namaqualand to Piketberg.

Nemesia versicolor Benth. *bont Leeubekkie, Weeskindertjies*
Annual, often branched from the base. Leaves opposite, narrow or broad and usually toothed. Flowers crowded at the tips of the branches, the back white or pink with red streaks and the front white, yellow, blue or mauve, the lower lip with a yellow velvety mound at the base and a slender hanging spur. *Flowering* June to November, greatly depending on the rains. Common in sandy areas from southern Namaqualand to Knysna.

Nemesia bicornis

Nemesia strumosa

Nemesia barbata

Nemesia ligulata

Nemesia versicolor

*Nemesia
versicolor*

185

Hemimeris racemosa (Houtt.) Merrill   *Geelgesiggie*
Soft, sparsely hairy annual, branching from the base. Leaves almost hairless,
toothed. Flowers pouched, bright yellow, the upper two lobes spotted with brown.
Flowering July to October. On sandy lower slopes and flats from Namaqualand to
Knysna.

Hemimeris sabulosa L.f.   *sand Geelgesiggie*
Softly hairy annual, more or less erect, branched. Leaves shortly hairy, ovate.
Flowers pouched with the stamens concealed by two pockets, pale canary yellow,
the upper two lobes spotted with brown. *Flowering* August to October. On sandy
coastal flats from Clanwilliam to Caledon.

Diascia capensis (L.) Britten   *langneus Horinkie*
Spreading annual, branching from the base. Leaves regularly lobed. Flowers on
long pedicels, wine red with two yellow pouches, stamens arching. *Flowering*
August to September. On sandy soil from Piketberg to Still Bay.

*Diascia collina K.E. Steiner   *Saldanha Horinkie*
Spreading annual branching from the base. Leaves regularly lobed. Flowers on
long pedicels, with two very short, blunt spurs, purple with yellow pouches.
Flowering August to September. Restricted to sandy soils near Langebaan.

Diascia diffusa Benth.   *eenoog Horinkie*
Low annual. Leaves broad and bluntly toothed. Flowers on long pedicels, red-pur-
ple with two yellow pouches and a central yellow bump, stamens with two knobs.
Flowering August to September. On granite or limestone outcrops from Piketberg
to the Peninsula.

Diascia longicornis (Thunb.) Druce   *bok Horinkie*
Low annual, branching from the base. Leaves lobed. Flowers on long pedicels,
salmon-pink, maroon in the centre with yellow flecks and two long, slender spurs.
Flowering August to September. On clay soils from Darling to Piketberg.

Hemimeris racemosa

Hemimeris sabulosa

Diascia capensis

Diascia collina

Diascia diffusa

*Diascia
longicornis*

187

Harveya squamosa (Thunb.) Steud. *Jakkalskos*
Root-parasite with a dense, pagoda-like spike of hairy, tubular flowers produced at
ground level, bright orange. *Flowering* August to December. On sandy soil from
Clanwilliam to Bredasdorp, parasitic on the roots of *Othonna* and *Willdenowia*.

Hyobanche sanguinea L. *Katnaels, Wolwekos*
Root-parasite with a conical spike of velvety, tubular flowers at ground level,
bright carmine red. *Flowering* July to November. Widespread in the wetter parts of
South Africa, often in sandy soils, parasitic on the roots of various shrubs.

APIACEAE

Arctopus echinatus L. *Platdoring, Platannadoring*
Stemless perennial with a rosette of three-lobed and toothed, prickly leaves pressed
to the ground and a long taproot. Flowers white or pinkish. Female flowers with
the bracts keeled and bearing three large spines. *Flowering* May to August. On clay
or granite slopes or rocky limestone flats from Nieuwoudtville to Uitenhage.

Torilis arvensis (Huds.) Link. *Wildewortel*
Soft perennial with carrot-like leaves. Flowers small, in radiating clusters, white.
Fruits covered with maroon barbs. *Flowering* August to January. Widespread in
damp, shaded situations throughout Africa and Europe.

Stoibrax capense (Lam.) B.L. Burtt *Tandpynwortel*
Annual, branching from the base, stem with a white bloom. Leaves finely divided,
carrot-like. Flowers in radiating clusters, minute, white. *Flowering* September to
November. On sandy flats and slopes from the Gifberg to Caledon.

Dasispermum suffruticosum (Bergius) B.L. Burtt *Duineseldery*
Perennial, branching from the base, stems finely ribbed, with a white bloom.
Leaves finely divided, parsley-like, slightly fleshy. Flowers in radiating clusters,
white. *Flowering* August to April. On coastal sand dunes from Saldanha Bay to
Kwazulu/Natal.

Harveya squamosa

Hyobanche sanguinea

Arctopus echinatus ♂♀

Torilis arvensis

Stoibrax capense

Dasispermum suffruticosum

189

Roella arenaria Schltr. *Prikkelster*
Perennial with erect or sprawling, woody stems. Leaves rigid and crowded, narrow and stiffly hairy. Flowers surrounded by rather rigid and toothed bracts resembling the leaves, cup-shaped with the lobes longer than the tube, white or pale blue. *Flowering* November to January. In sandy soils near the coast from Darling to Bredasdorp.

Prismatocarpus fruticosus L'Hér. *Steelvrug*
Diffuse shrublet with a woody base and slender, naked flowering stems. Leaves narrow and crowded on the lower parts of the stems. Flowers on slender, leafless branchlets, cup-shaped, white but often brown on the outside. *Flowering* in summer, most freely in open places. Widespread and common on dry mountain slopes in the Western Cape.

Wahlenbergia longifolia (A. DC.) Lammers *Suikerpoppie*
Shrublet with slender, erect branches leafy below. Leaves narrow, more or less erect. Flowers in small axillary clusters in the upper parts of the stems, pale mauve, darker in the centre and on the back, fading brownish, the style covered with pollen at the tip. *Flowering* November to February. On sandy soils from Hopefield to Caledon.

Wahlenbergia capensis (L.) A. DC. *beetle Blue*
Slender annual, roughly hairy. Leaves coarsely toothed, roughly hairy. Flowers solitary on long naked stalks, blue with a furry brown centre. *Flowering* October to November. Common on sandy soils from Piketberg to Swellendam.

Wahlenbergia paniculata (Thunb.) A. DC. *Bobby Blue*
Slender annual, branching from near the base, with shortly hairy stems. Leaves small and narrow, more or less clasping the stems, hairy. Flowers in loose clusters at the ends of the stems, tubular with spreading petals, blue. *Flowering* September to November. On sandy soil from Piketberg to Worcester.

Microcodon glomeratum A. DC. *blou Pompoms*
Dwarf, roughly hairy annual. Leaves crowded above, narrow and roughly hairy. Flowers sessile at the tips of the branches, funnel-shaped, mauve. *Flowering* September to November. On sandy flats and slopes from Namaqualand to Caledon.

Roella arenaria

Prismatocarpus fruticosus

Wahlenbergia longifolia

Wahlenbergia capensis

Wahlenbergia paniculata

Microcodon glomeratum

191

Lobelia alata Labill. *vlei Lobelia*
Perennial with creeping stems rooting at the nodes but erect at the ends, winged at the angles. Leaves usually sparsely toothed, bright green and slightly fleshy. Flowers solitary in the axils of the leaves, lilac or blue. *Flowering* December to June. Common in vleis and damp places near the coast in the Western and Eastern Cape and Kwazulu/Natal; also native to Chile and Australia.

Lobelia setacea Thunb. *skraal Lobelia*
Slender, weak perennial with narrow, thread-like leaves scattered along the stem. Flowers in the axils of long thread-like bracts, pale blue. *Flowering* September to December. On sandy flats from Langebaan to Caledon.

Lobelia comosa L. *Lobelia*
Perennial with more or less erect, ridged stems, woody and leafy below. Leaves narrow and sparsely toothed. Flowers in open clusters, bright mauve or pale pink with yellow and white flashes on the lower three petals. *Flowering* November to May. On sandy soils near the coast and on lower slopes from Piketberg to Still Bay.

Lobelia coronopifolia L. *kussing Lobelia*
Tufted perennial with slender, wiry, leafless flowering stems. Leaves divided, clustered at the base of the plant. Flowers dark blue. *Flowering* September to December. On sandy and stony slopes and flats from Clanwilliam to Kwazulu/Natal.

Monopsis simplex (L.) E. Wimmer *pers Lobelia*
Fleshy annual with sprawling stems. Leaves narrow, toothed in the upper half. Flowers solitary on long pedicels, purple with a black, velvety centre, cleft to the base between the two upper lobes. *Flowering* September to November. On damp sandy or loam flats throughout the Western Cape.

Monopsis lutea (L.) Urb. *geel Lobelia*
Perennial with creeping or trailing stems, somewhat woody below. Leaves rather crowded beneath the flowering stems, narrow and toothed. Flowers among the leaves, bright yellow and cleft to the base between the two upper lobes. *Flowering* November to April. In damp, sandy places and vleis near the coast but also recorded inland from Nieuwoudtville to Albertinia.

Lobelia alata

Lobelia setacea

Lobelia comosa

Lobelia coronopifolia

Monopsis simplex

Monopsis lutea

CAMPANULACEAE

Cyphia phyteuma (L.) Willd. *Baroe*
Erect geophyte with a basal rosette of undivided and lightly toothed leaves.
Flowers crowded in a spiral spike, tubular and two-lipped, drab lilac or brownish.
Flowering August to October. On stony and sandy flats from Clanwilliam to
Riversdale.

Cyphia bulbosa (L.) Bergius *fraai Baroe*
Erect, usually unbranched geophyte with the lower leaves deeply divided. Flowers
crowded in a spike, tubular and two-lipped, white or pale lilac. *Flowering* August
to October, especially after fire. On clay or granite from Clanwilliam to the Eastern
Cape.

Cyphia crenata (Thunb.) Presl. *klein Bokkies*
Twining perennial. Leaves narrowly triangular, toothed, held upright, usually with a
tuft of axillary leaflets. Flowers solitary or few in the axils of the upper leaves,
nodding, corolla tube swollen at the base, slit to the base underneath, mauve.
Flowering July to October. On sandy soil from Nieuwoudtville to the Peninsula.

Cyphia digitata (Thunb.) Willd. *Bokkies*
Twining perennial. Leaves deeply three to five divided, toothed. Flowers in the
axils of the upper leaves, with a short tube, two-lipped, slit to the base underneath,
pale mauve or white. *Flowering* July to November. On rocky slopes or clay flats
from Namaqualand to Ladismith.

RUBIACEAE

Galium tomentosum Thunb. *Kleefgras*
Perennial with soft, scrambling branches closely covered with minute, hooked
hairs. Leaves in whorls, with hooked hairs on the margins. Flower in branched
clusters with four greenish petals. *Flowering* September to December. On sandy
soils from Namibia to the Eastern Cape.

DIPSACACEAE

*Scabiosa incisa Mill. *Scabious*
Tufted perennial with finely divided leaves. Flowers crowded in dense, flattened
heads solitary on erect, naked stalks, mauve. *Flowering* September to December. In
coastal scrub on deep sands from Piketberg to the Peninsula.

Cyphia phyteuma

Cyphia bulbosa

Cyphia crenata

Cyphia digitata

Galium tomentosum

Scabiosa incisa

Elytropappus rhinocerotis (L.f.) Less.   *Renosterbos*
Fine shrub with rather slender, weeping branches, white-woolly when young.
Leaves reduced to minute scales. Flower heads insignificant, solitary in the axils of
the upper leaves, cylindrical, straw-coloured with three tubular, purple disc florets.
Flowering March to September. The dominant shrub on drier clay soils and epony-
mous component of renosterveld in the Northern, Western and parts of the Eastern
Cape.

Eriocephalus africanus L.   *Kapokbossie*
Shrublet with opposite or tufted, greyish leaves. Leaves needle-like or three-lobed,
channelled, thickish, sparsely silky. Heads with two to three conspicuous, white ray
florets. *Flowering* May to September. Widespread in the Western Cape on clay flats
and slopes.

Eriocephalus racemosus L.   *Kapkoppie*
Shrublet with tufts of greyish, leathery leaves, needle-like and silky, smelling of
thyme. Heads mostly pendulous, with the rays apparently absent. *Flowering* July to
September. On dunes and sandy flats near the coast from Piketberg to Humansdorp.

Stoebe plumosa Thunb.   *Slangbos*
Intricately-branched shrub with branchlets at right angles. Leaves minute, closely
appressed to the stems, grey and woolly. Flower heads in globose clusters arranged
in long spikes at the end of the branches, with pale brown bracts surrounding purple disc florets. *Flowering* mainly April to May but also in the spring. On clay flats
and lower slopes from Angola to Port Elizabeth.

Stoebe capitata Bergius   *knoppies Slangbos*
Rounded intricately branched shrublet. Leaves small and usually twisted, woolly
above. Flower heads crowded into dense globose clusters containing pink or sometimes white tubular disc florets. *Flowering* December to March. On sandy flats and
lower slopes from Ceres to the Eastern Cape.

Trichogyne repens (L.) A. Anderb.   *wit Naaldebossie*
Straggling shrublet with woolly branches. Leaves minute, woolly below, twisted
and with the margins rolled under. Flower heads in rounded clusters at the tips of
the branchlets, creamy white. *Flowering* July to October. Sandy flats from
Vredenburg to Bredasdorp.

Elytropappus rhinocerotis

Eriocephalus africanus

Eriocephalus racemosus

Stoebe plumosa

Stoebe capitata

Trichogyne repens

197

Metalasia muricata (L.) D. Don   *Blombos*
Metalasia densa (Lam.) P.O. Karis
Shrubs or shrublets, sparingly or much-branched, with clusters of smaller leaves in
the axils of the leaves which are stiff, twisted and thinly cobwebby. Flower heads
densely clustered in branched heads, without ray florets, innermost bracts white to
pink. The two species are very alike but can be separated as follows:
M. muricata Leaves curved or hooked at the tips, with a distinct midvein at least at
the base; papery floral bracts thicker at the tips and faintly keeled.
M. densa Leaves usually straight, sometimes with an indistinct midvein; papery
floral bracts thinner at the ends and flat.
 Flowering April to September. Both species are common and widespread. *M.
muricata* occurs along the coast from Paternoster to the Eastern Cape and grows
mainly on sand, often in dunes. *M. densa* ranges from Namaqualand to the
Northern Province and is often found along roadsides or in disturbed ground but
not in renosterveld. Both species may form dense thickets.

Plecostachys serpyllifolia (Bergius) Hilliard & B.L. Burtt   *Vaaltee*
A much-branched, straggling shrublet with slender branches and all parts greyish-
woolly. Leaves round with the tips downcurved and margins wavy. Flower heads
small, congested in rounded clusters at the tips of the branchlets, with small, milky
white floral bracts. *Flowering* November to August with a peak in April. In damp
sandy places, often near the sea from Melkbosstrand to southern Kwazulu/Natal.

Petalacte coronata D. Don   *wilde Sewejaartjie*
Tufted shrublet with white-woolly stems and leaves. Leaves grey, narrow, overlapping. Flower heads in crowded, flat-topped clusters at the ends of the stems, with
papery, white bracts. *Flowering* June to November. In deep coastal sands from
Clanwilliam to Bredasdorp.

Helichrysum stellatum (L.) Less.   *pienk Sewejaartjie*
Shrublet branching from the base with whitish-woolly stems and leaves. Leaves
narrow, crisped, whitish-woolly. Flower heads in flat-topped clusters, with papery,
pink to white bracts. *Flowering* September to November. On sandy or granite soils
from Calvinia to Swellendam.

Helichrysum cochleariforme DC.   *Gold-and-silver*
Much-branched annual with grey, woolly leaves and branchlets. Leaves narrow and
folded. Flower heads in branched clusters at the ends of the branchlets, bracts
papery, outer golden brown, inner white. *Flowering* September to December. On
deep sandy soils near the coast from Aurora to Mossel Bay.

Metalasia muricata

Metalasia densa

*Plecostachys
serpyllifolia*

Petalacte coronata

Helichrysum stellatum

*Helichrysum
cochleariforme*

Helichrysum revolutum (Thunb.) Less.   *strand Sewejaartjie*
Bushy shrublet with whitish-woolly stems and leaves. Leaves narrow with the margins conspicuously rolled under, whitish-woolly especially below, slightly eared at the base. Flower heads in dense, flat-topped clusters, yellowish. *Flowering* July to October. Widespread in rocky or sandy places from southern Namibia to Montagu.

Helichrysum moeserianum Thell.   *geel Sewejaartjie*
Annual, branching from the base, densely grey-cobwebby. Leaves broadest near the tips, slightly eared at the base, margins wrinkled and curled under. Flower heads in branched, flat-topped clusters at the ends of the stems, with yellow disc florets only. *Flowering* August to February. On sandy flats and slopes from Vanrhynsdorp to Mossel Bay.

*Athanasia rugulosa DC.   *Hopefield Klaaslouwbos*
Erect shrublet, bare below and closely leafy above. Leaves overlapping, slightly spreading, narrow and rough below, covered with grey, powdery wax. Flower heads clustered in flat-topped heads at the tips of the branches, containing yellow disc florets. *Flowering* in the spring and summer. Restricted to sandy flats from Hopefield to Malmesbury.
    Athanasia trifurcata (L.) L. (klaaslouwbos) is similar but the leaves are coarsely toothed at the tips. It is widespread on clay soils.

Athanasia crithmifolia L.   *draadblaar Klaaslouwbos*
Erect shrub, bare below and closely leafy above. Leaves overlapping, divided into three slender segments, soft and leathery. Flower heads in tight, flat-topped clusters at the tip of the branches. *Flowering* November. On sandy soils from Piketberg to Riviersonderend.

Nidorella foetida (L.) DC.   *Vleikruid*
Roughly hairy shrublet with slightly woody stems. Leaves narrow and channelled, slighty fleshy, roughly hairy, with tufts of small leaves in the axils, aromatic. Flower heads in dense, branched clusters, containing numerous yellow disc florets. *Flowering* mostly in the summer. Along streams or in sandy seepage areas near the sea from Lambert's Bay to Bredasdorp.

Chrysocoma ciliata L.   *Beesbossie*
Shrublet. Leaves narrow, spreading to erect, greyish. Flower heads solitary or few at the ends of the branchlets, with yellow disc florets only. *Flowering* June to December. Widespread in southern Africa, usually on clay soils.

Helichrysum revolutum

Helichrysum moeserianum

*Athanasia
rugulosa*

Athanasia crithmifolia

Nidorella foetida

*Chrysocoma
ciliata*

201

Pteronia uncinata DC.   *strand Gombos*
Rounded, many-stemmed bushes, stems naked below. Leaves often in whorls of
three, narrow and succulent with the tips sharply downcurved and hooked. Flower
heads in flat-topped clusters at the ends of the branches, narrow and containing
four or five yellow disc florets with a honey-like scent. *Flowering* February to
March. On coastal sands from Malmesbury to Clanwilliam (also Still Bay).

Pteronia divaricata (Bergius) Less.   *geel Gombos*
Twiggy shrublet, velvety on the young parts. Leaves rounded, velvety. Flower
heads several, clustered at the ends of the branchlets, with six or seven large yellow
disc florets only. *Flowering* September to November. On sandy and rocky soils
from Namibia to Hopefield.

Pteronia camphorata L.   *sand Gombos*
Shrub with erect branches. Leaves narrow, with white hairs on the margins. Flower
heads solitary and grouped at the ends of the branches, with several large yellow
disc florets. *Flowering* September to November. On sandy coastal and mountain
slopes from Namaqualand to Uniondale.

Pteronia onobromoides DC.   *Sab*
Rounded aromatic shrub. Leaves leathery and succulent, narrow and slightly downcurved at the tips, the margins bearing fine, white, cartilaginous bristles. Flower
heads solitary at the ends of the branches, large and egg-shaped, containing many
tubular yellow disc florets, opening in fruit to form fluffy pom-poms of seeds bearing a tuft of tawny hairs. *Flowering* in November. Common in deep sands near the
coast from Port Nolloth to Langebaan.

Pteronia ovalifolia DC.   *grys Gombos*
Twiggy shrub, thinly hairy on the young branches. Leaves opposite, grey-felted.
Flower heads solitary or paired at the end of the branchlets, with several large yel-
low disc florets. *Flowering* October to November. On stony soils from
Namaqualand to Worcester.

Cotula coronopifolia L.   *Eendekos*
Low herb with the longer stems trailing and rooting, sometimes perennial. Leaves
more or less irregularly toothed or even divided, somewhat fleshy, loosely clasping
the stem. Flower heads with bright yellow disc, often slightly nodding. *Flowering*
May to February. Widespread in damp, flat places throughout southern Africa.

Pteronia uncinata

Pteronia divaricata

Pteronia camphorata

Pteronia onobromoides

Pteronia ovalifolia

Cotula coronopifolia

203

Cotula turbinata L. *Ganskos*
Simple or branched, hairy annual with finely divided leaves. Flower heads solitary on slender, naked stalks, with button-shaped yellow disc and short, stubby yellow ray florets. *Flowering* June to December. Common on sandy and disturbed areas from Clanwilliam to Bredasdorp.

*Cotula duckittiae (L. Bolus) Bremer & Humphries *Buttons*
Similar to *C. turbinata* but the flower heads much larger, orange and with well-developed ray florets. *Flowering* September to October. Restricted to sandy coastal flats around Jakkalsfontein and Bokbaai.

Foveolina tenella (DC.) Källersjö *Kleinkruid*
Slender annual, sometimes branched, with finely divided leaves clustered at the base. Flower heads solitary on slender, naked stalks, with button-shaped yellow disc and a few white ray florets. *Flowering* June to September. Common on sandy hills and flats from Namaqualand to Malmesbury.

Oncosiphon suffruticosum (L.) Källersjö *Stinkkruid, Wurmbossie*
Slightly hairy annual, branching in the upper half, foetid-smelling when bruised. Leaves finely divided. Flower heads small, numerous, in rounded clusters at the branch tips, with yellow disc florets only, unpleasantly scented. *Flowering* September to January. On sandy flats and slopes, often coastal from Namibia to Caledon.

Oncosiphon grandiflorum (Thunb.) Källersjö *groot Stinkkruid*
Slightly hairy annual, branching in the upper half, aromatic when bruised. Leaves finely divided. Flower heads few, in flat-topped clusters at the branch tips, with yellow disc florets only, honey-scented. *Flowering* September to November. On sandy flats from southern Namibia to Jakkalsfontein.

*Oncosiphon glabratum (Thunb.) Källersjö *Wildekamille*
Annual, branching from the base. Leaves dark green, finely divided. Flower heads solitary, with white ray florets and a raised yellow disc. *Flowering* September to October. Restricted to damp sandy places from Aurora to Darling.

Cotula turbinata   *Cotula duckittiae*   *Foveolina tenella*

Oncosiphon suffruticosum   *Oncosiphon grandiflorum*   *Oncosiphon glabratum*

Gymnodiscus capillaris (L.f.) Less.   *Geelkruid*
Annual with a rosette of leathery, paddle-shaped leaves sometimes coarsely toothed or lobed. Flower heads small, in loose clusters on sparsely branched, naked stalks, yellow. *Flowering* June to October. Common on sandy soils in the Western Cape.

Gorteria personata L.   *Klitskruid*
Scruffy annual, branching from the base, the branches sprawling and roughly hairy. Leaves narrow, rougly hairy, the margins curled under, dark green above, white-cobwebby below. Flower heads solitary at the ends of the branchlets, bracts spine-tipped, with yellow disc and yellow ray florets, greenish black underneath. *Flowering* August to October. On sandy flats from Nieuwoudtville to Humansdorp.

Didelta carnosa (L.f.) Aiton var. **carnosa**
Didelta carnosa var. **tomentosa** (Less.) Roessler   *see Gousblom*
Rounded shrublet with slightly fleshy stems. Leaves narrow and fleshy with the margins rolled under, smooth or grey-cobwebby. Flower heads solitary on naked stalks, the outer five bracts broad and spreading, the inner narrow and toothed, with yellow disc and ray florets. *Flowering* July to December. On coastal dunes and sandy flats from Namaqualand to Darling.

Berkheya armata (Vahl.) Druce   *groot Disseldoring*
Tufted perennial. Leaves narrow, thistle-like, green and rough above, cobwebby below, the margins rolled under. Flower heads solitary on cobwebby stalks, with spiny bracts and bright yellow ray and disc florets. *Flowering* September to November. On sandy flats from Malmesbury to Mossel Bay.

Berkheya rigida (Thunb.) Adamson & T.M. Salter   *Disseldoring, Krammedik*
Stiff, slightly woody shrublet forming tussocks, somewhat cobwebby. Leaves much-lobed with each lobe spine-tipped, the margins rolled under, woolly below. Flower heads in branched clusters, with spiny bracts and tubular yellow disc flowers. *Flowering* August to February. Frequent on dry flats and hillslopes, along roadsides or watercourses from the West Coast to Riversdale.

206

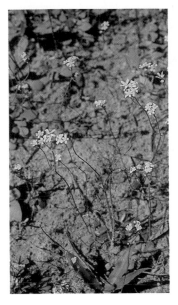

Gymnodiscus capillaris

Gorteria personata

Dıdelta carnosa var.
carnosa

Didelta carnosa var.
tomentosa

Berkheya armata

Berkheya rigida

207

Leysera gnaphalodes (L.) L. *skilpad Teebossie*
Shrublet with hairy stems. Leaves grey, narrow and thread-like, hairy. Flower heads loosely clustered at the ends of the branches, the bracts stiff and papery at the tips, with yellow disc and ray florets. *Flowering* September to December. On sandy flats and slopes from Namibia to Riversdale.

*Steirodiscus speciosus (Pillans) B. Nord. *Cabaroe*
Annual, branched above. Leaves deeply incised, with needle-like segments along the axis. Flower heads solitary on flexed, wiry stalks, the bracts fused into an urn-shaped cup, with vibrant yellow-orange ray and disc florets. *Flowering* September to October. On sandy flats around Mamre.

Tripteris clandestina Less. *Trekkertjie*
Erect, branching annual, sticky and roughly hairy. Leaves coarsely toothed. Flowers heads solitary among the upper leaves, with largely membranous bracts and blackish disc florets, the ray florets yellow with a reddish base. *Flowering* July to October. Common on sandy soils, often along roadsides and fallow lands from Namibia to Swellendam.

Osteospermum dentatum Burm.f. *jakkals Gousblom*
Straggling perennial, branching from the base, roughly hairy. Leaves leathery, coarsely toothed and eared at the base. Flowers in open clusters at the ends of the branches, with yellow ray and disc florets. *Flowering* September to December. On coastal sands from Langebaan to Caledon.

Chrysanthemoides incana (Burm.f.) Norlindh *grys Bietou*
Shrub, cobwebby on the young parts, the branch tips sometimes spiny. Leaves leathery, lightly toothed, cobwebby. Flower heads often solitary at the ends of branches, with yellow disc and ray florets. *Flowering* almost throughout the year. On sandy dunes or slopes from Namibia to Bredasdorp

Chrysanthemoides monilifera (L.) Norlindh *Bietou*
Large shrub with cobwebby hairs on the young parts. Leaves leathery, mostly slightly toothed. Flower heads clustered at the ends of the branches, cobwebby in bud, with yellow disc and several yellow ray florets. Fruits thinly fleshy, glossy black when ripe. *Flowering* throughout the year but especially in winter and spring. Common and widespread on sands along the seaboard of southern and tropical Africa.

Leysera gnaphalodes

Steirodiscus speciosus

Tripteris clandestina

Osteospermum dentatum

Chrysanthemoides incana

*Chrysanthemoides
monilifera*

Euryops multifidus (Thunb.) DC. *hanepoot Harpuisbos*
Open shrublet with bare, pale grey branches with scaly bark. Leaves crowded at the tips of the branchlets, fleshy, cylindrical below and three- to five-forked at the tips, dull green. Flower heads solitary, on slender greyish-powdery stalks set among the leaves, with yellow disc and ray florets. *Flowering* May to September. Frequent on rocky outcrops from near Steinkopf to Worcester.

Oedera uniflora (L.f.) Anderb. & Bremer *vierkant Gombos*
Much-branched, rounded shrublet, the branches bare below but closely leafy above. Leaves small, rough, overlapping and four-ranked at the ends of the branchlets. Flower heads solitary and sessile at the tips of the branchlets, with yellow ray and disc florets. *Flowering* November to January. On sandy soils or limestone outcrops from Saldanha Bay to Albertinia.

Cineraria alchemilloides DC. *Cineraria*
Loosely branched perennial with slender, green branches. Leaves round and irregularly toothed. Flower heads in branched terminal clusters, with yellow disc and ray florets, honey-scented. *Flowering* August to September. Widespread in damp, shaded ravines throughout southern Africa.

Othonna filicaulis Jacq. *Bobbejaankoolklimop*
Branched, sprawling herb with a greyish bloom and tuberous root. Leaves broad, round and leathery, clasping the stem and eared at the base. Flower heads few, on distinct stalks, with yellow or white disc florets only and mauve pappus bristles. *Flowering* June to August. On sandy slopes and granite outcrops from Namaqualand to the Peninsula.

Othonna coronopifolia L. *sand Bobbejaankool*
Shrub with pale, naked stems. Leaves crowded at the ends of the branches, narrow and leathery, usually irregularly toothed. Flower heads solitary or a few, on distinct stalks, with yellow disc and ray florets. *Flowering* May to December. On sandy soils and dunes from Clanwilliam to the Peninsula.

Othonna arborescens L. *Bobbejaankool*
Shrub with shining brown, naked stems. Leaves crowded at the ends of the branches, broad and leathery, often with the margins slightly rolled under. Flower heads solitary, on distinct stalks, with yellow disc and ray florets. *Flowering* May to September. Among rocks or sand along the coast from Langebaan to Humansdorp.

Euryops multifidus

Oedera uniflora

*Cineraria
alchemilloides*

Othonna filicaulis

Othonna coronopifolia

*Othonna
arborescens*

Othonna cylindrica (Lam.) DC.   *dikblaar Bobbejaankool*
Densely branched shrublet with pale grey, naked stems. Leaves crowded at the tips
of the branchlets, succulent and cylindrical, covered with a white bloom. Flower
heads in sparsely branched clusters, on distinct stalks, with yellow disc and ray
florets. *Flowering* May to September. Often on rocky outcrops from Vioolsdrift to
Malmesbury.

Senecio aloides DC.   *groot Dikblaar*
Shrublet with smooth, greyish, somewhat fleshy branches. Leaves clustered at the
ends of the branches, fleshy and cylindrical with a slight groove above. Flower
heads one or two, on naked stalks twice as long as the leaves, large (bracts c. 15
mm long), with yellow disc and ray florets, fragrant. *Flowering* July to October. In
sandy soils near the coast from Namibia to the Peninsula.

Senecio sarcoides C. Jeffrey   *soetkop Dikblaar*
Similar to *S. aloides* but with several flower heads clustered on short stalks about
as long as the leaves, and the flower heads much smaller (bracts c. 10 mm long).
Flowering July to October. In rocky places on shale or granite from Namibia to
Robertson.

Senecio pubigerus L.   *Skraalbossie*
Shrub with slender, spreading, closely-ribbed branches, yellowish green. Leaves
reduced to triangular scales. Flowers heads one to three, clustered on short, thinly
white-woolly shoots in the axils of the scale-leaves, with yellow disc and two to
four yellow ray florets. *Flowering* March to June. Common on flats and lower
slopes from Piketberg to Worcester.

Senecio halimifolius L.   *Tabakbos*
Robust, erect shrub. Leaves leathery, coarsely toothed near the tips, somewhat
undulate, cobwebby in the axils. Flower heads in branched, flat-topped clusters at
the ends of the stems, with yellow ray and disc florets. *Flowering* November to
January. Common in damp sandy places near the coast from Lambert's Bay to
Hermanus.

Senecio rosmarinifolius L.f.   *grys Hongerblom*
Perennial shrublet with slender, erect flowering branches. Leaves narrow and weakly toothed, cobwebby, with the margins rolled under. Flower heads several, in flat-
topped clusters, with yellow disc and short yellow ray florets. *Flowering* November
to April. On flats and slopes, usually in drier places but occasionally in marshes
from Hopefield to the Eastern Cape.

Othonna cylindrica

Senecio aloides

Senecio sarcoides

Senecio pubigerus

Senecio halimifolius

Senecio rosmarinifolius

213

Senecio maritimus L.   *strand Hongerblom*
Annual, branching below. Leaves slightly succulent, broadest in the upper half,
hairy below, the margins lightly toothed and rolled under. Flower heads in
branched clusters. with yellow disc and ray florets. *Flowering* August to December.
On coastal dunes and rocks from Yzerfontein to Caledon.

Senecio burchellii DC.   *Gifbossie*
Perennial herb or shrublet with slender flowering branches. Leaves narrow, with
the margins rolled under, half-clasping and minutely eared and toothed at the base.
Flower heads few in loose clusters, with yellow disc and conspicuous yellow ray
florets. *Flowering* throughout the year. Common on sandy and disturbed ground,
especially roadsides, throughout the Western Cape. Many species of *Senecio* are
toxic to stock and especially horses and this is one of them. The danger of poisoning is highest in early spring when the young plants are cropped along with grass.

Senecio littoreus Thunb.   *geel Hongerblom*
Hairless annual. Lower leaves deeply lobed, eared at the base, the margins rolled
under. Flowers several in open clusters, with bright yellow disc and ray florets.
Flowering July to September. On sandy coastal flats from Namaqualand to the
Peninsula.

*Senecio foeniculoides Harv.   *Vinkelbossie*
Many-stemmed shrublet with closely leafy stems. Leaves much-divided with nar-
row lobes. Flower heads borne in much-branched, flat-topped clusters at the end of
the stems, each head containing twelve to sixteen yellow disc florets. *Flowering*
December to January. Rare in deep sandy soil in fynbos between Twenty Four
Rivers and Milnerton.

Senecio scapiflorus (L'Hér.) C.A. Sm.   *Perskoppie*
Perennial, producing annual branches from the base, with cobwebby stems and
leaves. Leaves clustered at the base, variously lobed, on long petioles. Flower
heads solitary on long, slender stalks, with mauve or white disc florets only, the
anthers purple. *Flowering* September to November. On sandy coastal flats from
Namaqualand to the Peninsula.

Senecio radicans (L.f.) Sch. Bip.   *Bobbejaantoontjies, Necklace plant*
Stems creeping, rooting at intervals, with short erect branches. Leaves succulent,
ellipsoid and slightly channelled above, striped with purple. Flower heads solitary
or few, containing several white disc florets with conspicuous purple anthers.
Flowering April to July. On granite outcrops and karroid hills throughout the country.

Senecio maritimus

Senecio burchellii

Senecio littoreus

Senecio foeniculoides

Senecio scapiflorus

Senecio radicans

215

Senecio arenarius Thunb. *Hongerblom*
Glandular-hairy annual with branching stem. Leaves more or less clasping at the base, variously lobed or toothed. Flower heads in branched clusters, with yellow disc and magenta ray florets, involucre cylindrical, hairy, with one to three small bracts at the base. *Flowering* August to October. Common on sandy flats from Namibia to Bredasdorp.

Senecio elegans L. *veld Cineraria*
Robust annual with roughly hairy stems. Leaves deeply divided and crisped, the margins rolled under, roughly hairy. Flower heads in flat-topped, branched clusters at the end of the stem, with yellow disc and magenta ray florets, involucre globose, hairless, with many black-tipped bracts at the base. *Flowering* September to November. On sandy coastal flats and lower slopes from Namaqualand to the Eastern Cape.

Corymbium villosum Less. *Heuningbossie*
Tufted perennial with woolly stems. Leaves in a basal tuft, tough and narrow, densely woolly below. Flowers in branched, flat-topped clusters at the tip of the stem, with white or mauve disc florets only. *Flowering* September to November, mostly after fire. On rocky sandstone or granite from Cedarberg to Swellendam.

Amellus tenuifolius Burm. *grys Asterjie*
Shrublet with erect, thinly hairy stems. Leaves grey, narrow and twisted, thinly hairy. Flower heads solitary on leafy stalks, loosely clustered at the ends of the branches, with yellow disc and blue-mauve ray florets. *Flowering* October to December. On sandy soils from Namaqualand to Caledon.

Felicia hyssopifolia (Bergius) Nees *bos Astertjie*
Much-branched shrublet with leaves clustered on new growth. Leaves narrow. Flower heads on naked stalks, with yellow disc and pale blue or white ray florets. *Flowering* almost throughout the year. Widespread on clays or rocky soils in Namibia and South Africa.

Senecio arenarius

Senecio elegans

Corymbium villosum

Amellus tenuifolius

Felicia hyssopifolia

Felicia tenella (L.) Nees   *Astertjie*
Annual, sometimes branching from the base. Leaves narrow, hairy. Flower heads
solitary on more or less leafy stalks, with yellow disc and blue or lilac ray florets.
Flowering mainly September to February. On sandy soils throughout the Western
Cape.

Felicia bergeriana (Spreng.) O. Hoffm.   *breëblaar Astertjie*
Annual, mostly branching above. Leaves soft, broadest near the apex, roughly
hairy. Flower heads solitary on more or less naked stalks, with yellow disc and blue
ray florets. *Flowering* July to September. On sandy soil from Nieuwoudtville to
Caledon.

Felicia heterophylla (Cass.) Grau   *bloublom Astertjie*
Sparsely branched annual. Leaves soft, broadest near the apex, roughly hairy.
Flower heads solitary on more or less naked stalks, with blue disc and ray florets.
Flowering August to October. On sandy flats and lower slopes from Clanwilliam to
the Peninsula.

Dimorphotheca pluvialis DC.   *Reënblommetjie*
Annual, sparsely hairy, with narrow, bluntly toothed leaves. Flower heads large,
with ray florets white above and purple underneath and the disc florets black,
drooping in fruit. *Flowering* July to October. Widespread on sandy soils from
Namibia to Riversdale.

Ursinia anthemoides (L.) Poir.   *Magriet*
Erect annual, sometimes branching from the base. Leaves finely divided, aromatic
when bruised. Flower heads solitary at the ends of the branches, on naked stalks,
with orange, yellow or salmon ray florets sometimes black at the base and yellow
or black disc florets. *Flowering* August to October. On sandy soils from Namibia to
Port Elizabeth.

Arctotheca calendula (L.) Levyns   *Cape weed*
Herb with basal rosette of leaves variously incised along the margins, hairy and
whitish underneath. Heads large, solitary on roughly hairy stalks conspicuously
ridged lengthways, with pale yellow ray florets darker at the base and yellow or
black disc florets. *Flowering* July to November. Widespread along roadsides, old
lands and other disturbed places in the Western Cape and extending to Natal.

Felicia tenella

Felicia bergeriana

Felicia heterophylla

Dimorphotheca pluvialis

Ursinia anthemoides

Arctotheca populifolia

Arctotheca populifolia (Bergius) Norlindh   *Seepampoen*
Sprawling perennial with ridged, cobwebby stems, forming thick mats. Leaves grey
and thickly white-woolly. Flower heads solitary on erect stalks, with yellow ray
and disc florets. *Flowering* thoughout the year. On coastal dunes from Saldanha
Bay to Mozambique.

Arctotis angustifolia L.   *smalblaar Gousblom*
Sprawling perennial with cobwebby branches. Leaves narrow, coarsely toothed,
grey-cobwebby. Flower heads solitary, on erect stalks, with white or orange ray florets black at the base and reddish beneath, and black disc florets. *Flowering* August
to November. On sandy soils from Clanwilliam to Caledon.

Arctotis breviscapa Thunb.   *sandveld Gousblom*
Stemless annual. Leaves in a basal tuft, variously incised along the margins, white-
woolly below and roughly hairy above. Heads large, on roughly hairy stalks, the
ray florets orange (sometimes black at the base) and the disc florets black.
Flowering August to January. On sandy flats and slopes from Clanwilliam to the
Peninsula.

Arctotis acaulis L.   *renoster Gousblom*
Similar to *A. breviscapa* but the leaves with a large, spade-shaped segment at the
tip. *Flowering* July to September. On clay soils from Namaqualand to Swellendam.

Arctotis hirsuta (Harv.) Beauv.   *Gousblom*
Annual with branched stem. Leaves stiffly hairy, variously incised along the margins. Heads large, on stalks covered with rough, reddish hairs, the ray florets white,
yellow or orange and the disc florets sometimes blackish. *Flowering* July to
October. On sandy soils along the west coast.

Arctotheca calendula

Arctotis angustifolia

Arctotis breviscapa

Arctotis acaulis

Arctotis hirsuta

Arctotis hirsuta

*Arctotis candida Thunb. *Malmesbury gousblom*
Stemless annual with the leaves mostly basal but extending up the stems. Leaves regularly lobed, densely white-woolly below and roughly hairy above. Heads large, at the end of the stems, the ray florets white (rarely orange), maroon underneath and the disc florets black. *Flowering* August to October. Restricted to clay soils around Malmesbury.

Arctotis stoechadifolia Bergius *kus Gousblom*
Mat-forming perennial with sprawling, cobwebby branches. Leaves deeply lobed, narrowed below, silvery-cobwebby. Flower heads large, solitary, on erect stalks, ray florets cream or pale yellow with a black basal mark edged in bright yellow, disc florets black. *Flowering* September to December. On coastal sand dunes and flats from Langebaan to the Peninsula.

Arctotis revoluta Jacq. *krulblaar Gousblom*
Shrub with cobwebby branches. Leaves deeply divided and strongly crisped along the margins, white-woolly below. Heads large, on woolly stalks, the ray florets yellow or orange above and maroon underneath and the disc florets yellow. *Flowering* August to November. On granite outcrops and coastal sands from Saldanha Bay to the Breede River mouth.

Gazania pectinata (Thunb.) Spreng. *Kaapse rooi Gousblom*
Stemless perennial. Leaves in a basal tuft, narrow or deeply divided, grey-woolly below and more or less roughly hairy above. Flower heads solitary, on woolly stalks, inner bracts drawn into a slender point, disc florets orange and ray florets orange with a brown or black mark at the base. *Flowering* almost thoughout the year. Roadsides, flats or lower slopes from Hopefield to Bredasdorp.

Gazania krebsiana Less. *rooi Gousblom*
Similar to *G. pectinata* but the inner bracts blunt. *Flowering* almost throughout the year. Widespread throughout southern and tropical Africa.

Arctotis candida

Arctotis stoechadifolia

Arctotis revoluta

Gazania pectinata

Gazania krebsiana

INDEX OF COMMON NAMES

225

INDEX OF SCIENTIFIC NAMES

About the Botanical Society of South Africa

Founded in 1913 at the same time as Kirstenbosch Botanic Gardens, the Botanical Society aims to interest the people of South Africa and other countries in the National Botanic Gardens. We also aim to educate members of the public in the cultivation, conservation and awareness of our unique indigenous flora.

ARE YOU A MEMBER?
The Botanical Society of South Africa is one of the largest, most effective organisations working to safeguard our veld and flora. If you are not already a member we invite you to join. There is something for everyone in the Society's wide range of activities, from hikes and walks to illustrated lectures, tours and conservation activism. Members receive the colourful and informative "Veld & Flora" magazine, free seeds of your choice annually from the Kirstenbosch seed list, as well as free admission to all the national botanic gardens in South Africa.

By joining the Society you support those members who are willing to invest their time and expertise to protect our natural heritage for this and future generations. We need your membership and support. To join, please contact the Executive Secretary, Botanical Society of South Africa, Kirstenbosch, Claremont 7735 RSA or telephone Cape Town (021) 797-2090.

If you have enjoyed the wild flower guides in this series and wish to support us in our programme of producing guides for other areas of South Africa, donations may be sent to the Botanical Society of South Africa for its publication programme. Any donations or bequests made to the Botanical Society or its Flora Conservation Committee are free of donations and estate duty tax.

Plants are protected by Ordinance 19 of 1974 as amended which prohibits the picking of any plant within 90 m of the middle of the road, or the picking of any plant without the written permission of the landowner, or the picking of any species that are proclaimed endangered or protected without the necessary permits. Permits are obtainable on written application from:

The Chief Director
Cape Nature Conservation
Private Bag X9086
8000